세상이 변해도
배움의 즐거움은
변함없도록

시대는 빠르게 변해도
배움의 즐거움은
변함없어야 하기에

어제의 비상은
남다른 교재부터
결이 다른 콘텐츠
전에 없던 교육 플랫폼까지

변함없는 혁신으로
교육 문화 환경의 새로운 전형을
실현해왔습니다.

비상은 오늘, 다시 한번
새로운 교육 문화 환경을 실현하기 위한
또 하나의 혁신을 시작합니다.

오늘의 내가 어제의 나를 초월하고
오늘의 교육이 어제의 교육을 초월하여
배움의 즐거움을 지속하는 혁신,

바로, 메타인지 기반 완전 학습을.

상상을 실현하는 교육 문화 기업 비상

메타인지 기반 완전 학습
초월을 뜻하는 meta와 생각을 뜻하는 인지가 결합한 메타인지는
자신이 알고 모르는 것을 스스로 구분하고 학습계획을 세우도록 하는
궁극의 학습 능력입니다. 비상의 메타인지 기반 완전 학습 시스템은
잠들어 있는 메타인지를 깨워 공부를 100% 내 것으로 만들도록 합니다.

READING TAPA

How to Study

구성과 특장

Pre-Study

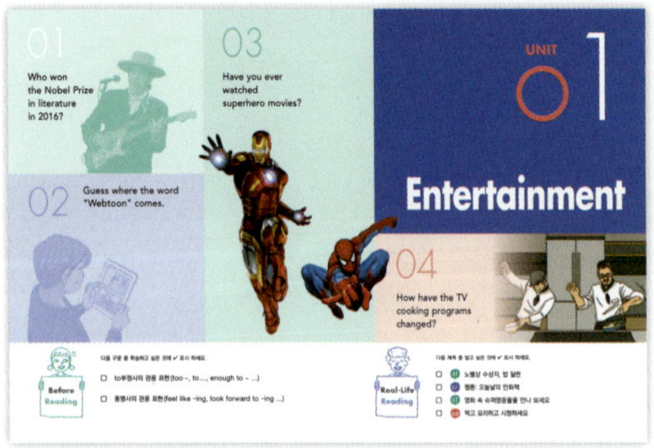

UNIT의 독해 소재와 관련 구문을 파악하세요!
흥미로운 이미지와 관련 내용을 살펴보면 학습할 내용에
대한 기대가 한껏 부풀어 오를 거예요.

Main Study

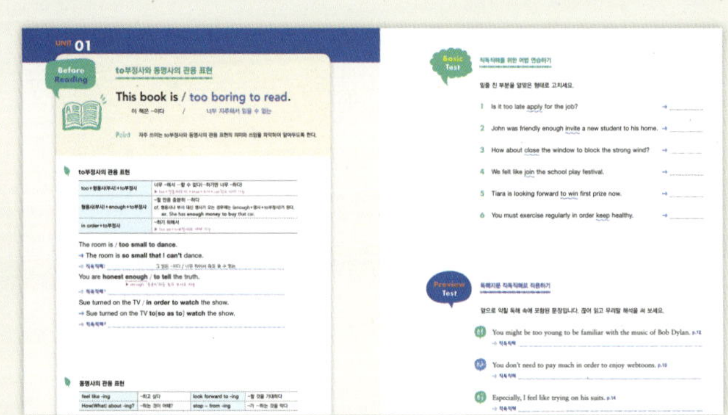

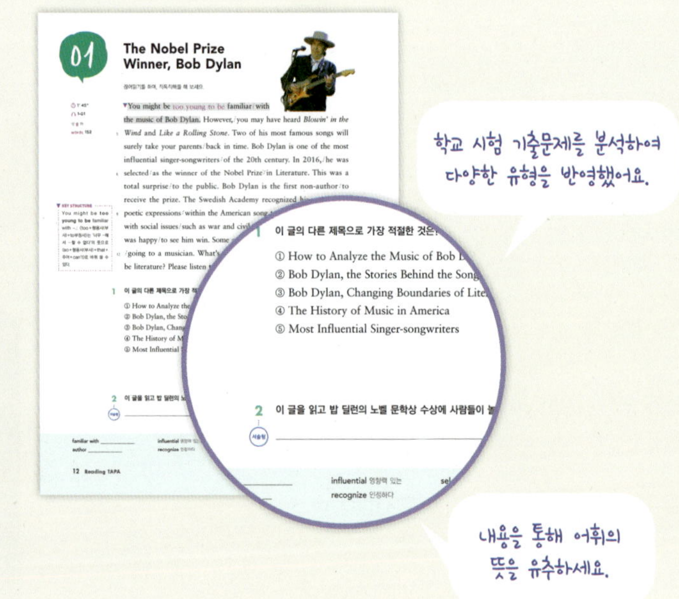

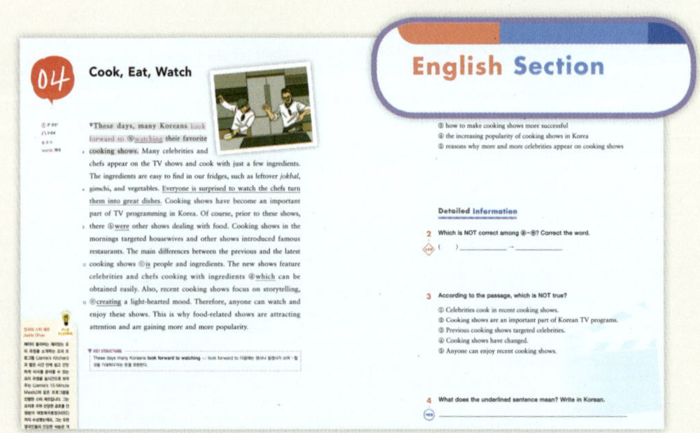

Step 1

독해의 기본, 구문을 익히세요!

중학교에서 배우는 핵심 구문들을 분석하여 **중학생이 반드시 알아야 하는 구문 10가지**로 구성했습니다. 독해 문제를 풀기 전에 핵심 구문부터 확실히 익힌다면 한결 쉽게 해석을 할 수 있답니다!

Step 2

흥미로운 소재의 독해를 공부하세요!

사회, 문화, 과학, 연예 등의 다양한 분야에서 지식을 쌓을 수 있는 참신한 소재들로 구성했답니다. MP3로 원어민 선생님이 읽어주는 독해지문을 들어보는 것도 잊지 마세요!

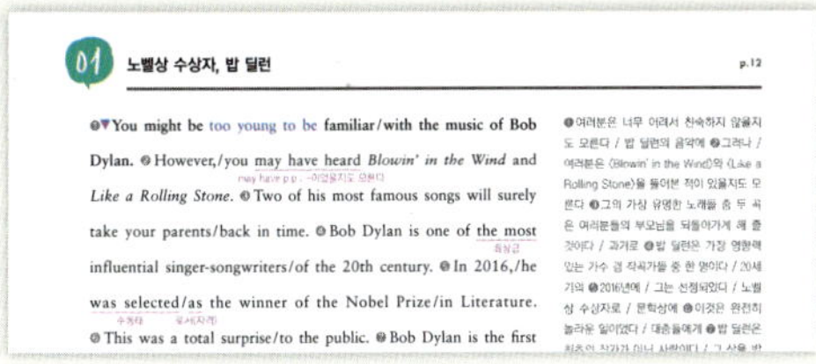

정답과 해설에서
정확한 해석과 문장 구조를
확인하세요!

Step 3

영어로 생각하고 영어로 해결해 보세요!

Unit마다 영어로만 구성된 English Section 코너를 제공합니다. **영어로 사고하면서 문제를 해결**하다 보면, 어느새 실력이 향상되어 있을 거예요!

After Study

Workbook도 활용하세요!

Unit이 끝날 때마다 Workbook으로 배운 내용을 복습하세요!

Word Test를 통해
핵심 어휘를 학습하세요.

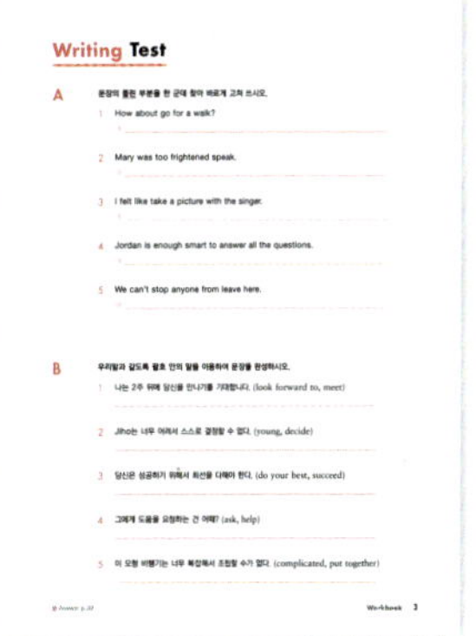

Writing Test를 통해
문장 단위의 쓰기 연습을
해 보세요.

Translation Test를 통해
필수 구문이 포함된 문단을
끊어 읽고 직독직해하세요.

Contents

차례

01

Who won
the Nobel Prize
in literature
in 2016?

02

Guess where the word
"Webtoon" comes.

03

Have you ever
watched
superhero movies?

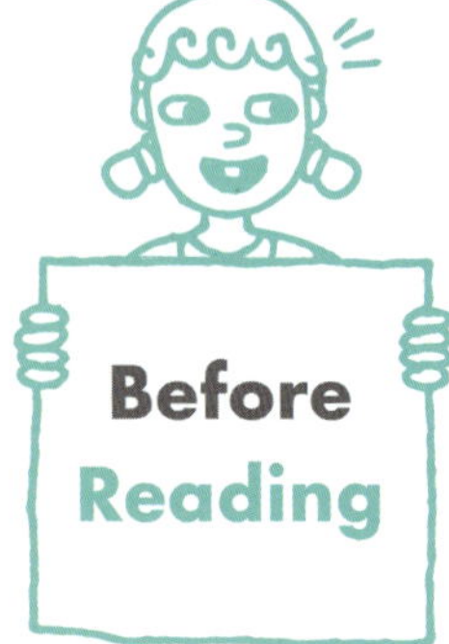

다음 구문 중 학습하고 싶은 것에 ✔ 표시 하세요.

- ☐ to부정사의 관용 표현 (too ~, to ..., enough to ~ ...)

- ☐ 동명사의 관용 표현 (feel like -ing, look forward to -ing ...)

**Before
Reading**

Entertainment

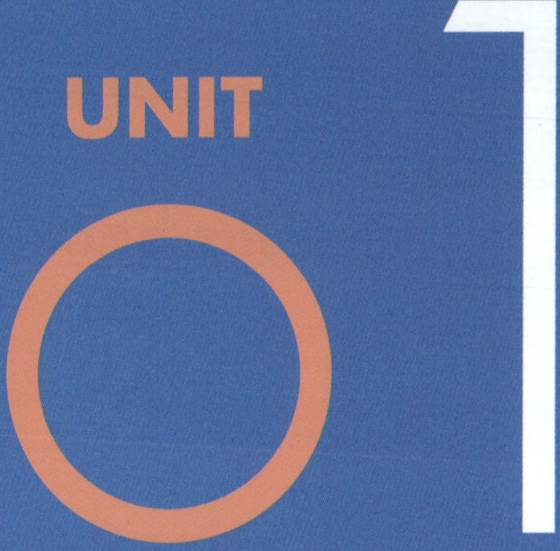

04

How have the TV cooking programs changed?

다음 제목 중 알고 싶은 것에 ✔ 표시 하세요.

- ☐ **01** 노벨상 수상자, 밥 딜런
- ☐ **02** 웹툰: 오늘날의 만화책
- ☐ **03** 영화 속 슈퍼영웅들을 만나 보세요
- ☐ **04** 먹고 요리하고 시청하세요

Before Reading

to부정사와 동명사의 관용 표현

This book is / too boring to read.
이 책은 ~이다 / 너무 지루해서 읽을 수 없는

Point 자주 쓰이는 to부정사와 동명사의 관용 표현의 의미와 쓰임을 파악하여 알아두도록 한다.

 **to부정사의 관용 표현**

too+형용사(부사)+to부정사	너무 ~해서 …할 수 없다(…하기엔 너무 ~하다) ▶ 〈so+형용사(부사)+that+주어+can't〉로 대체 가능
형용사(부사)+enough+to부정사	~할 만큼 충분히 …하다 *cf.* 형용사나 부사 대신 명사가 오는 경우에는 〈enough+명사+to부정사〉가 된다. 　　*ex.* She has **enough money to buy** that car.
in order+to부정사	~하기 위해서 ▶ 〈so as+to부정사〉로 대체 가능

The room is / **too small to dance**.

→ The room is **so small that I can't** dance.

⇨ **직독직해:** ────────── 그 방은 ~이다 / 너무 작아서 춤을 출 수 없는 ──────────

You are **honest enough** / **to tell** the truth.
　　　　　　▶ enough: '충분히'라는 뜻의 부사로 사용

⇨ **직독직해¹** ──────────────────────────────

Sue turned on the TV / **in order to watch** the show.

→ Sue turned on the TV **to[so as to] watch** the show.

⇨ **직독직해²** ──────────────────────────────

 **동명사의 관용 표현**

feel like -ing	~하고 싶다	look forward to -ing	~할 것을 기대하다
How(What) about -ing?	~하는 것이 어때?	stop ~ from -ing	~가 …하는 것을 막다

I **feel like going** home / now.

⇨ **직독직해³** ──────────────────────────────

We **look forward to working** / with her.

⇨ **직독직해⁴** ──────────────────────────────

직독직해를 위한 어법 연습하기

밑줄 친 부분을 알맞은 형태로 고치세요.

1 Is it too late <u>apply</u> for the job? → ....

2 John was friendly enough <u>invite</u> a new student to his home. → ....

3 How about <u>close</u> the window to block the strong wind? → ....

4 We felt like <u>join</u> the school play festival. → ....

5 Tiara is looking forward <u>to win</u> first prize now. → ....

6 You must exercise regularly in order <u>keep</u> healthy. → ....

Preview Test

독해지문 직독직해로 적용하기

앞으로 익힐 독해 속에 포함된 문장입니다. 끊어 읽고 우리말 해석을 써 보세요.

01 You might be too young to be familiar with the music of Bob Dylan. **p.12**
⇨ 직독직해 ....

02 You don't need to pay much in order to enjoy webtoons. **p.13**
⇨ 직독직해 ....

03 Especially, I feel like trying on his suits. **p.14**
⇨ 직독직해 ....

04 These days many Koreans look forward to watching their favorite cooking shows. **p.16**
⇨ 직독직해 ....

01 The Nobel Prize Winner, Bob Dylan

끊어읽기를 하며, 직독직해를 해 보세요.

⏱ 1′ 45″
🎧 1-01
상 **중** 하
words 152

▼You might be too young to be familiar/with the music of Bob Dylan. However,/you may have heard *Blowin' in the Wind* and *Like a Rolling Stone*. Two of his most famous songs will surely take your parents/back in time. Bob Dylan is one of the most influential singer-songwriters/of the 20th century. In 2016,/he was selected/as the winner of the Nobel Prize/in Literature. This was a total surprise/to the public. Bob Dylan is the first non-author/to receive the prize. The Swedish Academy recognized his creation of poetic expressions/within the American song tradition. His songs deal with social issues/such as war and civil rights. However,/not everyone was happy/to see him win. Some authors complained/about the award /going to a musician. What's your opinion/on this? Can song lyrics be literature? Please listen to some of his songs/before you decide.

1 이 글의 또 다른 제목으로 가장 적절한 것은? (제목 추론)

① How to Analyze the Music of Bob Dylan
② Bob Dylan, the Stories Behind the Songs
③ Bob Dylan, Changing Boundaries of Literature
④ The History of Music in America
⑤ Most Influential Singer-songwriters

2 이 글을 읽고 밥 딜런의 노벨 문학상 수상에 사람들이 놀란 이유를 우리말로 쓰시오. (세부 내용 파악)

(서술형) ____

---

familiar with ____________ influential 영향력 있는 select ____________ literature 문학
author ____________ recognize 인정하다 creation 창작(물) tradition ____________

Webtoons: Today's Comic Books

⏱ 1' 30"
🎧 1-02
상 중 하
words 109

Webtoon is a combination of the words "web" and "cartoon." These days, the number of people enjoying webtoons has greatly increased. Why are webtoons gaining popularity? First, webtoons guarantee more artistic freedom. Webtoon artists have more control over their work than comic book artists. They are their own editors and publishers. They are free to express what they imagine. (A) Second, webtoons can be viewed instantly. (B) Anyone with an Internet connection has easy access to webtoons. (C) ▼Third, you don't need to pay much in order to enjoy webtoons. (D) In general, webtoons are cheaper than printed comic books because production costs are lower. Webtoons might be part of your daily routine. (E)

1 이 글의 주제로 가장 적절한 것은? (주제 추론)

① the origin of the word "webtoon"
② how to succeed as a webtoon artist
③ how comic books developed into webtoons
④ reasons why webtoons are becoming popular
⑤ similarities between webtoons and comic books

2 이 글의 (A)~(E) 중 다음 문장이 들어갈 곳으로 알맞은 것은? (글의 흐름)

> But don't get too absorbed in them.

① (A)   ② (B)   ③ (C)   ④ (D)   ⑤ (E)

greatly _____________   guarantee _____________   artistic 예술적인   editor 편집자
publisher _____________   imagine 상상하다   instantly 즉시, 곧바로   daily routine 일상

Meet Superheroes in the Movies

⏱ 2' 55"
🎧 1-03
상 중 하
words 171

Nowadays, we often see many superheroes in Hollywood movies. Who is your favorite superhero and why? Here are some answers from around the world.

Tom Batman is my hero. He saved his hometown in the dark. ▼Especially, I feel like trying on his suits. And I want to drive his Batmobile, too. They're cool!

Jihun My favorite superhero changes often. Currently, my favorite is Iron Man. _____ⓐ_____, he wasn't a superhero, but a mad scientist. However, he tried to keep the world safe, so he became a real hero to me. _____ⓑ_____, I love his high-tech inventions, and the actor Robert Downey Jr. is so funny.

Sarah Spider-Man is wonderful. He is super strong, super fast, and has super senses like a spider. He climbs up high buildings to <u>defeat</u> bad men. But, unlike other heroes, Spider-Man lives a lonely life, because he is an orphan. So, he had to learn how to use his great powers alone, which impresses me a lot.

Now, it's your turn. Who is your superhero?

> ▼ **KEY STRUCTURE** ----------------------------
> Especially, I **feel like trying on** his suits.: 〈feel like -ing〉는 동명사의 관용적 표현으로 '~하고 싶다'의 의미를 나타낸다. 이 표현에서 like는 전치사로 쓰였으므로 to부정사는 쓸 수 없음에 유의한다.

superhero 슈퍼영웅　　　nowadays _____________　　　hometown 고향　　　suit 옷, 정장
favorite 매우 좋아하는　　　currently 현재, 지금　　　mad 정신 이상인　　　safe _____________

Main Idea

1 이 글의 중심 소재로 알맞은 것은? 〔소재 추론〕

① my favorite action star
② how to become a superhero
③ the most popular superhero
④ my favorite superhero
⑤ superhero's incredible suits

Detailed Information

2 이 글의 빈칸 ⓐ, ⓑ에 들어갈 말이 알맞게 짝지어진 것은? 〔연결사 파악〕

	ⓐ	ⓑ		ⓐ	ⓑ
①	Moreover	– By the way	②	In fact	– Besides
③	As a result	– However	④	First of all	– Therefore
⑤	Therefore	– In addition			

3 이 글의 내용과 일치하는 것은? 〔내용 일치·불일치〕

① Tom wants to buy Superman's suits.
② Jihun has not decided on his hero yet.
③ Jihun likes Iron Man because he is a mad inventor.
④ Robert Downey Jr. plays Spider-Man.
⑤ Spider-Man grew up without his parents' help.

4 이 글의 밑줄 친 defeat과 의미가 가장 가까운 것은? 〔어휘 추론〕

① beat   ② embarrass   ③ yield
④ surprise   ⑤ avoid

invention 발명(품)	sense 감각	climb up ~에 오르다	unlike ~와 달리
lonely 외로운, 쓸쓸한	orphan 고아	alone ___________	impress ___________

Cook, Eat, Watch

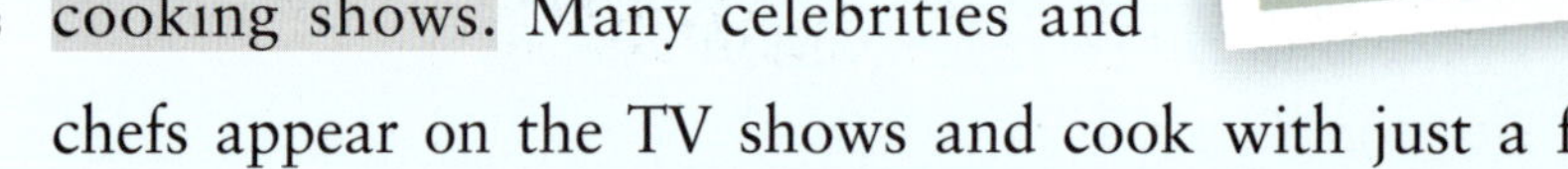

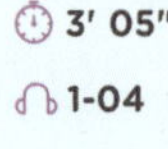

⏱ 3' 05"
🎧 1-04
상 중 하
words **160**

제이미 올리버는 재미있는 요리 과정을 소개하는 요리 프로그램 〈Jamie's Kitchen〉과 짧은 시간 안에 쉽고 간단하게 식사를 준비할 수 있는 요리 과정을 실시간으로 보여주는 〈Jamie's 15-Minute Meals〉와 같은 프로그램을 진행한 스타 셰프입니다. 그는 요리로 국위 선양한 공로를 인정받아 대영제국훈장(MBE)까지 수상했는데요, 그는 또한 영국인들의 건강한 식습관 개선 활동에 앞장서는 사회운동가로도 유명하답니다.

▼These days, many Koreans look forward to ⓐ watching their favorite cooking shows. Many celebrities and chefs appear on the TV shows and cook with just a few ingredients. The ingredients are easy to find in our fridges, such as leftover *jokbal*, gimchi, and vegetables. Everyone is surprised to watch the chefs turn them into great dishes. Cooking shows have become an important part of TV programming in Korea. Of course, prior to these shows, there ⓑ were other shows dealing with food. Cooking shows in the mornings targeted housewives and other shows introduced famous restaurants. The main differences between the previous and the latest cooking shows ⓒ is people and ingredients. The new shows feature celebrities and chefs cooking with ingredients ⓓ which can be obtained easily. Also, recent cooking shows focus on storytelling, ⓔ creating a light-hearted mood. Therefore, anyone can watch and enjoy these shows. This is why food-related shows are attracting attention and are gaining more and more popularity.

▼ **KEY STRUCTURE**

These days many Koreans **look forward to watching** ~.: look forward to 다음에는 명사나 동명사가 쓰여 '~할 것을 기대하다'라는 뜻을 표현한다.

ingredient ____________	leftover 남은 음식	prior to ____________
target ~을 대상으로 하다	previous ____________	obtain 얻다

Main Idea

1 **What is the best topic of the passage?**

① effective ways to reduce food wastes

② secrets to turn leftovers into great dishes

③ how to make cooking shows more successful

④ the increasing popularity of cooking shows in Korea

⑤ reasons why more and more celebrities appear on cooking shows

Detailed Information

2 **Which is NOT correct among ⓐ~ⓔ? Correct the word.**

신경향

(   ) ________________ → ________________

3 **According to the passage, which is NOT true?**

① Celebrities cook in recent cooking shows.

② Cooking shows are an important part of Korean TV programs.

③ Previous cooking shows targeted celebrities.

④ Cooking shows have changed.

⑤ Anyone can enjoy recent cooking shows.

4 **What does the underlined sentence mean? Write in Korean.**

서술형 ____

recent __________	light-hearted 편안한 마음의	mood __________	therefore 그러므로
attract 끌다	attention 관심	gain 얻다	popularity __________

01

What do the students around the world usually eat for lunch?

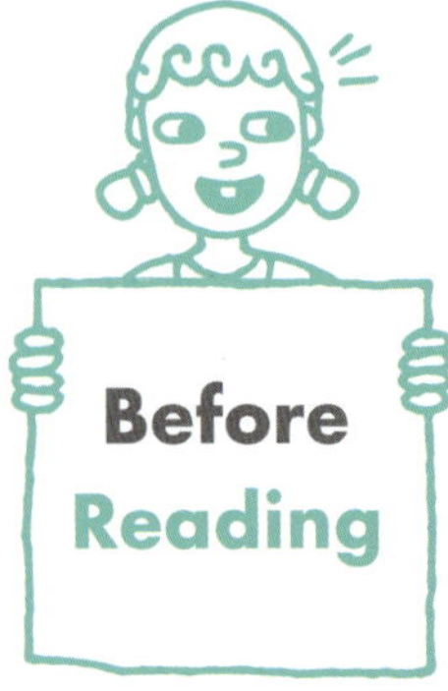

다음 구문 중 학습하고 싶은 것에 ✔ 표시 하세요.

☐ 현재분사의 쓰임과 형태

☐ 과거분사의 쓰임과 형태

☐ 감정을 나타내는 분사

02

What is your favorite for a painting tool?

03

Have you ever tried a unique transportation?

04

The standard of beauty changes all the time!

분사의 쓰임과 형태

Look / at the broken vase.
봐라 / 저 깨진 꽃병을

Point 분사와 분사의 수식을 받는 (대)명사의 의미 관계를 생각하며 해석한다.

🍃 **분사의 개념:** 분사는 동사를 변형하여 (대)명사의 앞 또는 뒤에서 수식하거나 감정을 나타내는 역할을 하며, 동사원형에 -ing를 붙인 현재분사와 -ed를 붙인 과거분사가 있다.

🍃 **현재분사:** 〈동사원형+-ing〉의 형태로 능동, 진행의 의미를 나타낸다.

[능동] The **burning** candles / on the cake / are very beautiful.
⇨ **직독직해** [1] ____

[진행] They are the only guests / **staying** / at the hotel.
⇨ **직독직해** [2] ____

🍃 **과거분사:** 〈동사원형+-ed〉의 형태로 수동, 완료의 의미를 나타낸다.

[수동] My mother bought / me / a new purse / **made** in Italy.
⇨ **직독직해** [3] ____

[완료] Can you help me / find / my **lost** dog?
⇨ **직독직해** [4] ____

🍃 **감정을 나타내는 분사**

[현재분사] '~한 감정을 느끼게 만드는'이라는 의미로 사람이나 사물이 기분 또는 감정을 유발할 때 주로 쓴다.
The comedy movie was / really **exciting**.
⇨ **직독직해** [5] ____

[과거분사] '~한 감정을 느끼는'이라는 뜻으로 사람이 기분이나 감정을 느낄 때 주로 쓴다.
Robert got **excited** / at the party.
⇨ **직독직해** [6] ____

» 정답과 해설 p.06

밑줄 친 부분을 알맞은 형태로 고치세요.

1 Tiffany saw the slept bear at a zoo. → ....

2 The dog is barked in the lobby. → ....

3 The cheese making in France is delicious. → ....

4 Mr. Lee is reading a novel writing in English. → ....

5 Look at the man climbed the mountain. → ....

6 John was frightening by the horror movie. → ....

Preview Test   독해지문 직독직해로 적용하기

앞으로 익힐 독해 속에 포함된 문장입니다. 끊어 읽고 우리말 해석을 써 보세요.

01 Do you ever wonder what children are eating for lunch? **p.22**
⇒ 직독직해 ....

02 One of the most unexpected tools is the human body. **p.23**
⇒ 직독직해 ....

03 In Cambodia, you'll find an interesting train called the bamboo train. **p.24**
⇒ 직독직해 ....

04 Defining beauty is interesting because it is something seen differently in different times and places. **p.26**
⇒ 직독직해 ....

01 School Lunches Around the World

끊어읽기를 하며, 직독직해를 해 보세요.

⏱ 1′ 35″
🎧 2-01
상 중 하
words 115

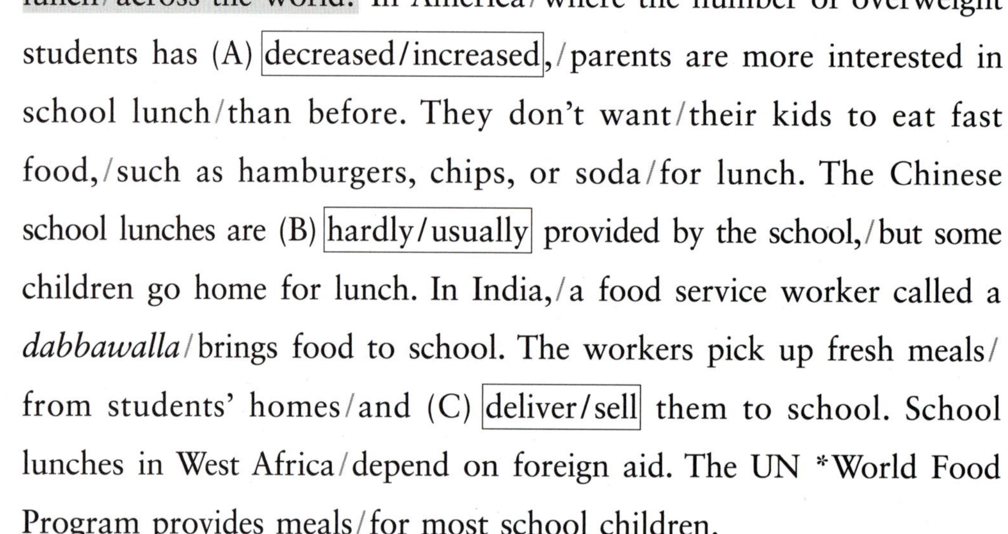

▼Do you ever wonder/what children are eating for lunch/across the world? In America/where the number of overweight students has (A) decreased/increased,/parents are more interested in school lunch/than before. They don't want/their kids to eat fast food,/such as hamburgers, chips, or soda/for lunch. The Chinese school lunches are (B) hardly/usually provided by the school,/but some children go home for lunch. In India,/a food service worker called a *dabbawalla*/brings food to school. The workers pick up fresh meals/from students' homes/and (C) deliver/sell them to school. School lunches in West Africa/depend on foreign aid. The UN *World Food Program provides meals/for most school children.

*World Food Program 세계식량계획(UN의 식량문제 국제 협력체)

▼ KEY STRUCTURE

Do you ever wonder what children are **eating** ~?: 현재분사 eating은 '진행'의 의미를 나타내고, what 이하는 wonder의 목적어로 쓰인 절이다.

1 이 글의 내용과 일치하지 <u>않는</u> 것은? (내용 일치·불일치)

① 미국의 부모들은 학교 급식에 대해 전보다 관심이 늘었다.
② 미국의 부모들은 간편한 패스트푸드를 급식으로 선호한다.
③ 중국에서는 집에 가서 점심을 먹는 학생들도 있다.
④ 인도에서는 음식 배달부가 학교로 음식을 가지고 온다.
⑤ 서아프리카에서는 UN이 지원해 준 음식으로 급식을 한다.

2 이 글의 (A), (B), (C)에 들어갈 말이 알맞게 짝지어진 것은? (어휘 추론)

신경향

① decreased – hardly – deliver
② increased – usually – deliver
③ decreased – usually – sell
④ increased – usually – sell
⑤ increased – hardly – sell

wonder ____________
pick up 줍다, 수거하다

overweight 과체중의
fresh ____________

soda 탄산음료
depend on ~에 의존하다

provide ____________
aid 도움, 원조

≫ 정답과 해설 p.06

Try Unique Painting Tools

1' 40"
2-02
상 **중** 하
words 137

Think about painting. You're probably imagining an artist ⓐ<u>holding</u> a brush. But there are actually more interesting ways of painting a picture. Creative artists use all kinds of different painting tools. ▼One of the most unexpected tools is the human body. Finger painting is the oldest way of using the body to paint. For example, look at the very old paintings ⓑ<u>made</u> by cavemen. They were probably done by using fingers. These days, some famous artists also paint with their fingers. A French artist ⓒ<u>named</u> Yves Klein decided to ______________________. He hired models to be his "human paintbrushes". He had these models ⓓ<u>covering</u> in blue and gold paint. Then he asked them to rub themselves against the white canvas. Surprisingly, the paintings ⓔ<u>made</u> in this way became very famous and expensive.

▼ **KEY STRUCTURE**
One of the most **unexpected** tools is the human body.: 과거분사 unexpected는 '수동'의 의미를 나타내며 뒤에 나온 tools를 수식한다.

1 이 글의 빈칸에 들어갈 말로 알맞은 것은? (빈칸 추론)

① retire because of age
② sell one of his paintings
③ paint with his fingers
④ use more than just his fingers
⑤ buy the best paints and canvas

2 이 글의 ⓐ~ⓔ 중 어법상 <u>어색한</u> 것은? (어법성 판단)

① ⓐ
② ⓑ
③ ⓒ
④ ⓓ
⑤ ⓔ

tool ___________
hold ___________
unexpected 예상치 못한
caveman 원시인

hire ___________
rub ___________
canvas 캔버스
surprisingly 놀랍게도

Unique Travel Transportation

⏱ 3' 10"
🎧 2-03
상 중 하
words **191**

I'm Chris Kim and a world traveler.

When you travel, what kinds of transportation do you use? Buses, subways, trains, and taxies are the most popular forms of transportation. How about going from place to place in a unique way while abroad?

▼In Cambodia, you'll find an interesting train called the bamboo train. As its name suggests, it is made of bamboo. Although slow, it is one of the cheapest rides in the country. While ⓐ travel Peru, I explored Lake Titicaca on a boat ⓑ name *Barco de Totora*. It is a dragon-shaped boat made of *reed. It was an amazing experience. In Thailand, taking a ride in a *tuk-tuk* is a must. It is a kind of a small three-wheeled taxi. You can find them moving quickly around the streets of many cities in Thailand. Moreover, I remember a different kind of taxi that can be found in Cuba. Its name is *Coco Taxi* because the vehicle looks like the shell of a coconut. It is a bit noisy but cheaper than a regular taxi. Next time you visit Havana in Cuba, I recommend traveling the city in a *Coco Taxi*.

*reed 갈대

▼ **KEY STRUCTURE**
In Cambodia, you'll find an **interesting** train ~.: 현재분사는 수식하는 대상이 감정을 느끼는 존재가 아니라 감정을 유발하는 존재일 때 사용한다.

필리핀의
'지프니(jeepney)'

PLUS READING

지프니(jeepney)는 다양한 색과 장식으로 치장된 필리핀의 이색 교통수단입니다. 지프니는 제2차 세계대전이 끝난 후 미군이 남겨두고 간 군용 차량을 개조한 것인데요, 각 차량마다 개성이 다 다르답니다. 지프니는 정류장 없이 택시처럼 어디서나 타고 내릴 수 있는 게 특징이랍니다.

unique ____________   transportation ____________   abroad 해외에서
suggest 시사하다   be made of ~로 만들어지다   bamboo ____________

Main Idea

1 이 글의 중심 소재로 알맞은 것은? (소재 추론)

① 해외의 독특한 여행 교통수단
② 해외여행 유의 사항
③ 해외 교통수단의 오래된 역사
④ 각국의 교통과 관련된 직업
⑤ 대중교통과 대기 오염에 관한 연구

Detailed Information

2 이 글의 ⓐ와 ⓑ에 주어진 동사를 알맞은 형태로 고쳐 쓰시오. (어법성 판단)

ⓐ ________________   ⓑ ________________

3 이 글의 내용과 일치하지 <u>않는</u> 것은? (내용 일치·불일치)

① 대나무 기차는 캄보디아의 운송 수단 중 가장 저렴하다.
② *Barco de Totora*는 대나무로 만들어졌다.
③ 툭툭은 작은 바퀴 세 개가 달린 택시이다.
④ 쿠바의 코코 택시는 코코넛 껍질처럼 생겼다.
⑤ 쿠바의 코코 택시는 일반 택시보다 더 저렴하다.

4 이 글을 읽고, 다음 질문에 대한 답변을 찾아 영어로 쓰시오. (세부 내용 파악)

(서술형)

> What does *Barco de Totora* look like?

____

---

although 비록 ~하지만   **amazing** 놀라운   **must** 필수(품)   **wheeled** 바퀴가 달린
vehicle 차량, 운송 수단   **shell** __________   **noisy** __________   **recommend** __________

Different Ideas About Beauty

⏱ 3' 10"
🎧 2-04
상 중 하
words 176

▼Defining beauty is interesting because it is something seen differently in different times and places. For example, in the 19th century England, most women didn't like very strong men. Farming and factory work were ______ⓐ______ jobs requiring strong workers. Rich people looked down on the strong men doing these jobs. Rich men didn't do physical work. They read books and discussed business indoors. So, women usually thought strong and athletic men lacked style and grace. That's why weak and thin men were preferred and they were satisfied with their figure.

In some cultures, fat women are considered beautiful. One example is the Annang tribe of Nigeria. The women from rich families are fat because they can afford a lot of food. So, Annang men prefer big women. Rich Annang parents actually send their daughters to special fattening rooms. The girls in these places are fed a very fatty diet. They live there for about six months. Once they are big enough, they are ready to get married. The bridegroom hopes his bride is ______ⓑ______!

▼ **KEY STRUCTURE**

Defining beauty is **interesting** because it is something **seen** differently ~.: Defining beauty는 감정을 유발하는 것이므로 현재분사 interesting이 쓰였고, something은 '다르게 보이는 것'이므로 과거분사 seen이 쓰였다.

---

define 정의하다　　**look down on** ~을 무시하다　　**discuss** ____________　　**indoors** ____________
athletic 강건한　　**lack** ~이 없다, 결핍되다　　**grace** 품위　　**weak** ____________

Main Idea

1 **What is the main idea of this passage?**

① Women should be stronger than men.
② Athletic men don't match the standard of beauty.
③ Fat women are considered beautiful in some cultures.
④ Beauty is seen differently in different times and places.
⑤ Working-class men were popular in 19th century England.

Detailed Information

2 **Which is right for the blank ⓐ?**

① simple   ② free   ③ hard
④ quick   ⑤ exciting

3 **What can you guess from the Annang tribe?**

① Fat women usually don't get married.
② Most women try to lose weight.
③ Women prefer weak and thin men.
④ Women from poor families may not be fat.
⑤ All women live in special fattening rooms for six months.

4 **Which is right for the blank ⓑ?**

① getting thinner   ② taller than him
③ going on a diet   ④ going to be a vegetarian
⑤ as big as possible

---

figure 몸매   **afford** ____________   **fatten** 살찌우다   **fatty** 기름진
diet 음식물, 식이요법   **get married** 결혼하다   **bridegroom** ____________   **bride** ____________

01
Can you guess what a trouble tree is?

03
What is the meaning of the sentence, "Where is the god?"

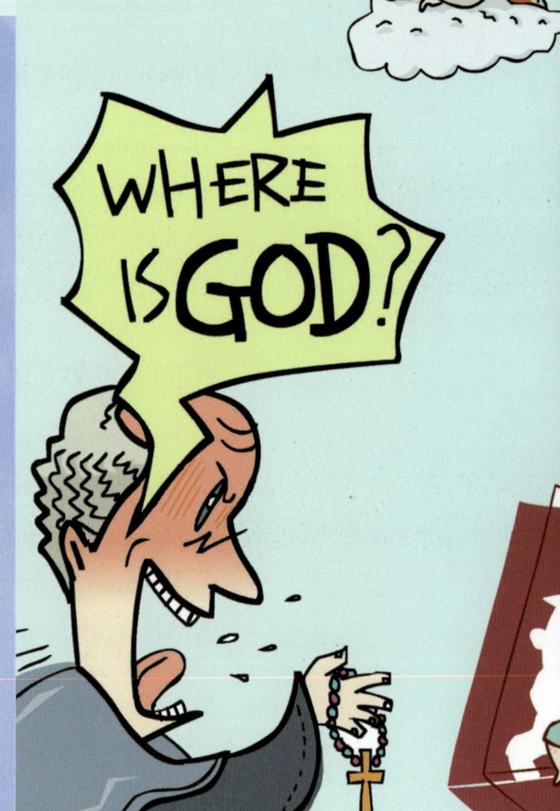

02
Have you heard of Lorenzo's Oil?

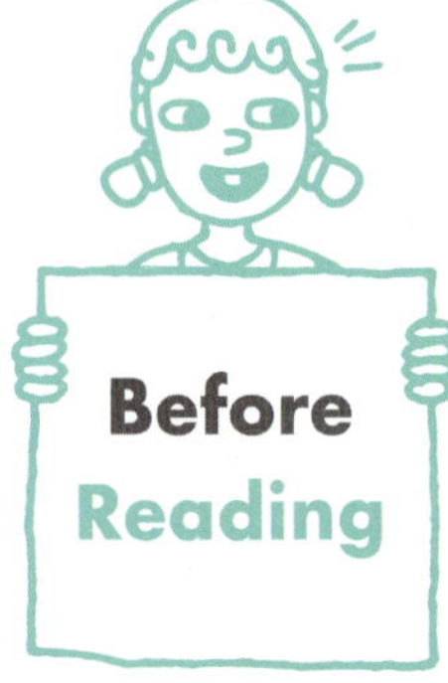

다음 구문 중 학습하고 싶은 것에 ✔ 표시 하세요.

Before Reading

- ☐ 평서문의 간접화법
- ☐ 의문사 없는 의문문의 간접화법
- ☐ 의문사 있는 의문문의 간접화법
- ☐ 명령문의 간접화법

04

Imagine you jump from the edge of the space!

다음 제목 중 알고 싶은 것에 ✔ 표시 하세요.

- ☐ **01** 걱정 나무
- ☐ **02** 로렌조 오일
- ☐ **03** 두 소년들
- ☐ **04** 우주에서 뛰어내린 사람

Before Reading

다양한 화법

Eric told me / that he loved me.

Eric은 나에게 말했다 / 그가 나를 사랑한다고

Point 문장 안에서 절이 의미하는 바를 파악하여 해석한다.

화법은 다른 사람의 말을 전달하는 표현 방법으로 다른 사람의 말을 그대로 전하는 직접화법과, 전달자의 입장으로 바꿔 전달하는 간접화법이 있다.

평서문 간접화법: 전달동사 say to는 tell로 바꾸고 " " 안의 말을 that절로 바꾼다.

Tom said to me, "I have to go to school." ▶ 직접화법

→ Tom **told** me / **that he had to** go to school. ▶ 간접화법

⇨ **직독직해[1]** --

▶ 직접화법을 간접화법으로 변환 시 동사의 시제를 일치시키고 인칭이나 지시대명사와 부사도 알맞게 바꿔야 한다.

의문사가 없는 의문문의 간접화법: 전달동사 say 또는 say to는 주로 ask로 바꾸고 " " 안의 말은 〈if(whether)+주어+동사〉의 순서로 나타낸다.

Kate said to me, "Can you ride a bike?" ▶ 직접화법

→ Kate **asked** me / **if(whether) I could ride** a bike. ▶ 간접화법

⇨ **직독직해[2]** --

의문사가 있는 의문문의 간접화법: 전달동사 say 또는 say to를 주로 ask로 바꾸고 " " 안의 말은 〈의문사+주어+동사〉의 순서로 나타낸다.

Mr. Brown said to Maria, "Where does she live?" ▶ 직접화법

→ Mr. Brown **asked** Maria / **where she lived.** ▶ 간접화법

⇨ **직독직해[3]** --

명령문의 간접화법: 명령문에 어울리는 전달동사와 함께 〈전달동사+목적어+to부정사〉의 어순으로 나타낸다.

I said to Erica, "Open the window." ▶ 직접화법

→ I **told** Erica / **to open** the window. ▶ 간접화법

⇨ **직독직해[4]** --

▶ 명령문의 간접화법은 주로 tell, order, ask, advise 등의 전달동사를 활용한다.

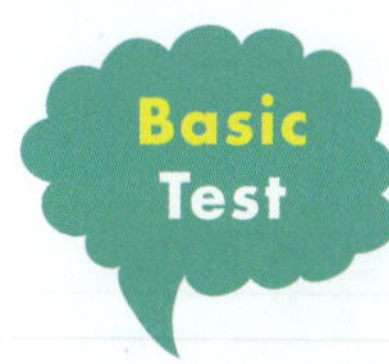

직독직해를 위한 어법 연습하기

간접화법은 직접화법으로 직접화법은 간접화법으로 바꿔 써 보세요.

1 John asked me whether I could give him a hand.

→ ____

2 Peter said, "I am watching a movie with Mina."

→ ____

3 I said to Lisa, "Clean your room."

→ ____

4 Ronald asked me where I bought my clothes.

→ ____

5 Linda said to Jinho, "When do you want to leave?"

→ ____

Preview Test

독해지문 직독직해로 적용하기

앞으로 익힐 독해 속에 포함된 문장입니다. 끊어 읽고 우리말 해석을 써 보세요.

01 I asked him, "What does the tree mean to you?" **p.32**

⇨ 직독직해 ____

02 Augusto asked himself whether he could let Lorenzo die without any effort. **p.33**

⇨ 직독직해 ____

03 The parents asked a minister in town what they should do. **p.34**

⇨ 직독직해 ____

04 He told us to go up really high to understand how small we are. **p.36**

⇨ 직독직해 ____

A Trouble Tree

끊어읽기를 하며, 직독직해를 해 보세요.

⏱ 1' 30"
🎧 3-01
상 중 하
words 135

On Monday,/the carpenter finished/a rough first day.
3 First,/he got a flat tire/while driving to my farm. Then/his electric saw stopped working/and his old truck refused to start. So,/I offered/to drive him home. He seemed to be in a bad mood. As he
6 walked up to his house,/he stopped briefly/in front of <u>a small tree</u>. He touched the tips of the branches/with his hands/and then opened the door. Surprisingly,/he became a totally different person. Smiling
9 brightly,/he hugged his children/and gave his wife a kiss. ▼I asked him,/"What does the tree mean/to you?" He said,/"Oh, it's my trouble tree. I always hang my worries/on that tree/whenever I come
12 home. In the morning/I pick them up again."

> ▼ **KEY STRUCTURE** --------------------------------
> I **asked** him, **"What does the tree mean to you?"**: 이 문장은 직접화법 구문으로, 간접화법인 I asked him what the tree meant to him.으로 바꿔 쓸 수 있다.

1 이 글의 밑줄 친 <u>a small tree</u>의 사용법으로 알맞은 것은? (세부 내용 파악)

① 가족의 소원을 적어서 걸어 둔다.　　② 일과 관련된 걱정거리를 걸어 둔다.
③ 집을 짓기 위한 목재로 사용한다.　　④ 내일 해야 할 일들을 써서 걸어 둔다.
⑤ 다른 사람이 집안을 들여다보는 것을 막는다.

2 이 글의 carpenter의 심경 변화로 알맞은 것은? (심경 추론)

① cheerful → regretful　　② worried → embarrassed
③ unhappy → bored　　④ angry → positive
⑤ relieved → nervous

---

carpenter ___________　　rough 혹독한, 고된　　flat tire 바람 빠진 타이어　　saw ___________
refuse ___________　　briefly 잠시　　tip 끝, 끝 부분　　branch 나뭇가지

Lorenzo's Oil

1' 40"
3-02
상 중 하
words 135

Augusto had a 5-year-old son, Lorenzo. One day, Lorenzo got sick with a disease called *ALD. Augusto said to doctors, "Can you cure my son?" All of the doctors said, "Nothing can be done about ALD. Lorenzo will die soon." But Augusto asked himself whether he could let Lorenzo die without any effort. He answered, "No! He is only 5 years old. I'm his father." To find a medicine, Augusto started to study ALD. Finally, he discovered a certain kind of oil and Lorenzo took it. It worked on him! Lorenzo was able to live much longer than everyone expected. He died at 30 years old in 2008 and Augusto died in 2013. The medicine has been named "Lorenzo's Oil" to remember the father's great love. Lorenzo's Oil is helpful for all ALD patients now.

*ALD 부신백질이영양증

> **▼ KEY STRUCTURE**
> But Augusto **asked** himself **whether he could let** Lorenzo die without any effort.: 접속사 whether와 간접의문문 어순을 이용한 의문사가 없는 의문문의 간접화법 구문으로, 직접화법 문장인 But Augusto said to himself, "Can I let Lorenzo die without any effort?"로 바꿀 수 있다.

1 이 글을 통해 답할 수 있는 질문이 **아닌** 것은? (세부 내용 파악)

① Was ALD easy to cure?
② What did Augusto do to save his son?
③ What worked on Lorenzo?
④ How old was Augusto when he passed away?
⑤ Why did people call the medicine Lorenzo's Oil?

2 이 글의 밑줄 친 문장을 간접화법으로 바꿔 쓸 때, 빈칸에 알맞은 말을 쓰시오. (어법성 판단)

(서술형)

Augusto asked doctors ______________________________________.

---

get sick 병에 걸리다	**disease** 질병	**cure** __________	**effort** __________
discover 발견하다	**certain** 어떤, 특정의	**work on** ~에 효과가 있다	**expect** __________

03 Two Little Boys

⏱ 3' 10"
🎧 3-03
상 중 하
words **174**

A couple had two bad little boys. They were 8 and 10 years old, and they got

3 into trouble a lot. If there was any trouble in their town, the two young boys were always there. ▼The parents asked a minister in town what they should do. They asked him for help because he helped bad

6 children become good. The minister agreed to speak with the boys, but he asked to see them one by one. The ⓐ8-year-old boy went to meet with him first. (A) The minister sat the boy down and asked

9 him ⓑsincerely, "Where is God?" (B) The boy did not answer. (C) So, the minister repeated the question in a louder voice, "Where is God?" (D) So the minister raised his voice even more and shook his finger in

12 front of the boy's face, "WHERE IS GOD?" (E) The boy jumped up and ran directly home. His older brother followed him and asked what happened. The younger brother replied, "We are in BIG trouble

15 this time. God is missing and people think we did it."

▼ **KEY STRUCTURE**
The parents **asked** a minister in town **what they should do**.:
의문사가 있는 의문문의 간접화법 구문으로 직접화법으로 고치면 The parents said to a minister in town, "What should we do?"가 된다.

couple 부부, 커플	**get into trouble** 말썽을 일으키다	**minister** _______	**agree** 동의하다
one by one 차례로	**repeat** 반복하다	**voice** _______	**raise** ~을 올리다

1 이 글의 분위기로 알맞은 것은? (분위기 추론)

① critical   ② informative
③ poetic   ④ humorous
⑤ romantic

Detailed Information

2 이 글의 (A) ~ (E) 중 다음 문장이 들어갈 곳으로 알맞은 것은? (글의 흐름)

> Again, the boy was quiet.

① (A)   ② (B)   ③ (C)
④ (D)   ⑤ (E)

3 이 글의 밑줄 친 ⓐ는 목사님의 질문인 "Where is God?"을 어떻게 이해했는가? (세부 내용 파악)

① God is in your mind.
② Please be a good boy.
③ You made God go missing.
④ Will you help me find God?
⑤ You have to believe in God.

4 이 글의 밑줄 친 ⓑ sincerely와 의미가 가장 가까운 것은? (어휘 추론)

① uselessly   ② seriously   ③ softly
④ continually   ⑤ happily

---

shake __________	jump up 뛰어오르다	directly 곧장	follow __________
happen 발생하다	reply 대답하다	be in trouble 곤경에 처하다	missing __________

A Space Jumper

⏱ 3' 20"
🎧 3-04
상 중 하
words 182

Have you ever dreamed of skydiving from the edge of space? Felix Baumgartner has. He finally made his dream come true. Born in Austria, Baumgartner imagined flying through the air when he was a child. He began skydiving at the age of 16. And he has set many records in the field of skydiving. Baumgartner set his most <u>significant</u> record on October 14, 2012. He jumped down from a small space capsule at the height of about 38.6 km. It was the highest skydiving ever. On that day, Baumgartner was pulled up to the second layer of Earth's atmosphere in a small space capsule carried by a large *helium balloon. Finally, he jumped down from the capsule wearing a spacesuit and helmet. After nine minutes, he touched down safely on the ground. He became the first human to travel faster than the speed of sound without a vehicle. Now, do you know what Baumgartner said? ▼He told us to go up really high to understand how small we are. ⓐHe also told us not to hesitate in making your dreams come true.

*helium balloon 헬륨 가스로 채운 기구

▼ **KEY STRUCTURE**

He **told** us **to go up** really high to understand how small we are.: 명령문의 간접화법을 직접화법으로 바꾸면 He said to us, "Go up really high to understand how small we are."이다.

드론 스카이다이빙

스카이다이버 잉거스 어그스트칸스(Ingus Augstkalns)는 라트비아의 드론 제조사가 개발한 대형 드론에 매달려 약 330m 고공까지 올라갔다가 낙하산을 이용해 안전하게 지상에 착륙했어요. 이 도전은 가까운 미래에 우리 드론 기술이 화재 등 재난이 발생했을 시 인명 구조에 활용될 수 있음을 입증해 보인 사례가 되었답니다.

edge 끝, 가장자리
field ＿＿＿＿＿＿＿＿＿

come true 실현되다
height ＿＿＿＿＿＿＿＿＿

record 기록
pull 끌어당기다

직독직해를 위한 어법 연습하기

괄호 안에서 알맞은 말을 고르세요.

1 Linda saw Jack (pay / to pay) with credit card.

2 Can you help me (washing / to wash) my dog?

3 Mary made him (clean / cleaning) the room.

4 I heard a baby (cried / crying) in the living room.

5 My father won't let me (is / be) alone.

6 Ian helped his mom (cook / cooking) dinner.

Preview Test

독해지문 직독직해로 적용하기

앞으로 익힐 독해 속에 포함된 문장입니다. 끊어 읽고 우리말 해석을 써 보세요.

01 They really make you feel cool and refreshed. **p.42**
⇨ 직독직해 ____

02 Only one *gimbap* can help them to feel full. **p.43**
⇨ 직독직해 ____

03 If these trends continue, we can expect to see **the growth rate of the** *dosirak* **market speed up.** **p.44**
⇨ 직독직해 ____

04 Have you seen someone making or eating *miyeokguk*? **p.46**
⇨ 직독직해 ____

Stay Cool on Hot Days

끊어읽기를 하며, 직독직해를 해 보세요.

⏱ 1' 50"
🎧 4-01
상 중 하
words **147**

Cold desserts are perfect / for hot summer days. ▼They really make / you / ⓐfeel cool and refreshed. In Korea, / we eat *patbingsu* / on hot days. It's a dessert / ⓑmade of crushed ice, red beans, chopped fruits, milk, and strawberry syrup. Koreans are not the only ones / ⓒwho love cold desserts. In Malaysia and Singapore, / you can find people / ⓓeating a similar cold dessert / named *Ais Kacang*. It means "bean ice" / in English. In India, / people eat *Kulfi*, / ⓔthat is made with milk, nuts, flour, and dried fruits. In the old days, / it was made with ice / from the mountains in the Himalayas. At that time, / it was enjoyed only / by royalty. In Mexico, / people enjoy eating *Paletas*, / which are made with fresh fruits. They are similar / to *popsicles. If you visit the city of Tocumbo in Mexico, / look for a statue of a huge *Paleta*. It greets visitors / there.

*popsicle 아이스캔디

---

1 이 글의 주제로 알맞은 것은? 〔주제 추론〕

① various cold desserts in the world
② the best foods for a cold
③ the history of ice cream
④ how to make cold desserts at home
⑤ health problems caused by cold foods

2 이 글의 ⓐ~ⓔ 중 어법상 어색한 것을 찾아 고쳐 쓰시오. 〔어법성 판단〕

(   ) ____________ → ____________

---

refreshed 상쾌한   crushed 분쇄된   red bean 팥   chopped (음식 재료를) 썬[다진]
similar ____________   flour ____________   royalty 왕족   statue ____________

Don't Skip Breakfast!

1' 55"
4-02
상 중 하
words 138

Today, a busy life makes more people eat out for breakfast than before. As a result, the number of new breakfast options is increasing rapidly.

At fast food restaurants In 2013, a new morning combination set menu came out. This is very popular for two reasons: it is a hot meal for early birds and is sold at a low price for young people.

At major supermarkets Lately, the number of "*home meal replacements" has been growing! They are not exactly homemade foods, but working moms and office workers welcome them. As for healthy food, several sorts of organic cereals and powder made of mixed grains are found at many supermarkets.

At convenience stores Super triangular *gimbaps* catch consumers' eyes. They are larger than the earlier version by 36%. Only one *gimbap* can help them to feel full.

*home meal replacement 가정식 대체식품

> **▼ KEY STRUCTURE**
> Only one *gimbap* can **help them to feel** full.: 5형식 문장으로 동사 help는 목적격보어 자리에 동사원형 또는 to부정사가 둘 다 올 수 있다.

1 이 글의 종류로 알맞은 것은? (글의 종류)

① recipe ② article ③ diary
④ travel essay ⑤ science report

2 이 글의 내용과 일치하지 <u>않는</u> 것은? (내용 일치·불일치)

① 최근에 많은 사람들은 아침 식사를 밖에서 사 먹는다.
② 패스트푸드점의 모닝 콤보 세트 메뉴는 저렴한 가격으로 판매된다.
③ 대형 슈퍼마켓의 가정식 대체식품은 실제로 집에서 만든 음식이다.
④ 유기농 시리얼과 곡물 선식은 아침 식사로 먹는 건강식이다.
⑤ 슈퍼 삼각 김밥 하나만 먹어도 포만감을 느낄 수 있다.

---

combination 조합, 결합
organic ____________
come out 출시되다
mixed 혼합된
early bird 일찍 일어나는 사람
grain ____________
homemade 집에서 만든
triangular 삼각형의

The Growth of *Dosirak* Market

⏱ 3' 10"
🎧 4-03
상 중 하
words 194

In Korea, the *dosirak* market is growing rapidly. Recently, the sales of *dosirak* at convenience stores increased by over 50 percent on average, as compared to the previous year. A *dosirak* is a box lunch, and you can easily find it for sale. Convenience stores on every street corner ⓐ carries a variety of box lunches. The growth of the *dosirak* market ⓑ is directly related to the increase of single-person households. The proportion of single-person households is now over 26 percent and still growing. Especially, customers in their 20s and 30s show a high satisfaction with the cheap price of *dosirak*. A *dosirak* is not a new concept in Korea. *Dosiraks* ⓒ have taken up space in convenience stores for a long time. But they have recently changed. They used to be relatively low-quality meals for quick lunches. However, today's *dosisaks* are healthy and diverse options are offered at reasonable prices. Some *dosiraks* offer a taste of ⓓ as many as 11 side dishes. Another secret of their success is ⓔ that they offer the feeling of having home-cooked meals. ▼If these trends continue, we can expect to see the growth rate of the *dosirak* market speed up.

혼밥족

1인 및 맞벌이 가구의 증가와 함께 혼자서 간단히 식사를 하는 사람이 늘어나고 있는데, 이들을 '혼밥족(혼자 밥 먹는 사람들)'이라는 신조어로 불러요. 혼밥족들은 간편하고 빠르게 먹을 수 있는 음식을 선호하는데, 그 수요에 따라 혼밥족들을 위한 식품과 식재료를 판매하는 오프라인 시장뿐만 아니라 온라인 쇼핑몰의 시장도 매년 급성장하고 있답니다.

▼ **KEY STRUCTURE**

If ~, we can expect to **see the growth rate of the *dosirak* market speed up.**: 〈지각동사＋목적어＋목적격보어(동사원형)〉의 구조가 to부정사구에 포함된 문장으로, 지각동사의 목적격보어로 동사원형이 쓰였다.

growth 성장	rapidly 빠르게	sale 판매
convenience store 편의점	increase _______	a variety of _______

» 정답과 해설 p.16

Main Idea

1 이 글의 주제로 알맞은 것은? 〔주제 추론〕

① the necessity of eating home-cooked meals
② the influences of low-quality meals on health
③ the introduction of a new menu for *dosirak*
④ secrets of the popularity of Korean food
⑤ reasons why the *dosirak* market is growing in Korea

Detailed Information

2 이 글의 ⓐ~ⓔ 중 어법상 어색한 것을 찾아 고쳐 쓰시오. 〔어법성 판단〕

(   ) _________________ → _________________

3 이 글을 읽고, 다음 질문에 대한 답변을 찾아 완성하시오. 〔세부 내용 파악〕

> What is the main difference between today's *dosiraks* and the previous ones?

→ Today's *dosiraks* are healthy and _____________ options are offered while the previous ones were relatively _____________ meals for quick lunches.

4 이 글에서 도시락 시장의 성장과 관련된 요인으로 언급되지 <u>않은</u> 것은? (2개) 〔세부 내용 파악〕

① 편의점의 다양화　　② 건강에 대한 인식 변화　　③ 1인 가구의 증가
④ 저렴한 가격　　⑤ 메뉴의 다양성 증가

---

proportion 비율　　　　take up space 자리를 차지하다　　relatively _____________　　diverse 다양한
reasonable _____________　　side dish 밑반찬　　　　trend _____________　　growth rate 성장률

Let's Make *Miyeokguk!*

[A] ▼Have you seen someone making or eating *miyeokguk*? ① This soup has ⓐspecial meaning for Koreans. In the Korean culture, mothers traditionally eat this soup for several days after they give birth. ② It is also usually the soup that Koreans eat to celebrate birthdays.

[B] Now you know what *miyeokguk* is. Then how about making ③it yourself? Let me tell you about how to make it. First, put the *miyeok* in water to soften it. When ④it becomes soft, take it out and cut it into pieces. After that, it's time to heat up a pot. Add some chopped beef with a little bit of sesame oil, soy sauce, and salt, and cook it for 1 minute. Next put the *miyeok* and 1 spoon of soy sauce into the pot and cook it for 1 more minute. Remember to stir it often. After that, pour in 6 cups of water and boil it. Then you can reduce the heat. Lastly, cook it for 20 minutes, and add some salt. That's all. Isn't it simple? Now serve ⑤it to your family or friends. I'm sure you'll see them enjoy it very much.

▼ **KEY STRUCTURE**

Have you **seen someone making** or eating *miyeokguk*?: 지각동사를 사용한 5형식 문장으로, 진행의 의미를 강조할 때는 목적격보어 자리에 현재분사가 쓰이기도 한다.

traditionally ____________   give birth 출산하다   soften 부드럽게 하다
heat up 데우다, 가열하다   pot 냄비   add 첨가하다

Main Idea

1 **What is the best topic of the passage [B]?**

① some kinds of healthy food
② the origin of *miyeokguk*
③ benefits of Korean traditional food
④ how to make *miyeokguk*
⑤ the meaning of *miyeokguk* to Koreans

Detailed Information

2 **Which is NOT true about *miyeokguk*?**

① Koreans feel it is a special meal to them.
② You should cut *miyeok* into pieces before it becomes soft.
③ Some sesame oil is needed for it.
④ You need to add some salt in the last step.
⑤ It's not difficult to make it.

3 **Among ①~⑤, which does NOT mean *miyeokguk*?**

①   ②   ③   ④   ⑤

4 **What does the underlined ⓐ mean? Write two things in Korean.**

• ____

• ____

beef _____________	sesame oil 참기름	soy sauce 간장	stir 젓다
pour _____________	boil 끓이다	reduce _____________	serve 제공하다

01
Why don't you travel to tropical islands?

03
What can we see in Chicago?

02
What can you advise to solo travelers?

다음 구문 중 학습하고 싶은 것에 ✔ 표시 하세요.

☐ 현재완료 1(계속 / 완료)

☐ 현재완료 2(경험 / 결과)

☐ 과거완료

05

Travel

04

It is important to have a dream.

다음 제목 중 알고 싶은 것에 ✔ 표시 하세요.

- ☐ 01 열대 섬 관광
- ☐ 02 혼자 여행하는 사람들을 위한 조언
- ☐ 03 시카고에서의 신나는 하루
- ☐ 04 나의 꿈

Before Reading

완료시제의 이해

When I returned, / he **had** already **gone** to bed.

내가 돌아왔을 때 / 그는 이미 잠자리에 들어 있었다

Point 현재, 과거시제와 각각의 완료시제의 시간 차이에 대해 생각하며 해석한다.

완료시제는 어떤 사건의 시점이 다른 시점보다 앞서 있음을 나타낼 때 사용하며 현재완료, 과거완료가 있다.

현재완료(계속 / 완료): ⟨have + p.p.⟩의 형태로 '~해오고 있다'의 뜻으로 과거에 시작된 동작이나 상태가 현재까지도 계속될 때 사용하거나 '(지금 막) ~했다'의 뜻으로 과거에 일어난 일이 완료되었을 때 쓴다.

[계속] Susan **has lived** / in Canada / since 2015.

⇨ 직독직해 [1] ____

[완료] Jack **has finished** / his homework.

⇨ 직독직해 [2] ____

현재완료(경험 / 결과): ⟨have + p.p.⟩의 형태로 '~한 적이 있다'의 뜻으로 경험을 나타낼 때 사용하거나 '~해 버렸다'의 뜻으로 과거의 일로 현재의 결과가 나온 경우에 쓴다.

[경험] My brother **has been** / to Europe.

⇨ 직독직해 [3] ____

[결과] I **have lost** / my bag.

⇨ 직독직해 [4] ____

과거완료: ⟨had + p.p.⟩의 형태로 과거의 어느 시점보다 더 먼저 발생한 동작이나 상태를 나타낼 때 사용한다.

Mark **had** never **eaten** / hamburgers / until he was 10 years old.

⇨ 직독직해 [5] ____

They **had gone** already / when Tom arrived.

⇨ 직독직해 [6] ____

» 정답과 해설 p.18

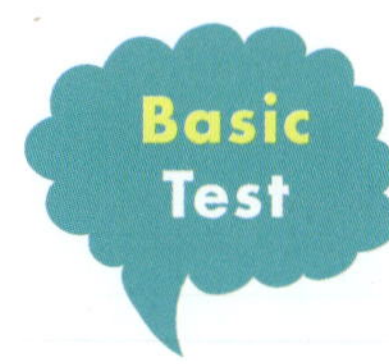

직독직해를 위한 어법 연습하기

밑줄 친 부분을 알맞은 형태로 고치세요.

1 Minho and Jihun have learn Chinese for 5 years. → ....

2 Mr. Brown has cooking chicken soup since 10 a.m. → ....

3 Ruth have knew the truth for 3 years. → ....

4 Yuri and Eric have be to the city before. → ....

5 Matt said that he has never seen Ann before. → ....

6 Cathy have lived there for 2 years when she was 10 years old.

→ ....

독해지문 직독직해로 적용하기

앞으로 익힐 독해 속에 포함된 문장입니다. 끊어 읽고 우리말 해석을 써 보세요.

01 Have you had cold weather since last winter? **p.52**
⇨ 직독직해 ....

02 I have heard from a tour guide that he had barely seen so many solo travelers before. **p.53**
⇨ 직독직해 ....

03 On the previous day, we had visited so many places. **p.54**
⇨ 직독직해 ....

04 She had started to tour around the world before she was 19. **p.56**
⇨ 직독직해 ....

Tropical Islands Tours

끊어읽기를 하며, 직독직해를 해 보세요.

⏱ 1' 25"
🎧 5-01
상 중 **하**
words **116**

▼Have you had cold weather / since last winter? Then you should call *Paradise Travel*. We offer wonderful
3 tours / to beautiful areas. If you join our popular tours, / you can see lovely tropical islands / like Bali, Phuket, and the Maldives. It's a great way / to relax. You can lie on the beach / and enjoy the sun.

6 • **Duration:** 4 days 3 nights

• **Hotel:** five-star hotels / with great swimming pools and comfortable rooms

9 • **Activities:** scuba diving, sailing, and nature walking

• **Price:** $500 (including a hotel bill for 3 nights, American breakfast, equipment fee)

12 Call us at 636-0000 / to reserve a *Paradise Travel* tour. If you want to know more information, / please visit *www.paradisetravel.com*. It will be a great decision!

▼ **KEY STRUCTURE**

Have you **had** cold weather since last winter?: 현재완료 구문으로 '계속'의 의미를 나타낸다. last winter라는 시점 앞에 since가 쓰여 '지난겨울부터 쭉'의 의미를 나타낸다.

---

1 이 글을 읽고 Tropical Islands Tours에 대해 알 수 <u>없는</u> 것은? (세부 내용 파악)

① 여행 기간   ② 숙박 시설   ③ 여가 활동
④ 항공권 가격   ⑤ 연락처

2 이 글의 밑줄 친 <u>reserve</u>와 의미가 가장 가까운 것은? (어휘 추론)

① recommend   ② cancel   ③ book
④ introduce   ⑤ advertise

---

tropical 열대의　　　　offer ____________　　　　relax 안정을 취하다, 쉬다　　　lie 눕다
comfortable ____________　　sailing 요트 타기　　　equipment ____________　　decision 결정

　　　　　　　　　　　　　　　　　　》 정답과 해설 p.18

Tips for Solo Travelers

⏱ 1' 30"
🎧 5-02
상 중 하
words 155

▼I have heard from a tour guide that he had barely seen so many solo travelers before. But not now. Why? With the help of Internet, people can easily get information about the parts of the unknown world to them. Here are some tips for solo travelers. First, keep in touch with your friends and family by e-mail, text, social media or phone so they can lend a hand if needed. Second, don't be afraid to let plans change. Solo travelers don't have to worry about someone else's desires. Some of the best travel stories come from unexpected adventures and last-minute decisions to go somewhere new. Be brave! Third, keep your most important things in one place. Then you can find them easily when you need them. Last but not least, open up to others. If you smile and talk to others first, you will learn a lot from these strangers in a strange land.

▼ **KEY STRUCTURE**
I **have heard** from a tour guide that ~.: 현재완료 시제를 이용하여 '경험'의 의미를 나타낸다.

1 이 글의 밑줄 친 **some tips**의 내용과 일치하지 <u>않는</u> 것은? (내용 일치·불일치)

① 친구들과 지속적으로 연락하라.　　② 일정 변경을 두려워하지 마라.
③ 중요한 물건은 한 곳에 보관하라.　　④ 물과 약간의 간식을 휴대하라.
⑤ 다른 사람들에게 마음을 열어라.

2 이 글을 쓴 목적으로 알맞은 것은? (목적 추론)

① to advise　　② to complain　　③ to appreciate
④ to advertise　　⑤ to criticize

---

solo ____________　　barely 거의 ~ 아닌　　unknown ____________　　lend a hand 도움을 주다
desire ____________　　com from ~에서 나오다　　adventure 모험　　stranger ____________

An Exciting Day in Chicago

⏱ 3' 00"
🎧 5-03
상 중 하
words **190**

Saturday was my second day in Chicago. I had to get up early even though I was very tired. ▼On the previous day, we had visited so many places. I went to Northerly Island Park, the Willis Tower, etc. Willis Tower, the second highest building in the U.S., was especially an exciting place to me. I was so scared ___ⓐ___ excited while walking on the sky deck.

This morning I went to Millennium Park after finishing my breakfast. I saw 'The Bean' there. It was a huge bean-shaped sculpture. After that, I went to the Navy Pier. It is a large pier on Lake Michigan. There were so many must-see places, such as the Ferris Wheel, Shedd Aquarium, the Michigan Museum, and so on. When leaving the Navy Pier, I felt hungry. Thanks to my smartphone, I was able to find a popular restaurant. I tried a Chicago deep-dish pizza for lunch. It was the best pizza I have ever eaten. After lunch, I enjoyed the boat tour of the Chicago River. On the boat, I could not only enjoy the view of Chicago ___ⓑ___ also learn about the city itself.

미국에서 세 번째로 큰 도시, 시카고

PLUS READING

시카고는 가장 미국적인 도시이자 현대 건축물로 유명한 곳이기도 합니다. 1871년 시카고 대화재로 도시의 3분의 1이 불에 탄 이후 재건 과정에서 지금과 같은 멋지고 개성 있는 현대 건축물들이 들어섰습니다. 그래서 시카고 여행에서는 배를 타고 시카고를 대표하는 50여 개의 건물에 대한 안내를 받을 수 있는 '건축물 투어 크루즈'를 해 보는 것을 추천한답니다.

▼ **KEY STRUCTURE**

On the previous day, we **had visited** so many places.: 과거 시점 이전에 일어난 일을 나타내므로 과거완료(대과거)시제가 쓰였다.

especially 특히
bean 콩

scared 겁먹은, 무서워하는
huge ___________

deck 갑판
sculpture 조형물, 조각상

Main Idea

1 이 글의 종류로 알맞은 것은? 〔글의 종류〕

① 논설문　　　　② 광고문　　　　③ 기행문
④ 희곡　　　　　⑤ 전기문

Detailed Information

2 이 글의 내용과 일치하지 <u>않는</u> 것은? 〔내용 일치·불일치〕

① 글쓴이는 피곤했지만 일찍 일어났다.
② 글쓴이는 시카고에서의 첫째 날에 Willis Tower에 갔다.
③ Navy Pier는 미시간 호수에 있다.
④ Navy Pier에는 콩 모양의 조형물이 있다.
⑤ 글쓴이는 스마트폰으로 유명한 식당을 찾을 수 있었다.

3 이 글의 빈칸 ⓐ, ⓑ에 공통으로 들어갈 말로 알맞은 것은? 〔빈칸 추론〕

① or　　　　　　② so　　　　　　③ for
④ and　　　　　⑤ but

4 이 글의 밑줄 친 문장에서 어법상 <u>어색한</u> 부분을 고쳐 문장을 다시 쓰시오. 〔어법성 판단〕

(서술형) → ____

---

pier 부두　　　　　　　lake ____________　　　　must-see 꼭 봐야 할　　　　aquarium ____________
and so on 기타 등등　　be able to ~을 할 수 있다　　deep-dish (피자가) 두꺼운　　view ____________

My Dream

⏱ 3' 10"
🎧 5-04
상 중 하
words **190**

(A) Like my cousin, I want to learn a lot from the experience. By the time I
3 return, I will have seen many different cultures. I think the experience will have changed me. It will be a great <u>opportunity</u> for me.

6 (B) I have a dream. After I finish high school, I want to travel around the world for a year. I will buy a "round-the-world" ticket. It's a special ticket that lets me visit many places. By the end of the trip, I
9 will have visited 5 continents. I will have stayed in over 20 different countries.

(C) I first got the idea from my cousin, Sarah. ▼She had started to
12 tour around the world before she was 19. She visited many exciting places. She saw the *Taj Mahal* in India, and enjoyed shopping in markets for tourists. She traveled through Europe by train, so she
15 could take pictures of lots of beautiful landscapes. She stayed in guest houses around the world and spent some time with new people. She also volunteered to teach children at an orphanage in Kenya. Through
18 these experiences, she told me that she could learn a lot.

▼ **KEY STRUCTURE**

She **had started** to tour around the world before she was 19.: 과거완료 시제로 '그녀가 19살 이었을 때' 보다 더 먼저 발생한 일을 나타내고 있다.

---

cousin 사촌
opportunity _____________

experience 경험; 경험하다
round-the-world 세계 일주(의)

return _____________
ticket 티켓, 표

culture 문화
continent _____________

직독직해를 위한 어법 연습하기

우리말과 같도록 괄호 안의 말을 배열하여 문장을 완성하세요.

1 이 공을 네가 가능한 멀리 던져라. (as / far / throw / can / the ball / as / you)

→ ____

2 Aron은 Tim만큼 무게가 나가지 않는다. (heavy / Aron / not / as / is / Tim / as)

→ ____

3 더 많이 베풀면 베풀수록 더 많이 되돌려 받는다. (the / give / you / more / the / you / more / get back)

→ ____

4 낮 시간이 점점 더 길어진다. (the / and / longer / daytime / grows / longer)

→ ____

Preview Test

독해지문 직독직해로 적용하기

앞으로 익힐 독해 속에 포함된 문장입니다. 끊어 읽고 우리말 해석을 써 보세요.

01 The architect of Seokguram was carving the central ceiling stone as carefully as he could. **p.62**

⇨ 직독직해 ____

02 The @ symbol, before the introduction of e-mail, was not as popular as it is these days. **p.63**

⇨ 직독직해 ____

03 It led popcorn to become more and more popular. **p.64**

⇨ 직독직해 ____

04 Making symbols for everything got harder and harder as time passed. **p.66**

⇨ 직독직해 ____

A National Treasure, Seokguram

끊어읽기를 하며, 직독직해를 해 보세요.

⏱ 1′ 35″
🎧 6-01
상 중 하
words 142

Seokguram is the 24th national treasure/in Korea. There is an interesting legend/about Seokguram. ▼The architect of Seokguram was carving/the central ceiling stone/as carefully as he could. Suddenly, it cracked/before his eyes/and he fell down. In a dream,/he saw gods/descending from heaven/and they repaired the ceiling stone. When he awoke,/he found the ceiling surface fixed/but for the faint traces of cracks. Small cracks/on the ceiling stone/can still be seen today. Whether the legend is true or not,/Seokguram had been abandoned/for centuries/until it was rediscovered/in 1909. A local postman was/in a rainstorm,/so he found shelter/in the nearest cave. He lit a candle/in the dark/and found a large stone *Buddha! Later,/he brought others/to show the cave/and it became __________.

*Buddha 불상

> **▼ KEY STRUCTURE**
> The architect of Seokguram ~ **as carefully as he could.**: 〈as+원급+as+주어+can(could)〉는 '가능한 ~한(하게)'이라는 뜻으로 〈as+원급+as possible〉과 바꿔 쓸 수 있다.

---

1 이 글의 내용과 일치하지 <u>않는</u> 것은? 〔내용 일치·불일치〕

① 석굴암은 한국의 국보이다.
② 석굴암의 천장에 관련된 전설이 전해 내려온다.
③ 석굴암의 천장에는 균열한 부분의 자국이 남아 있다.
④ 석굴암은 여러 번의 재건 작업을 통해 완성되었다.
⑤ 석굴암을 1909년에 재발견한 것은 집배원이다.

2 이 글의 빈칸에 들어갈 말로 알맞은 것은? 〔빈칸 추론〕

① famous　　② luxurious　　③ ordinary
④ normal　　⑤ expensive

| national treasure 국보 | legend 전설 | architect __________ | carve 조각하다 |
| crack 갈라지다; 금 | descend __________ | faint 희미한 | trace __________ |

02 The @ Symbol

⏱ 1' 35"
🎧 6-02
상 중 하
words 139

▼The @ symbol, before the introduction of e-mail, was not as popular as it is these days. It was just used to show the cost or weight of something. For example, if you bought 10 apples, you might write it as 10 apples @ $1.10 each. But that changed when Ray Tomlinson created the world's first e-mail system. Since then, the @ symbol has been used more than ever. <u>Surprisingly, however, the symbol's name is not as official as we think.</u> Actually, there is no official name for the sign. There are dozens of strange names for it. For instance, it is called a monkey's tail by Germans. In China, they call it a mouse. In France, people see a snail. It is called the "meow" in Finland, for they think of it as a cat that curls up.

▼ KEY STRUCTURE

The @ symbol, ~, was **not as popular as** it is these days.: 〈not+as+원급+as〉는 '~만큼 …하지 않은(않게)'의 뜻으로 〈not+so+원급+as〉로 바꿔 쓸 수 있다.

---

1 이 글에서 @의 다양한 명칭의 예로 언급되지 않은 것은? （세부 내용 파악）

① 원숭이 꼬리 　　② 쥐 　　③ 달팽이
④ 코끼리 코 　　⑤ 웅크린 고양이

2 이 글의 밑줄 친 부분을 우리말로 해석하시오. （어법상 판단）

（서술형） → ________________________________

---

symbol 상징, 기호 　　**official** __________ 　　**sign** 기호 　　**dozens of** 수많은
tail __________ 　　**snail** 달팽이 　　**meow** (고양이 울음소리) 야옹 　　**curl up** (몸을) 웅크리다

Where Did Popcorn Come From?

2' 50"
6-03
상 중 하
words 182

(A) Do you know the history of popcorn? Popcorn was Native Americans' local food and used for decoration. They made it a long time ago. Native Americans knew there were three kinds of corn. These were sweet corn for eating, corn for animal feed, and corn for popping. The following is how Native Americans introduced corn to the first settlers, *Pilgrims who came to America in 1620.

(B) Soon movie theaters started to sell popcorn to make more money. ▼It led popcorn to become more and more popular. Today Americans still enjoy popcorn at the movies.

(C) One year after they came to America, the Pilgrims had a Thanksgiving dinner. They invited some Native Americans to the dinner. The Native Americans brought food with them and one of them brought popcorn. The Pilgrims liked the taste of popcorn, so they learned how to make popcorn from the Native Americans.

(D) Since then, Americans have continued to make popcorn at home. But, in 1945, there was a new machine that changed the history of popcorn. This electric machine enabled people to make popcorn outside the home.

*Pilgrim 1620년 아메리카 대륙에 건너가 정착한 영국 청교도단

▼ **KEY STRUCTURE**

It led popcorn to become **more and more popular.**: 〈비교급＋and＋비교급〉은 '점점 더 ~한(하게)'이라는 뜻의 비교 구문으로 상태 변화를 표현한다.

Native American 아메리카 원주민
pop 튀기다

local 지역의, 현지의
following 다음에 언급되는 것

decoration ____________
introduce ____________

Main Idea

1 이 글의 성격으로 알맞은 것은? 분위기 추론

① humorous ② poetic ③ scientific
④ romantic ⑤ informative

Detailed Information

2 이 글의 단락 (A)에 이어질 순서로 알맞은 것은? 글의 흐름

① (B) – (C) – (D) ② (B) – (D) – (C)
③ (C) – (D) – (B) ④ (D) – (B) – (C)
⑤ (D) – (C) – (B)

3 이 글에서 1945년 즈음 팝콘의 역사에 변화를 가져온 것으로 알맞은 것은? 세부 내용 파악

① corn for popping ② settlers in America
③ an electric popcorn machine ④ a lot of theaters
⑤ three kinds of corn

4 이 글의 내용을 바르게 이해한 아이들로 알맞게 짝지어진 것은? 세부 내용 파악

• 소미: 팝콘은 원주민들이 추수감사절 만찬에 가지고 와서 청교도들에게 알려졌대.

• 다혜: 청교도들은 옥수수로 만든 음식을 즐겨 먹었다고 해.

• 병호: 영화관에서는 더 많은 돈을 벌기 위해 팝콘을 팔기 시작했지.

• 석재: 오늘날에는 팝콘보다는 다른 간식들이 더 인기가 많아.

① 소미, 다혜 ② 소미, 병호 ③ 다혜, 병호
④ 다혜, 석재 ⑤ 소미, 석재

---

settler ＿＿＿＿＿＿＿ make money 돈을 벌다 Thanksgiving 추수감사절 continue 계속하다
machine ＿＿＿＿＿＿＿ electric ＿＿＿＿＿＿＿ enable 가능하게 하다 outside ~ 밖에서

The Origin of the Alphabet

3′ 00″
6-04
상 중 하
words 190

How did we get the modern alphabet? It took thousands of years, and as much effort as any other invention. The first people to write things down carved symbols onto rocks or shells. These symbols usually <u>represented</u> people or things. ________________, a drawing of a person might mean a person. People who lived a long time ago led simple lives. They used very easy symbols because they used them only to express their simple needs. One of the most basic needs was food. To tell each other about how to hunt animals or where to find food, people drew on cave walls. Soon, people could grow their own food. So, they needed to use more symbols for more than just people, places, and things. ▼Making symbols for everything got harder and harder as time passed. (A) <u>So, many people started to feel the need to invent a set of letters, an alphabet.</u> (B) <u>Egyptians tried to make one and did it.</u> (C) <u>And it became common in Egypt.</u> (D) <u>There are many historical sites in Egypt.</u> (E) <u>Other countries that traded with or fought against Egypt knew this alphabet, and it was spread.</u>

▼ **KEY STRUCTURE**

Making symbols for everything got **harder and harder** as time passed.: 〈비교급＋and＋비교급〉은 '점점 더 ~한'이라는 뜻으로 주로 get, become, grow 등의 동사와 함께 쓰인다.

그림문자

사물의 형태를 본떠 만든 상형문자를 인류의 가장 오래된 문자로 보지만, 그림문자는 상형문자 앞 단계의 것으로 볼 수 있어요. 이런 그림문자는 북아메리카의 인디언들 사이에서 널리 사용되어 동물의 껍질, 뼈, 뿔, 바위 등에 조각하거나 그려졌답니다.

origin ____________	alphabet 알파벳	modern 현대의
write ~ down ~을 적다	carved 조각된	mean ____________

Main Idea

1 What kind of writing is this?

① travel plan
② travel diary
③ tips for hotel reservation
④ historical article
⑤ guide to Egypt

Detailed Information

2 What is the closest meaning of <u>represented</u>?

① expressed   ② changed   ③ introduced
④ found   ⑤ thought

3 Which is right for the blank?

① Nevertheless   ② For instance   ③ However
④ Moreover   ⑤ On the contrary

4 Which sentence is NOT needed in the passage?

① (A)   ② (B)   ③ (C)
④ (D)   ⑤ (E)

express ____________   basic 기본적인   hunt 사냥하다   cave 동굴
common 흔한   site ____________   trade ____________   spread 퍼지다

01

What are three things that represent Jejudo?

03

Here are tips for your part-time job.

02

What's good about a mobile payment system?

다음 구문 중 학습하고 싶은 것에 ✔ 표시 하세요.

- ☐ 관계대명사의 격
- ☐ 관계대명사의 용법
- ☐ 관계대명사 what
- ☐ 전치사 + 관계대명사

04

You are beautiful
just the way you are.

다음 제목 중 알고 싶은 것에 ✔ 표시 하세요.

- ☐ **01** 무형 문화유산 '해녀'
- ☐ **02** 현금이 필요 없는 미래
- ☐ **03** 부당한 대우를 받는 청소년 근로자들
- ☐ **04** 수정된 모델의 이미지

관계대명사

He is reading a book / which I like.

그는 책을 읽고 있다　　　　　/　　　내가 좋아하는

Point　선행사와 관계대명사의 격을 확인하며 해석한다.

관계대명사는 두 문장을 연결하는 접속사와 대명사의 역할을 하며 형용사절을 이끈다.

🌿 **관계대명사의 격**: 선행사와 격에 따라 who, which, whose, whom, that을 쓴다.

[주격] Look at the man / **who** is playing soccer.
⇨ **직독직해 1** ____

[소유격] I met a boy / **whose** name is Robert.
⇨ **직독직해 2** ____

[목적격] This is the bike / **that**[**which**] I bought yesterday.
⇨ **직독직해 3** ____

🌿 **관계대명사의 용법**: 선행사를 수식할 때는 관계대명사의 제한적 용법으로, 보충 설명을 할 때는 계속적 용법
으로 나타낸다.

[제한적 용법] Nuri has a brother / **who** is a middle school student.
⇨ **직독직해 4** ____

[계속적 용법] Nuri has a brother, / **who** is a middle school student.
　　　　　　　　　　　　　　▶ 콤마 + 관계대명사
⇨ **직독직해 5** ____

cf. 관계대명사 that 앞에는 콤마를 쓸 수 없다.

🌿 **관계대명사 what**: 선행사를 포함할 때 관계대명사 what을 쓰며 the thing(s) that의 의미를 지닌다.

Tell me / **what** you want to do.
⇨ **직독직해 6** ____

🌿 **전치사 + 관계대명사**: 관계대명사가 전치사의 목적어일 때 관계대명사 앞에 전치사가 올 수 있다.

Seoul is the city / **in which** I was born.
⇨ **직독직해 7** ____

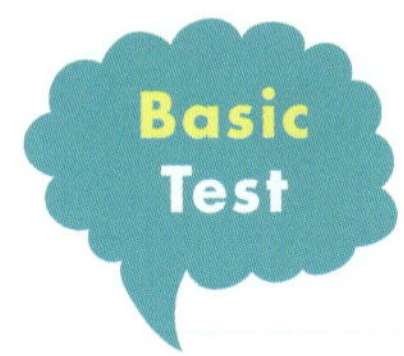

직독직해를 위한 어법 연습하기

괄호 안에서 알맞은 것을 고르세요.

1 The girl (who / whom) is next to Matt is my best friend.

2 Tony knows the man (who / whose) job is a doctor.

3 The policeman found (which / what) Serena had lost.

4 I met the boy (of whom / of which) you are speaking.

5 Susan borrowed the book (in which / what) she is interested.

6 Piona has a sister, (that / who) is an actress.

독해지문 직독직해로 적용하기

앞으로 익힐 독해 속에 포함된 문장입니다. 끊어 읽고 우리말 해석을 써 보세요.

01 *Haenyeo* use a unique and eco-friendly way of harvesting , which protects the marine environment. **p.72**
⇨ 직독직해 ....

02 In Korea, you can even use a credit card to buy newspapers that homeless people sell. **p.73**
⇨ 직독직해 ....

03 Here's what teens have to remember before getting a part-time job. **p.74**
⇨ 직독직해 ....

04 We all have seen some images , in which models have been photoshopped, to appear extremely skinny. **p.76**
⇨ 직독직해 ....

Intangible Cultural Heritage, *Haenyeo*

끊어읽기를 하며, 직독직해를 해 보세요.

⏱ 1' 45"
🎧 7-01
상 중 하
words 142

In 2016,/*Haenyeo*,/female divers on Jejudo,/ had a reason to celebrate. They were listed/as Korea's 19th ³*intangible cultural heritage of humanity by UNESCO. *Haenyeo* are women/who dive deep into the sea/with no scuba gear. They can hold their breath for two or three minutes,/and sometimes even ten. ⁶Their job is/to collect various sea creatures. They once were supporting the family/and risked their lives/to <u>make ends meet</u>. According to the Cultural Heritage Administration,/the *Haenyeo* culture respects the ⁹ocean and represents the cultural identity of the island/where people/ in the past/heavily relied on the sea/to survive.▼*Haenyeo* use/a unique and eco-friendly way of harvesting/, which protects the marine ¹²environment. Also, they have passed down diving know-how/to younger generations. This helped *Haenyeo* to be listed as/a UNESCO cultural heritage.

*intangible cultural heritage of humanity 인류 무형 문화유산

▼ **KEY STRUCTURE**

Haenyeo uses ~ way of harvesting, **which** protects the marine environment.: 계속적 용법의 관계대명사로 관계사절 속에서 주어의 역할을 한다.

1 이 글의 또 다른 제목으로 가장 적절한 것은? (제목 추론)

① The Origin of *Haenyeo* in Jejudo
② World Heritage Sites to Visit in Korea
③ Tips To Become *Haeneyo*
④ How to Be Added to the UNESCO Heritage List
⑤ Jeju *Haeneyo* Added to UNESCO Heritage List

2 이 글의 밑줄 친 부분이 의미하는 것은? (어휘 추론)

① save money　　　　　② find unexpectedly
③ avoid the main topic　④ work late into the night
⑤ have money to live

---

female 여성인; 여성　　　celebrate ＿＿＿＿＿　　creature ＿＿＿＿＿　　administration 행정국
respect ＿＿＿＿＿　　　eco-friendly 친환경적인　　marine ＿＿＿＿＿　　know-how 비결, 노하우

A Future without Cash

⏱ 1' 45"
🎧 7-02
상 중 하
words **144**

A cashless society is coming. Scandinavians use cash for no more than 6% of all payments they make. In Denmark, the government has proposed ______ⓐ______ stores throw their cash registers away. ▼In Korea, you can even use a credit card to buy newspapers that homeless people sell. One of the reasons why cash is disappearing is the wide use of credit cards, but there's another. These days, many people carry digital wallets. A digital wallet turns smartphones into electronic wallets by using a mobile payment system. Customers can make payments at stores or online with their smartphones. A Bank of Korea report said ______ⓑ______ 41.8% of Koreans in their 30s use a mobile payment method. Koreans are also welcoming a cashless society. Do you still use cash? Then how about buying something with your smartphone? Cash is quickly becoming a thing of the past.

▼ **KEY STRUCTURE**

In Korea, ~ newspapers **that** homeless people sell.: that은 선행사인 newspapers를 수식하는 절을 이끄는 목적격 관계대명사이며, which로 대체 가능하다.

1 이 글의 주제로 알맞은 것은? (주제 추론)

① Koreans should learn how to spend money wisely.
② Cash will be replaced with mobile payment.
③ It is important to take care of digital security.
④ Mobile payment is convenient to use.
⑤ We should reduce our spending.

2 이 글의 빈칸 ⓐ, ⓑ에 공통으로 들어갈 접속사를 쓰시오. (어법성 판단)

____

---

cashless 현금이 없는   payment _______________   throw away 처분하다   cash register 금전 등록기

homeless people 노숙자   disappear _______________   electronic 전자의   customer _______________

Teen Workers Treated Unfairly

03

⏱ 3' 10"
🎧 7-03
상 중 하
words **189**

It is said that about 80% of Korean teens have work experience. But ① <u>fortunately</u>, many teens are treated unfairly at their workplace. In addition, they are far more ② <u>likely</u> than adults to be injured at work, even though they work fewer hours and are prohibited by law from working in high-risk jobs. <u>What</u>'s worse is that too many teens don't even know about their rights in the workplace. ▼Here's what teens have to remember before getting a part-time job. In Korea, teens who are 15 years old or over are allowed to work. If you are younger, you have to get a permit from *the Ministry of Labor. If you're paid less than the ③ <u>minimum</u> wage, ask the employer to pay you more. Also, teens' working hours are seven hours a day. However, if you wish to work more, it is ④ <u>possible</u> to work one more hour per day. When you do, you should be paid for any ⑤ <u>overtime</u> work. And be sure to sign a contract before starting a new job. If anything unfair happens at your workplace, just call the Ministry of Labor and get some help.

*the Ministry of Labor 노동부

열정페이

요즘 많이 사용하는 신조어 '열정페이'란 '열정+pay(급여)'의 합성어입니다. 이것은 현재 우리 사회 큰 문제인 어려운 취업 현실을 잘 드러내는 용어로 노동에 대한 정당한 대가를 지불하지 않으면서 열정을 빌미로 하여 무급 또는 최저시급에도 미치지 못하는 임금을 주고 과도한 업무를 시키는 것을 비꼬는 말입니다.

▼ **KEY STRUCTURE**

Here's **what** teens have to remember ~.: 관계대명사 what은 선행사를 포함한 것으로 the thing that(which)으로 바꿔 쓸 수 있다.

---

teen 청소년, 십대(= teenager)
injure ____________

treat 대우하다, 취급하다
prohibit 금지하다

workplace ____________
high-risk 위험성이 큰

1 이 글의 중심 소재로 알맞은 것은? (소재 추론)

① 청소년 아르바이트의 권리
② 청소년 아르바이트의 장점
③ 청소년 아르바이트에 대한 노동부의 규제
④ 청소년 아르바이트에 대한 찬성과 반대
⑤ 성인과 청소년의 아르바이트 비율

Detailed Information

2 이 글에서 청소년이 아르바이트를 할 때의 주의사항으로 언급되지 <u>않은</u> 것은? (세부 내용 파악)

① 연령　　　　　② 최저 임금　　　　　③ 초과근무 수당
④ 계약서　　　　⑤ 고용보험

3 이 글의 ①~⑤ 중 문맥상 단어의 쓰임이 적절하지 <u>않은</u> 것은? (어휘 추론)

① fortunately　　　　　② likely
③ minimum　　　　　　④ possible
⑤ overtime

4 이 글의 밑줄 친 What과 쓰임이 <u>다른</u> 것은? (어법성 판단)

① I can't believe <u>what</u> he said.
② James asked me <u>what</u> it was.
③ <u>What</u> she did today made me happy.
④ This pen is <u>what</u> I really wanted to buy.
⑤ Show me <u>what</u> you bought at the store.

---

right ＿＿＿＿＿	part-time job 아르바이트	allow 허락하다	permit 허가(증)
wage ＿＿＿＿＿	sign ＿＿＿＿＿	contract 계약(서)	unfair 부당한

Modified Model Images

For a long time, there has been a lot of pressure on women to be thin. ▼We all have seen some typical images, in which models have been photoshopped to appear extremely skinny. One research shows that women compare themselves with those images. This comparison can lead them to develop a poor self-image. In turn, this can increase their risk of developing an *eating disorder. Modified images can have a huge negative impact on women and even children. For this reason, some governments have legislated laws on modified images. __________, laws are being passed, like the "Photoshop Law" which requires models ⓐ have a minimum *BMI and advertisers to label retouched images. When a model's image is modified to make her smaller, that fact must be stated. Governments and industries must work together to help protect women's self-confidence and health. The fashion media and advertising industries need to show healthy images of women. It will take a long time for this change ⓑ occur, but the effort is surely worth it.

*eating disorder 섭식 장애   *BMI 체질량 지수(Body Mass Index)

▼ **KEY STRUCTURE**

We all have seen some typical images, **in which** models have been photoshopped ~.: 앞의 선행사 images 가 전치사 in의 목적어 역할을 하므로 목적격 관계대명사 which를 in과 쓰며, where로 바꿔 쓸 수도 있다.

---

modified 수정된	pressure 압박, 압력	extremely 극단적으로	skinny ____________
comparison ___________	in turn 결국	risk ____________	impact 영향

Main Idea

1 **What is the main idea of the passage?**

① Eating disorder is a serious illness.

② Women have been under the pressure to be thin.

③ Extreme diet can be dangerous to women.

④ The "Photoshop law" is the key solution of the health problem.

⑤ Government and industries should make an effort to show healthy images of women.

Detailed Information

2 **Which is right for the blank?**

① Conversely   ② Therefore   ③ For example

④ In addition   ⑤ On the other hands

3 **What does underlined <u>this reason</u> indicate? Write in Korean.**

서술형

____

4 **Correct the underlined ⓐ and ⓑ words.**

ⓐ ________________   ⓑ ________________

government ___________	legislate 입법하다	require ___________	minimum 최소한의
label 라벨을 붙이다	self-confidence 자신감	occur 발생하다, 일어나다	worth ___________

Society

Let's overcome the generation gap!

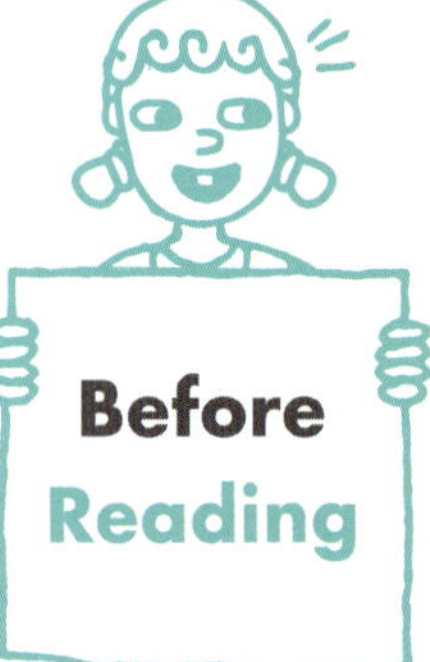

다음 구문 중 학습하고 싶은 것에 ✔ 표시 하세요.

- ☐ 관계부사 where
- ☐ 관계부사 when
- ☐ 관계부사 why
- ☐ 관계부사 how

02
Ancient Roman slaves could do anything!

03
Do you feel envy at others' posts on SNS?

04
What's special about Minangkabau society?

다음 제목 중 알고 싶은 것에 ✔ 표시 하세요.

- ☐ **01** 세대 차이
- ☐ **02** 고대 로마의 노예들
- ☐ **03** 온라인 세상은 실제가 아니에요!
- ☐ **04** 미낭카바우 부족 사회

Before Reading

관계부사의 다양한 쓰임

I know / how she made this pie.
나는 안다　/　　　그녀가 이 파이를 만든 방법을

Point　장소, 시간, 이유, 방법 등 선행사와 관계부사의 의미를 파악하여 해석한다.

관계부사는 두 문장을 연결하는 접속사와 부사의 역할을 하며 형용사절을 이끈다.

	선행사	관계부사
장소	the place, the house, the city …	where
시간	the time, the day, the month …	when
이유	the reason	why
방법	the way	how

관계부사 where: 선행사가 the place, the house ...와 같은 장소를 나타낼 때 사용한다.

This is *the bank* / **where** I visited yesterday.

⇨ 직독직해[1] ---

관계부사 when: 선행사가 the time, the day ...와 같은 시간을 나타낼 때 사용한다.

I don't know *the time* / **when** the baseball game will start.

⇨ 직독직해[2] ---

관계부사 why: 선행사가 the reason과 같은 이유를 나타낼 때 사용한다.

Tell me / *the reason* / **why** he got angry.

⇨ 직독직해[3] ---

관계부사 how: 선행사가 the way와 같은 방법을 나타낼 때 사용한다.

This is / **how** Susan solved the math problem.

⇨ 직독직해[4] ---

cf. 선행사 the way는 관계부사 how와 같이 쓸 수 없으므로 둘 중 하나를 생략해야 한다.

직독직해를 위한 어법 연습하기

두 문장을 관계부사를 이용하여 한 문장으로 쓰세요.

1 This is the place.   I met my boyfriend at the place.
→ This is the place ______________ I met my boyfriend.

2 I know the reason.   Lisa called him for the reason.
→ I know the reason ______________ Lisa called him.

3 Please tell me the time.   The train will depart at the time.
→ Please tell me the time ______________ the train will depart.

4 I remember the day.   I graduated on the day.
→ I remember the day ______________ I graduated.

5 I know the way.   The machine works in the way.
→ I know ______________ the machine works.

독해지문 직독직해로 적용하기

앞으로 익힐 독해 속에 포함된 문장입니다. 끊어 읽고 우리말 해석을 써 보세요.

01 We live in a different world where we cannot understand each other. p.82
⇨ 직독직해 ____

02 Do you know the reason why slaves were such an important part of ancient Rome? p.83
⇨ 직독직해 ____

03 Now let's find out how you can prevent those negative feelings. p.84
⇨ 직독직해 ____

04 There was a time when most societies were dominated by men. p.86
⇨ 직독직해 ____

A Generation Gap

끊어읽기를 하며, 직독직해를 해 보세요.

⏱ 1' 30"
🎧 8-01
상 중 하
words 147

Min Today,/I said Mom,/"Mom,/I was so *men-boong*/today." But, my mom didn't understand/the word "*men-boong*." It means/the feeling shocked/to the point of mental collapse. Even she warned me/that I should not use that kind of words. I have no idea/why my mom keeps me from saying those words. Most of my friends use the words/such as *men-boong*, *no-jem*, and so on. I think/we are facing a generation gap. Please let me know/how I can solve this problem.

Teacher Communication plays an important role/in bridging gaps/not only between parents and children but also in every relationship. _______________,/we should try to understand each other's world. ▼We have to accept/that we live in a different world/where we cannot understand each other. You have to make the effort/to understand and accept/your mother's perspectives and priorities.

> ▼ **KEY STRUCTURE**
> ~ we live in a different world **where** we cannot understand each other.: '장소'를 나타내는 선행사 another world가 있어서 관계부사 where가 사용되었으며 '우리는 ~하는 다른 세상에 살고 있다'라는 의미가 된다.

1 다음 빈칸에 알맞은 것은? (연결사 파악)

① Nevertheless　　② For instance　　③ In addition
④ Therefore　　⑤ As a result

2 이 글의 내용과 일치하지 <u>않는</u> 것은? (내용 일치·불일치)

① 민이의 엄마는 민이가 신조어를 사용하는 것을 좋아하지 않는다.
② 민이는 엄마와의 세대 차이 문제를 해결하고 싶어 한다.
③ 대화는 세대를 서로 연결해 주는 중요한 역할을 한다.
④ 세대 차이를 줄이기 위해 서로의 세계를 이해하려는 노력이 필요하다.
⑤ 어른들이 먼저 아이들의 세상을 이해하기 위해 노력해야 한다.

---

mental 정신의　　**collapse** 붕괴　　**warn** ____________　　**communication** ____________
bridge a gap 간극을 메우다　　**accept** ____________　　**perspective** 관점　　**priority** 우선 사항

Slaves in Ancient Rome

▼Do you know the reason why slaves were such an important part of ancient Rome? They were around 25% of the population of ancient Rome. Most had to do a lot of hard and tiring work because Rome was a slave-based society. In the countryside, for instance, slaves did most of the work on farms. They produced the food for everyone in the cities. Some slaves worked on big public projects, too. They helped build roads and big public buildings. But slaves didn't just do hard physical work. Some also did business and government work. They ran shops, kept accounts, and did paperwork. Some slaves even studied very hard and knew a lot about history, economics, math and science. Slave owners usually treated these educated slaves very well.

1 이 글을 쓴 목적으로 알맞은 것은? 〔목적 추론〕

① to discuss if keeping slaves is right
② to explain the role of slaves in ancient Rome
③ to criticize Romans for having slaves
④ to study the history of slavery
⑤ to talk about a few famous slaves in ancient Rome

2 이 글에서 노예의 임무로 언급되지 않은 것은? 〔세부 내용 파악〕

① 농장 일 하기　　② 공공건물 건설하기　　③ 상점 운영하기
④ 다른 노예들을 교육시키기　⑤ 서류 작업하기

---

slave ＿＿＿＿＿　　population 인구　　countryside 시골　　produce ＿＿＿＿＿
physical 육체적인, 신체의　account 회계, 거래　paperwork ＿＿＿＿＿　economics 경제학

Online World Is Not Real!

⏱ 3' 10"
🎧 8-03
상 중 하
words 185

(A) However, there's also a downside to this activity. According to some research, people who spend too much time on social networks often get depressed. <u>So what is the reason why they feel depressed?</u> It means that they feel less satisfied with their own life. When people were asked about this, most of them said they felt "envy" at others' posts. They kept comparing their lives with others, and believed that other people were living happier lives.

(B) More and more people are using social networks in their daily life. Using social networks is how you can easily find out personal things about other people. You can not only read about them, but also see their pictures.

(C) ▼Now let's find out how you can prevent those negative feelings. First, don't draw conclusions about other people from the web. Be sure to step away from your computer and get the full story about the other person. You can also try to meet the people in real life. When you are actually with others, you'll recognize that all of them live a normal life just like yours.

▼ **KEY STRUCTURE**

Now let's find out **how** you can prevent ~.: how는 관계부사로 선행사 the way를 수식하는 관계사절을 이끌지만, the way와 how는 동시에 쓰일 수 없어 둘 중 하나는 생략해야 한다.

PLUS READING

SNS의 장점

SNS는 여러 가지 장점을 가지고 있어요. 정보 공유가 신속하게 이뤄지고 인간관계도 폭넓게 유지할 수 있답니다. 또, 자신의 생각을 표현하는 수단이 되기도 해요. 유명인들과 같이 파급력이 큰 사람이라면 그 영향력이 굉장히 크답니다.

downside 부정적인 면　　research 연구, 조사　　depressed ___________
satisfied ___________　　envy 부러움, 질투, 시기　　compare A with B A와 B를 비교하다

Main Idea

1 이 글의 중심 소재로 알맞은 것은? 〔 소재 추론 〕

① 오프라인 대인관계의 중요성
② 소셜 네트워크의 사회적 기능
③ 소셜 네트워크의 문제점과 해결 방안
④ 소셜 네트워크의 장점과 단점
⑤ 현대 사회의 개인주의 현상

Detailed Information

2 이 글의 (A) ~ (C)를 순서대로 바르게 배열한 것은? 〔 글의 흐름 〕

① (A) – (C) – (B)　　② (B) – (A) – (C)　　③ (B) – (C) – (A)
④ (C) – (A) – (B)　　⑤ (C) – (B) – (A)

3 이 글의 내용을 바르게 이해한 아이들로 알맞게 짝지어진 것은? 〔 세부 내용 파악 〕

- 선우: 사람들은 소셜 네트워크에 등록된 친구의 수가 대인관계를 의미한다고 생각해.
- 유미: 소셜 네트워크를 통해 친구들의 소식을 쉽게 알 수 있어.
- 민영: 소셜 네트워크를 많이 하는 사람들은 자신의 삶에 만족하는 사람들이야.
- 진욱: 우리는 실생활에서 사람들을 만나도록 노력해야 해.

① 선우, 유미　　② 선우, 민영　　③ 유미, 민영
④ 민영, 진욱　　⑤ 유미, 진욱

4 이 글의 밑줄 친 부분을 관계부사의 쓰임에 유의하여 우리말로 해석하시오. 〔 어법성 판단 〕

→ ____

---

daily life 일상생활　　　　**personal** __________　　　　**prevent** 막다　　　　**negative** __________
draw (결론 등을) 이끌어내다　　**conclusion** 결론　　　　**recognize** 깨닫다　　　　**normal** 평범한, 정상의

The Minangkabau Society

⏱ 3' 15"
🎧 8-04
상 중 하
words 166

▶ There was a time when most societies were dominated by men. Men still hold most of the power in family and public life. For example, it was only a short time ago when women could not vote in most Western countries. Also, in many developing countries, women are still not equal to men.

However, the Minangkabau tribes, who live in the highlands of West Sumatra in Indonesia, have another way of running things. This is a society where women have traditionally held a lot of power. Most importantly, the oldest woman in the family is usually the head of the household. She controls the family's money and possessions. After she dies, her money and land are passed on to her daughter. But the Minangkabau society is not exactly the opposite of a traditional society. That's because women do not completely control society. Minangkabau men can't own land, but still have important roles to play. They usually take care of most of the religious and political affairs.

▼ **KEY STRUCTURE**

There was a time **when** most societies were ~.: 선행사인 a time이 '시간'을 나타내므로 관계부사 when이 쓰였으며, '~했던 때가 있었다'로 해석한다.

dominate 지배하다	public ＿＿＿＿＿
developing country 개발도상국	equal ＿＿＿＿＿

vote 투표하다	western ＿＿＿＿＿
tribe 부족, 종족	highland 고지대

» 정답과 해설 p.35

Main Idea

1 **What is the best topic of the passage?**

① the women's role in the Minangkabau tribe
② the power of men in most societies
③ the traditional society in Indonesia
④ the men's power in public life
⑤ the relationship between mother and daughter

Detailed Information

2 **According to the passage, which is NOT true?**

① Men have dominated most societies.
② Women in some countries are still treated unfairly.
③ The leader of the Minangkabau tribe is the oldest woman.
④ The Minangkabau society is similar to a traditional society.
⑤ The Minangkabau men also play important roles.

3 **Fill in the blank with the words in the passage.**

> When a Minangkabau woman, the head of the household, dies,
> _______________ normally inherits money.

4 **What is the closest meaning of <u>affairs</u>?**

① contacts   ② events   ③ beliefs
④ sides   ⑤ returns

---

head _______________   household 가족, 식구   control 통제하다   possession 소유물
opposite 반대의   completely 완전히, 전적으로   religious _______________   political 정치적인

01

Improve your concentration through puzzles!

02

Show off your beautiful handwriting!

03

Do you want to know what your stars do at home?

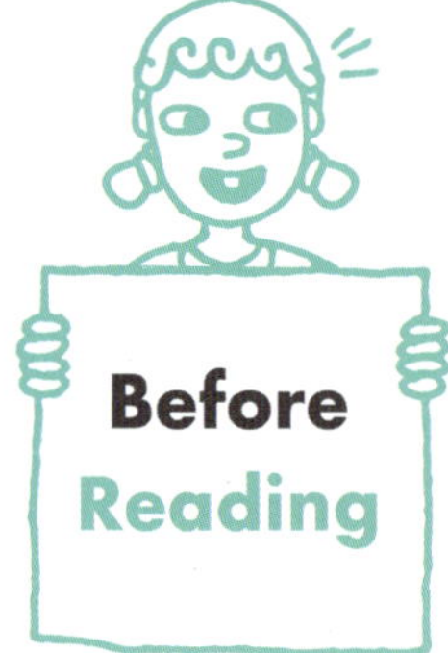

다음 구문 중 학습하고 싶은 것에 ✔ 표시 하세요.

Before Reading

- ☐ 명사절 접속사
- ☐ 시간, 양보의 접속사
- ☐ 조건, 이유의 접속사
- ☐ 상관접속사

09

Hobbies

04

Name any unusual
and unique hobbies
you know.

다음 제목 중 알고 싶은 것에 ✔ 표시 하세요.

- ☐ 01 재미있는 조각 그림 퍼즐
- ☐ 02 캘리그라피; 시각적 예술
- ☐ 03 유명인들은 집에서 무엇을 할까?
- ☐ 04 특이한 취미들

Before Reading

접속사의 다양한 쓰임

I listen to music / while I'm working.

나는 음악을 듣는다　　　/　　　일하는 동안에

Point　접속사의 다양한 기능과 의미를 파악하여 해석한다.

접속사에는 명사절과 부사절을 이끄는 접속사, 두 개 이상의 단어가 짝을 이루는 상관접속사가 있다.

명사절 접속사: 주어, 목적어, 보어 역할을 하는 절을 이끌며 that, if, whether 등이 있다.

I wonder / **if** David will come or not.

⇨ 직독직해 [1] ⋯⋯⋯⋯⋯⋯⋯⋯⋯⋯⋯⋯⋯⋯⋯⋯⋯⋯⋯⋯⋯⋯⋯⋯⋯⋯⋯⋯⋯⋯⋯

시간의 접속사: before(~ 전에), after(~ 후에), since(~ 이래로), when(~할 때), while(~하는 동안)

I could go outside / **after** I finished my homework.

⇨ 직독직해 [2] ⋯⋯⋯⋯⋯⋯⋯⋯⋯⋯⋯⋯⋯⋯⋯⋯⋯⋯⋯⋯⋯⋯⋯⋯⋯⋯⋯⋯⋯⋯⋯

양보의 접속사: though, although(비록 ~일지라도)

Though Ann is young, / she is very brave.

⇨ 직독직해 [3] ⋯⋯⋯⋯⋯⋯⋯⋯⋯⋯⋯⋯⋯⋯⋯⋯⋯⋯⋯⋯⋯⋯⋯⋯⋯⋯⋯⋯⋯⋯⋯

조건의 접속사: if(만약 ~라면), unless(만약 ~하지 않는다면)

Unless you hurry up, / you'll miss the bus.

⇨ 직독직해 [4] ⋯⋯⋯⋯⋯⋯⋯⋯⋯⋯⋯⋯⋯⋯⋯⋯⋯⋯⋯⋯⋯⋯⋯⋯⋯⋯⋯⋯⋯⋯⋯

이유의 접속사: because, since(~ 때문에)

Tom got angry / **because** Emily broke his cellphone.

⇨ 직독직해 [5] ⋯⋯⋯⋯⋯⋯⋯⋯⋯⋯⋯⋯⋯⋯⋯⋯⋯⋯⋯⋯⋯⋯⋯⋯⋯⋯⋯⋯⋯⋯⋯

상관접속사: 서로 관련된 두 개의 단어나 구를 이어 주는 역할을 한다.

both A and B	A와 B 둘 다	either A or B	A와 B 둘 중 하나
neither A nor B	A도 B도 아닌	not only A but also B	A뿐만 아니라 B도

Both Susan **and** Lea / are good at swimming.

⇨ 직독직해 [6] ⋯⋯⋯⋯⋯⋯⋯⋯⋯⋯⋯⋯⋯⋯⋯⋯⋯⋯⋯⋯⋯⋯⋯⋯⋯⋯⋯⋯⋯⋯⋯

직독직해를 위한 어법 연습하기

우리말과 뜻이 같도록 빈칸에 알맞은 말을 쓰세요.

1 나는 Mindy가 정답을 알고 있는지 아닌지 확신이 없다.
→ I'm not sure _______________ Mindy knows the answer.

2 비가 오지 않는다면, 나는 빨래를 할 거야.
→ _______________ it rains, I'll do my laundry.

3 Julie는 John이 집에 도착했을 때 TV를 보고 있는 중이었다.
→ Julie was watching TV _______________ John arrived at home.

4 Jim과 Noah 둘 다 사실을 이야기 했다.
→ _______________ Jim _______________ Noah told the truth.

5 비록 Maria는 다쳤지만 산 정상까지 올라갔다.
→ _______________ Maria got hurt, she reached the top of the mountain.

Preview Test

독해지문 직독직해로 적용하기

앞으로 익힐 독해 속에 포함된 문장입니다. 끊어 읽고 우리말 해석을 써 보세요.

01 It's because both sides of your brain work when you do jigsaw puzzles. **p.92**
⇨ 직독직해 ____

02 It is the art of both writing symbols beautifully by hand and arranging them well. **p.93**
⇨ 직독직해 ____

03 Do you play either the guitar or the piano? **p.94**
⇨ 직독직해 ____

04 It is a high-tech treasure hunt game because it is a game to find a hidden thing using GPS. **p.96**
⇨ 직독직해 ____

Fun, Fun Jigsaw Puzzles

끊어읽기를 하며, 직독직해를 해 보세요.

2' 10"
9-01
상 **중** 하
words **125**

Have you ever done/a *jigsaw puzzle? It's a game/in which pieces fit together/to form a picture.
3 Perhaps you've wondered/how jigsaw puzzles were first started. A printer from England, John Spilsbury decided/to stick a map onto a thin piece of wood. And he cut it/into strangely-shaped pieces. His
6 idea enabled children/to have a lot of fun. Later,/other printers began making jigsaw puzzles as well. Now people of all ages/enjoy putting jigsaw puzzles together. Putting puzzle pieces together is/a pleasant
9 and instructive way of relaxing. It is good for your brain.▼It's because/both sides of your brain work/when you do jigsaw puzzles. You can also improve your concentration/while you work on a puzzle.

*jigsaw puzzle 조각으로 된 그림을 맞추는 퍼즐

▼ **KEY STRUCTURE**
It's because ~ **when** you do jigsaw puzzle.: when은 시간, 때를 나타내는 접속사로 '~할 때'의 뜻을 표현한다.

1 이 글에서 jigsaw puzzles에 관한 장점으로 언급되지 <u>않은</u> 것은? 내용 일치·불일치

① 모두가 즐길 수 있다.　　　② 즐겁고 유익한 놀이이다.
③ 성취감을 느낄 수 있다.　　④ 두뇌 회전을 시킬 수 있다.
⑤ 집중력을 기를 수 있다.

2 이 글의 밑줄 친 부분을 접속사에 유의하여 우리말로 해석하시오. 어법성 판단

서술형 → ____

fit 끼우다, 맞추다　　　form ___________　　　perhaps 아마　　　printer 인쇄공
stick 붙이다　　　instructive ___________　　　improve ___________　　　concentration 집중(력)

Calligraphy;
the Visual Art

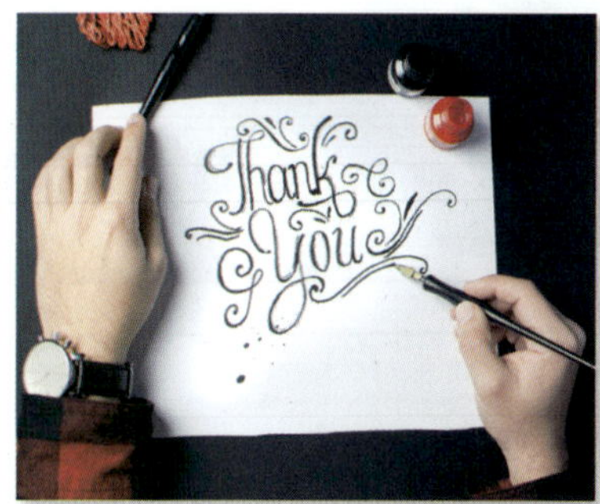

⏱ 2' 10"
🎧 9-02
상 중 하
words **145**

Calligraphy, ⓐ<u>which</u> means "beautiful handwriting," is a kind of visual art related to writing. Actually, calligraphy is more than that. ▼It is the art of both writing symbols beautifully by hand and ⓑ<u>arranging</u> them well. In calligraphy, you need skill to position words so that they show harmony, rhythm and creativity. Would you like to try calligraphy? You need a few tools to get started. You need a broad-tipped brush and ink, and of course paper to write on. Make sure you are sitting comfortably ⓒ<u>ago</u> you begin. Start by ⓓ<u>making</u> a vertical *stroke straight down. Then try making letters. Write anything you like such as the alphabet or your name. Once you build some confidence, try changing your letters. You can add curves. Even small changes will change the feel of your writing. Don't be afraid to get creative and remember ⓔ<u>to have</u> fun.

*stroke (글씨나 그림의) 획

▼ **KEY STRUCTURE**

It is the art of **both** writing symbols beautifully by hand **and** arranging them well: 〈both A and B〉의 상관접속사 형태로 'A와 B 둘 다'의 의미를 나타낸다.

1 이 글의 주제를 다음과 같이 쓸 때, 빈칸에 알맞은 것은? 주제 추론

> The ___________ of calligraphy and how to start it.

① origin　　　　② advantage　　　　③ popularity
④ evolution　　　⑤ definition

2 이 글의 밑줄 친 ⓐ~ⓔ 중 어법상 어색한 것을 찾아 고쳐 쓰시오. 어법성 판단

(　　) ________________ → ________________

---

visual 시각적인　　　related to ___________　　　arrange 배열하다　　　brush ___________
vertical 수직의　　　letter 글자　　　　　　　curve ___________　　　creative 창의적인

03 What Celebrities Do at Home

⏱ 3' 10"
🎧 9-03
상 중 하
words 185

What do you usually do in your spare time?

▼Do you play either the guitar or the piano? Do you dance or draw? Celebrities also have some ⓐ interest hobbies. Everyone knows Johnny Depp who stars in *Pirates of the Caribbean*. He usually shows a tough image, but at home he sometimes plays with dolls! Playing with Barbie dolls helped him develop the voices of Jack Sparrow and Willy Wonka in the movie. Academy award-winning actress Meryl Streep enjoys ⓑ knit. The hand-knit shawl she wore in the movie, *Doubt*, was made by herself. She has said that she gathers her thoughts while knitting. Furthermore, former CEO of the social network company Dick Costolo also has an interesting hobby. One of his favorite hobbies is beekeeping. He said to Bloomberg, "The whole way the hive works is fascinating. I love just hanging out and watching them." A lot of celebrities also __________________ as a hobby. Tom Hanks collects typewriters, Celine Dion collects shoes, and Nicolas Cage collects comic books. Celebrities have a wide variety of hobbies, and there are probably some who share your hobbies!

▼ **KEY STRUCTURE**
Do you play **either** the guitar **or** the piano?: 〈either A or B〉의 형태로 'A와 B 둘 중 하나'의 의미를 나타낸다.

spare time ___________	celebrity 유명인	pirate ___________	tough 거친
award-winning 상을 받은	actress 여배우	knit 뜨개질을 하다	shawl 숄

Main Idea

1 이 글의 중심 소재로 가장 적절한 것은? 〔주제 추론〕

① the movie industries
② playing with dolls
③ hobbies of celebrities
④ award-winning actresses
⑤ most popular hobbies

Detailed Information

2 이 글의 ⓐ와 ⓑ에 주어진 단어를 알맞은 형태로 고쳐 쓰시오. 〔어법성 판단〕

ⓐ _______________   ⓑ _______________

3 이 글의 내용과 일치하지 <u>않는</u> 것은? 〔내용 일치·불일치〕

① 조니 뎁은 바비 인형을 가지고 논다.
② 메릴 스트립은 뜨개질을 즐긴다.
③ Dick Costolo는 양봉을 한다.
④ 톰 행크스는 타자기를 수집한다.
⑤ 셀린 디옹은 만화책을 수집한다.

4 이 글의 빈칸에 알맞은 것은? 〔빈칸 추론〕

① read books
② love writing
③ build a collection
④ dislike having a hobby
⑤ are interested in fashion

---

former 이전의　　　　beekeeping 양봉　　　　whole ____________　　　　hive 벌떼; 벌집
fascinating 매혹적인, 재미있는　　　hang out ____________　　　collect 수집하다　　　typewriter 타자기

Unique Hobbies

Have you ever seen beetles fighting? Some people feel excited watching the fight. Their hobby looks a little cruel, but unique. Here are some other unique hobbies from foreign countries.

1. Tree Shaping: Gardening is a household chore, but many people enjoy shaping trees. Imagine a tree shaped like a dinosaur. As the tree is growing taller, the dinosaur is, too. It would be so interesting to see!

2. Extreme Ironing: Extreme ironing sounds funny, but it is an extremely active hobby. Some people climb mountains or surf waves as they iron something. It looks like ______ⓐ______.

3. Stone Skipping: Actually, this is a world-wide hobby. Have you ever thrown stones by a river or a pond? In Scotland, a stone skipping championship takes place every year. They compete how many times a stone skips before sinking.

4. Geocaching: Geocaching is *a compound word; "geo" means "earth," and "cache" means "a hiding place" or "a precious thing." ▼It is a high-tech treasure hunt game because it is a game to find a hidden thing using *GPS.

What is your unique hobby?

*a compound word 복합어, 합성어

*GPS(Global Positioning System) 인공위성으로 위치를 찾는 시스템

beetle 딱정벌레　　shape (모양을) 만들다

cruel ___________　　dinosaur 공룡

garden 정원 가꾸기를 하다　　extreme ___________

chore (정기적으로 하는) 일　　iron 다림질하다

Main Idea

1 **What is the main purpose of this passage?**

① to introduce a variety of unique hobbies
② to explain about dangerous hobbies
③ to share their unique experiences
④ to advertise the club activities
⑤ to criticize a unique hobbies

Detailed Information

2 **What cannot you guess from the passage?**

	Hobby	Strong Point
①	Beetles Fighting	Some think it is exciting.
②	Tree Shaping	You can express your imagination.
③	Extreme Ironing	It's very active.
④	Stone Skipping	It's hard to learn it.
⑤	Geocaching	It may be attractive to GPS users.

3 **Which is right for the blank ⓐ?**

① an exciting hide-and-seek game
② an easy and fun sports event
③ a wonderful circus performance
④ a famous off-line board game
⑤ a classical music concert

4 **What is the closest meaning of precious?**

① valuable   ② public   ③ common
④ popular   ⑤ useful

---

surf 파도타기를 하다   skip 물 수제비를 뜨다   pond 연못   take place 개최되다

compete ______________   sink 가라앉다   precious ______________   high-tech 최첨단의

10

Education

01

Guess what homeschooling is.

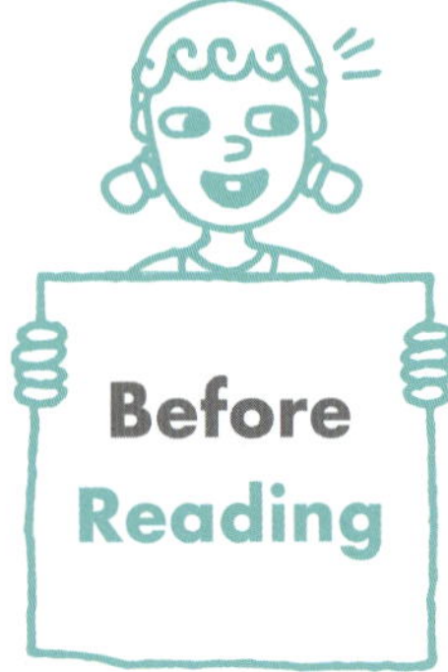

다음 구문 중 학습하고 싶은 것에 ✔ 표시 하세요.

Before Reading

- ☐ 조동사와 함께 쓰이는 수동태
- ☐ 진행형 수동태
- ☐ to부정사와 동명사의 수동태
- ☐ 동사구 수동태

02

Have you ever done volunteering?

03

K-Culture is booming globally!

04

How can we use VR (Virtual Reality) for education?

다음 제목 중 알고 싶은 것에 ✔ 표시 하세요.

- ☐  **01** 홈스쿨링
- ☐  **02** 교육 자원봉사 경험
- ☐  **03** 한국어의 인기
- ☐  **04** 교실에서의 가상현실 사용

수동태의 여러 가지 형태

The door might / be opened.
저 문은 ~일지도 모른다 / 열리다

Point 조동사와 함께 쓰인 수동태는 조동사의 의미에 유의하여 해석한다.

수동태는 〈be동사+p.p.(+by 행위자)〉의 형태로 나타내며 조동사와 함께 쓰거나 동사구를 수동태로 변환하는 등 다양한 형태로 쓸 수 있다.

조동사가 포함된 수동태: 〈조동사+be+p.p.(+by 행위자)〉의 형태이며 조동사에 따라 의미가 달라진다.

The computer **<u>can be repaired</u>** / by the engineer.
▶ 조동사와 함께 쓰일 때 동사는 항상 be

⇨ **직독직해¹** ____

진행형 수동태: 〈be동사+being+p.p.〉의 형태로 나타낸다.

The food **is being cooked** / in the kitchen / now.

⇨ **직독직해²** ____

to부정사와 동명사의 수동태: to부정사의 수동태는 〈to+be+p.p.〉, 동명사의 수동태는 〈being+p.p.〉의 형태로 나타낸다.

[to부정사] I expect the car / **to be sold** / before long.

⇨ **직독직해³** ____

[동명사] I don't like / **being asked** / to make a speech.

⇨ **직독직해⁴** ____

동사구 수동태: 〈동사+전치사〉나 〈동사+부사〉 등으로 이루어진 동사구는 하나의 단어처럼 취급하여 수동태로 전환한다.

The puppy / **is taken care of** / by my brother.

⇨ **직독직해⁵** ____

» 정답과 해설 p.42

직독직해를 위한 어법 연습하기

괄호 안의 말을 바르게 배열하여 문장을 완성하세요.

1 The letter ________________ to my friend, Jinny. (can / delivered / be)

2 The bridge ________________ now. (being / is / built)

3 I don't want ________________. (to / bothered / be)

4 People don't ________________ all the time. (being / like / watched)

5 The exhibition ________________ in France. (being / is / held)

독해지문 직독직해로 적용하기

앞으로 익힐 독해 속에 포함된 문장입니다. 끊어 읽고 우리말 해석을 써 보세요.

01 You will be protected from school violence. **p.102**
  ⇨ 직독직해 ____

02 While they were being taught, we helped them with various subjects. **p.103**
  ⇨ 직독직해 ____

03 We hear about lots of non-Koreans to be taught Korean in Korea. **p.104**
  ⇨ 직독직해 ____

04 VR technologies can be made use of in many areas. **p.106**
  ⇨ 직독직해 ____

Homeschooling

끊어읽기를 하며, 직독직해를 해 보세요.

⏱ 2' 10"
🎧 10-01
상 **중** 하
words **127**

Homeschooling is so advantageous/ that many people are becoming interested in it. It has many advantages. First, you'll get individual attention/in every class. Traditional schools have such a lot of students/that it's nearly impossible/for each student/to get attention from teachers. Second, you can learn/at your own speed. In this way,/you'll be less bored and distracted. ▼Third, you will be protected/from school violence. However,/homeschooling also has its disadvantages. You may have trouble making friends/because you will not have enough chances/to interact with other students. Also,/you may have trouble/comparing your academic ability/with others'. Therefore, you have to think about/how you like to study. Then you'll be able to choose/what will work best for you.

▼ **KEY STRUCTURE**

Third, you **will be protected** from school violence.: 〈조동사＋be동사＋p.p.〉의 형태로 조동사 will과 함께 쓰인 수동태 구문이다.

1 이 글의 홈스쿨링에 대한 내용과 일치하지 <u>않는</u> 것은? 〔 내용 일치·불일치 〕

① 개별적인 관심을 받을 수 있다.
② 학교에서 공부할 때보다 더 산만해질 수도 있다.
③ 학교 폭력으로부터 보호를 받을 수 있다.
④ 다른 사람들과 교류할 기회가 충분하지 않다.
⑤ 자신의 성향을 고려한 후 선택하는 것이 바람직하다.

2 이 글의 밑줄 친 부분을 우리말로 해석하시오. 〔 세부 내용 파악 〕

〔서술형〕 → ____

---

advantageous ______________ individual 개인적인 attention 관심 distracted 산만한
violence ______________ disadvantage ______________ interact with ~와 교류하다 compare 비교하다

  〉〉 정답과 해설 p.42

02 Education Volunteering Experience

2' 10"
10-02
상 중 하
words 154

When our group stepped into the classroom in Kenya, my heart started pounding. There were no desks and not even a blackboard. There were so many students in the classroom that I couldn't count them all! I was so shocked that I was speechless. There was curiosity on their faces. It was my first overseas volunteering experience, and I wanted to do my best. I met the group of children I was going to help. I was impressed by their interest and desire to learn. ▼While they were being taught, we helped them with various subjects. We also taught them about the culture and customs of Korea. They enjoyed learning and playing traditional Korean games. After just a week, it was time to leave. Was it easy? Of course it wasn't. Was it a worthy experience? Sure! They waved goodbye with smiles and tears. It was a meaningful experience that I will never forget.

1 이 글의 중심 소재로 가장 적절한 것은? (소재 추론)

① traditional Korean games
② interest and desire to learn
③ group activities in the classroom
④ the culture and customs of Korea
⑤ overseas volunteering experience

2 이 글의 내용과 일치하지 <u>않는</u> 것은? (내용 일치·불일치)

① 케냐의 교실에는 책상과 칠판이 없다.
② 소수의 학생들이 교실에서 기다리고 있었다.
③ 아이들의 배움에 대한 열망에 글쓴이는 감동을 받았다.
④ 한국의 문화와 관습에 대해서 가르쳤다.
⑤ 봉사활동은 일주일 동안 진행되었다.

---

step into ~에 발을 들여 놓다
volunteering 자원봉사
pound (심장이) 마구 뛰다
desire ______________
curiosity ______________
custom 관습
overseas 해외의
worthy ______________

03

The Popularity of the Korean Language

🕐 3' 10"
🎧 10-03
상 중 하
words 180

Have you ever heard that many K-pop fans are learning the Korean language? Maybe you have, because it's true. These days, the Korean language courses are paid attention to. Now in China, it's not difficult to see not only people learning Korean but also posters written in Korean. The popularity of the Korean music and entertainment has led to a great ①demand for the Korean language courses. The ②popularity of *TOPIK is soaring across the world thanks to the Korean Wave. When the test was first introduced in 1997, about 2,700 people from four countries (Korea, Japan, Uzbekistan, and Kazakhstan) applied. Now, the scale grew by more than 70 times over the last 20 years. ▼We often hear about lots of ③non-Koreans to be taught Korean in Korea or in other foreign countries. For example, the Korean classes in universities are filled with the students who want to learn Korean as ④exchange students. Also, they go to private academies to improve their Korean speaking skills. Now, we can ⑤hardly meet foreigners saying greetings in Korean or singing songs in Korean.

*TOPIK(Test of Proficiency in Korean) 한국어능력시험

▼ **KEY STRUCTURE**

We often hear about lots of non-Koreans **to be taught** Korean in Korea or in other foreign countries.: to 부정사의 수동태 형태로서 〈to+be+p.p.〉의 형태이며, '한국어를 가르침 받는(배우는) 비 한국인들'이라는 의미로 사용되었다.

TOPIK (한국어능력시험)

PLUS READING

한국어를 모국어로 하지 않는 외국인과 재외동포를 대상으로 한국어 사용 능력을 인증하는 시험으로 한국어의 학습 방향을 제시하고 한국어 보급을 확대하는 역할을 한답니다. 시험은 1~6급까지 6개 등급으로 구성되고 객관식 문항과 단답형으로 답하는 문장 완성형, 그리고 작문형 문제로 구성이 되어 있습니다.

popularity 인기
demand ____________

language ____________
soar (가치, 물가 등이) 치솟다

pay attention to ~에 주목하다
thanks to ~덕분에

≫ 정답과 해설 p.44

1 이 글의 중심 소재로 가장 적절한 것은? 소재 찾기

① 증가하는 한국어의 인기　　　　② 한국어의 변화
③ 한국어능력시험 소개　　　　　④ 한류열풍의 원인
⑤ 한국 문화의 전파

Detailed Information

2 이 글의 ①~⑤ 중 문맥상 단어의 쓰임이 적절하지 <u>않은</u> 것은? 어휘 추론

① popularity　　　② demand　　　③ non-Koreans
④ exchange　　　⑤ hardly

3 이 글을 읽고 알 수 있는 것은? 세부 내용 파악

① The popularity of Korean culture is not strong.
② TOPIK was hold in China in 1997.
③ The Korean singers affect the popularity of the Korean language.
④ The Korean universities have an excellent faculty.
⑤ The Korean speaking skills can be improved by various methods.

4 이 글의 밑줄 친 부분을 우리말로 해석하시오. 세부 내용 파악

서술형 → ____

introduce 도입하다　　　apply ___________　　　scale 규모　　　private ___________
academy 학원　　　　　improve ___________　　　skill 능력, 기술　　　greeting 인사

VR Usage in the Classroom

⏱ 3' 20"
🎧 10-04
상 중 하
words 173

Virtual reality(VR) was once regarded as a science fiction fantasy. But now a virtual environment is a very possible future. With the help of VR, the way students learn is expected to change dramatically. First, it will help them vividly remember what they've learned by creating a sense of presence. Let's take science classes as an example. Students raise their hands in the real world. Within a VR simulation, their avatars would make the same <u>movement</u>. In a chemistry class, they could interact with the *molecules by dragging them into position. In a biology class, they could separate *tissues with their hands and explore the human body. Second, VR will help make education available to everyone. VR hardware will become __________, so it can be supplied to the developing countries. This will allow students around the world to benefit from the same level of experience. ▼VR technologies can also be made use of in many areas other than education. Try to imagine how they will change your lives in the near future.

*molecules 분자   tissue 조직

▼ **KEY STRUCTURE**

VR technologies can also **be made use of** ~.: '~을 활용하다'의 의미인 make use of는 하나의 단어처럼 취급하여 수동태로 전환하면 be made use of로 쓴다.

VR(가상현실)   PLUS READING

가상현실(VR)이란 컴퓨터를 통해 현실의 특정한 환경이나 상황을 그대로 모방함으로써 마치 사용자가 실제 주변의 상황이나 환경과 상호 작용 하고 있는 것처럼 보이도록 만드는 기술입니다. 〈매트릭스〉나 〈아바타〉 등의 영화를 통해서 가상현실의 개념이 대중화되었고, 의학·생명과학·로봇공학·우주과학·교육학 등과 같은 다양한 분야에서 활용되고 있어요.

virtual 가상의   fiction 소설   fantasy ____________

vividly ____________   presence 실재, 존재   simulation 시뮬레이션, 모의실험

Main Idea

1 **What is the main topic of the passage?**

① the rise and fall of VR
② the future of interactive media
③ weakness of using VR in classroom
④ changes in education caused by VR
⑤ the importance of interaction in classroom

Detailed Information

2 **What are the two advantages of using VR for the education? Write in Korean.**

- ____
- ____

3 **Which is right for the blank?**

① smaller   ② cheaper   ③ harder
④ worse   ⑤ simpler

4 **What is the closest meaning of <u>movement</u>?**

① action   ② campaign   ③ transfer
④ progress   ⑤ development

drag ______________	position 자리, 위치	biology 생물학	separate ______________
explore 탐험하다	supply ______________	benefit 이익을 얻다	area 영역

UNIT 01

01

□ familiar with		~에 친숙한
□ influential [ìnfluénʃəl]	형	영향력 있는
□ select [silékt]	동	선발하다
□ literature [lítrətʃər]	명	문학
□ author [ɔ́:θər]	명	작가
□ recognize [rékəgnaiz]	동	인정하다
□ creation [kriéiʃən]	명	창작(물)
□ tradition [trədíʃən]	명	전통

02

□ greatly [gréitli]	부	대단히
□ guarantee [gæ̀rəntí:]	동	보장하다
□ artistic [ɑ:rtístik]	형	예술적인
□ editor [éditər]	명	편집자
□ publisher [pʌ́bliʃər]	명	출판업자
□ imagine [imǽdʒin]	동	상상하다
□ instantly [ínstəntli]	부	즉시, 곧바로
□ daily routine		일상

03

□ superhero [sú:pərhìrou]	명	슈퍼영웅
□ nowadays [náuədèiz]	부	요즘
□ hometown [hóumtaun]	명	고향

□ suit [su:t]	명	옷, 정장
□ favorite [féivərit]	형	매우 좋아하는
□ currently [kɛ́:rəntli]	부	현재, 지금
□ mad [mæd]	형	정신 이상인
□ safe [seif]	형	안전한
□ invention [invénʃn]	명	발명(품)
□ sense [sens]	명	감각
□ climb up		~에 오르다
□ unlike [ʌ̀nláik]	전	~와 달리
□ lonely [lóunli]	형	외로운, 쓸쓸한
□ orphan [ɔ́:rfn]	명	고아
□ alone [əlóun]	형	혼자
□ impress [imprés]	동	깊은 인상을 주다

04

□ ingredient [ingrí:diənt]	명	재료
□ leftover [léftouvər]	명	남은 음식
□ prior to		~ 이전에
□ target [tá:rgit]	동	~을 대상으로 하다
□ previous [prí:viəs]	형	이전의
□ obtain [əbtéin]	동	얻다
□ recent [rí:snt]	형	최근의
□ light-hearted [laìt-há:rtid]	형	편안한 마음의
□ mood [mu:d]	명	분위기
□ therefore [ðéərfɔ̀:(r)]	부	그러므로
□ attract [ətrǽkt]	동	끌다
□ attention [əténʃn]	명	관심
□ gain [gein]	동	얻다
□ popularity [pɑ̀:pjulǽrəti]	명	인기

□ wonder [wʌ́ndər]	동	궁금해하다
□ overweight [òuvərwéit]	형	과체중의
□ soda [sóudə]	명	탄산음료
□ provide [prəváid]	동	제공하다
□ pick [pik]	동	줍다, 수거하다
□ fresh [freʃ]	형	신선한
□ depend on		~에 의존하다
□ aid [eid]	명	도움, 원조

□ tool [tu:l]	명	도구
□ hold [hould]	동	잡다, 쥐다
□ unexpected [ʌ̀nikspéktid]	형	예상치 못한
□ caveman [kéivmæn]	명	원시인
□ hire [háiər]	동	고용하다
□ rub [rʌb]	동	문지르다
□ canvas [kǽnvəs]	명	캔버스
□ surprisingly [sərpráiziŋli]	부	놀랍게도

□ unique [ju:ní:k]	형	독특한
□ transportation [trænspɔːrtéiʃn]	명	교통수단
□ abroad [əbrɔ́:d]	부	해외에서
□ suggest [səgʤést]	동	시사하다

□ be made of		~로 만들어지다
□ bamboo [bæmbú:]	명	대나무
□ although [ɔ:lðóu]	접	비록 ~하지만
□ amazing [əméiziŋ]	형	놀라운
□ must [mʌst]	명	필수(품)
□ wheeled [hwí:ld]	형	바퀴가 달린
□ vehicle [ví:əkl]	명	차량, 운송 수단
□ shell [ʃel]	명	껍데기
□ noisy [nɔ́izi]	형	시끄러운
□ recommend [rèkəménd]	동	추천하다

□ define [difáin]	동	정의하다
□ look down on		~을 무시하다
□ discuss [diskʌ́s]	동	토론하다
□ indoors [ìndɔ́:rz]	부	실내에서
□ athletic [æθlétik]	형	강건한
□ lack [læk]	동	~이 없다, 결핍되다
□ grace [greis]	명	품위
□ weak [wi:k]	형	약한
□ figure [fígjər]	명	몸매
□ afford [əfɔ́:rd]	동	~할 여유가 있다
□ fatten [fǽtn]	동	살찌우다
□ fatty [fǽti]	형	기름진
□ diet [dáiət]	명	음식물, 식이요법
□ get married		결혼하다
□ bridegroom [bráidgrù(:)m]	명	신랑
□ bride [braid]	명	신부

UNIT 03

01

carpenter [kɑ́ːrpəntə(r)]	몡	목수
rough [rʌf]	혱	혹독한, 고된
flat tire		바람 빠진 타이어
saw [sɔː]	몡	톱
refuse [rɪfjúːs]	동	거부하다
briefly [bríːfli]	뷔	잠시
tip [tip]	몡	끝, 끝 부분
branch [bræntʃ]	몡	나뭇가지

02

get sick		병에 걸리다
disease [dizíːz]	몡	질병
cure [kjur]	동	치료하다
effort [éfərt]	몡	노력
discover [diskʌ́vər]	동	발견하다
certain [sɜ́ːrtn]	혱	어떤, 특정의
work on		~에 효과가 있다
expect [ikspékt]	동	예상하다

03

couple [kʌpl]	몡	부부, 커플
get into trouble		말썽을 일으키다
minister [mínistə(r)]	몡	목사
agree [əgríː]	동	동의하다

one by one		차례로
repeat [ripíːt]	동	반복하다
voice [vɔis]	몡	목소리
raise [reiz]	동	~을 올리다
shake [ʃeik]	동	흔들다
jump up		뛰어오르다
directly [diréktli]	뷔	곧장
follow [fáːlou]	동	따라가다
happen [hǽpən]	동	발생하다
reply [riplái]	동	대답하다
be in trouble		곤경에 처하다
missing [mísiŋ]	혱	사라진

04

edge [edʒ]	몡	끝, 가장자리
come true		실현되다
record [rékərd]	몡	기록
field [fiːld]	몡	분야
height [hait]	몡	높이
pull [pul]	동	끌어당기다
layer [léiə(r)]	몡	층
atmosphere [ǽtməsfìr]	몡	대기
spacesuit [spéissjːt]	몡	우주복
touch down		착륙하다
ground [graund]	몡	땅, 지면
travel [trǽvl]	동	이동하다
speed of sound		음속
hesitate [hézitèit]	동	망설이다

refreshed [rifréʃt]	ⓗ 상쾌한
crushed [krʌʃt]	ⓗ 분쇄된
red bean	팥
chopped [tʃá:pt]	ⓗ (음식 재료를) 썬(다진)
similar [símələ(r)]	ⓗ 유사한, 비슷한
flour [fláuə(r)]	ⓜ 밀가루
royalty [rɔ́iəlti]	ⓜ 왕족
statue [stǽtʃu:]	ⓜ 조각상, 동상

combination [kà:mbinéiʃn]	ⓜ 조합, 결합
come out	출시되다
early bird	일찍 일어나는 사람
homemade [hòumméid]	ⓗ 집에서 만든
organic [ɔːrgǽnik]	ⓗ 유기농의
mixed [mikst]	ⓗ 혼합된
grain [grein]	ⓜ 곡물; 알갱이
triangular [traiǽŋgjələ(r)]	ⓗ 삼각형의

| growth [grouθ] | ⓜ 성장 |
| rapidly [rǽpidli] | ⓤ 빠르게 |

sale [seil]	ⓜ 판매
convenience store	편의점
increase [ɪnkríːs]	ⓓ 증가하다
[ínkriːs]	ⓜ 증가
a variety of	다양한
proportion [prəpɔ́ːrʃən]	ⓜ 비율
take up space	자리를 차지하다
relatively [rélətivli]	ⓤ 비교적
diverse [dɑivə́ːrs]	ⓗ 다양한
reasonable [ríːznəbl]	ⓗ 합리적인; 비싸지 않은
side dish	밑반찬
trend [trend]	ⓜ 동향, 추세
growth rate	성장률

traditionally [trədíʃənəli]	ⓤ 전통적으로
give birth	출산하다
soften [sɔ́ːfn]	ⓓ 부드럽게 하다
heat up	데우다, 가열하다
pot [pɑːt]	ⓜ 냄비
add [æd]	ⓓ 첨가하다
beef [biːf]	ⓜ 소고기
sesame oil	참기름
soy sauce	간장
stir [stɜː(r)]	ⓓ 젓다
pour [pɔː(r)]	ⓓ 붓다
boil [bɔil]	ⓓ 끓이다
reduce [ridúːs]	ⓓ 줄이다
serve [sɜːrv]	ⓓ 제공하다

01

□ **tropical** [trɑ́:pikəl]	형 열대의
□ **offer** [ɔ́:fə(r)]	동 제공하다
□ **relax** [rilǽks]	동 안정을 취하다, 쉬다
□ **lie** [lai]	동 눕다
□ **comfortable** [kʌ́mftəbl]	형 편안한
□ **sailing** [séiliŋ]	명 요트 타기
□ **equipment** [ikwípmənt]	명 장비
□ **decision** [disíʒn]	명 결정

02

□ **solo** [sóulou]	형 혼자의
□ **barely** [bɛ́rli]	부 거의 ~ 아닌
□ **unknown** [ʌnnóun]	형 알려지지 않은
□ **lend a hand**	도움을 주다
□ **desire** [dizáiər]	명 바람
□ **come from**	~에서 나오다
□ **adventure** [ədvéntʃə(r)]	명 모험
□ **stranger** [stréindʒə(r)]	명 낯선 사람

03

□ **especially** [ispéʃəli]	부 특히
□ **scared** [skɛrd]	형 겁먹은, 무서워하는
□ **deck** [dek]	명 갑판
□ **bean** [bi:n]	명 콩
□ **huge** [hju:dʒ]	형 거대한

□ **sculpture** [skʌ́lptʃər]	명 조형물, 조각상
□ **pier** [pir]	명 부두
□ **lake** [leik]	명 호수
□ **must-see** [mʌ́st-sì:]	형 꼭 봐야 할
□ **aquarium** [əkwériəm]	명 수족관
□ **and so on**	기타 등등
□ **be able to**	~을 할 수 있다
□ **deep-dish** [dí:pdìʃ]	형 (피자가) 두꺼운
□ **view** [vju:]	명 풍경, 전망

04

□ **cousin** [kʌ́zən]	명 사촌
□ **experience** [ikspí(:)riəns]	명 경험 동 경험하다
□ **return** [ritə́:rn]	동 돌아오다
□ **culture** [kʌ́ltʃər]	명 문화
□ **opportunity** [àpərtú:nəti]	명 기회
□ **round-the-world** [ràundðəwə́:rld]	형 세계 일주(의)
□ **ticket** [tíkit]	명 티켓, 표
□ **continent** [kántɪnənt]	명 대륙
□ **stay** [stei]	동 머무르다
□ **tour** [tuər]	동 여행하다 명 여행
□ **market** [má:rkit]	명 시장
□ **tourist** [tú(:)ərist]	명 관광객
□ **landscape** [lǽndskeip]	명 풍경
□ **guest house**	게스트 하우스
□ **volunteer** [vàləntíər]	동 자원 봉사하다
□ **orphanage** [ɔ́:rfənidʒ]	명 고아원

01

national treasure	국보
legend [lédʒənd]	몡 전설
architect [á:rkitèkt]	몡 건축가
carve [kɑːrv]	통 조각하다
crack [kræk]	통 갈라지다 몡 금
descend [disénd]	통 내려오다
faint [feint]	혱 희미한
trace [treis]	몡 흔적

02

symbol [símbəl]	몡 상징, 기호
official [əfíʃəl]	혱 공식적인
sign [sain]	몡 기호
dozens of	수많은 ~
tail [teil]	몡 꼬리
snail [sneil]	몡 달팽이
meow [miáu]	몡 (고양이 울음소리) 야옹
curl up	(몸을) 웅크리다

03

Native American	아메리카 원주민
local [lóukəl]	혱 지역의, 현지의
decoration [dèkəréiʃən]	몡 장식품

pop [pɑp]	통 튀기다
following [fálouiŋ]	몡 다음에 언급되는 것
introduce [ìntrədú:s]	통 소개하다
settler [sétlər]	몡 정착인, 이주자
make money	돈을 벌다
Thanksgiving [θæŋsgíviŋ]	몡 추수감사절
continue [kəntínju(:)]	통 계속하다
machine [məʃí:n]	몡 기계
electric [iléktrik]	혱 전기의
enable [inéibl]	통 가능하게 하다
outside [àutsáid]	젠 ~ 밖에서

04

origin [ɔ́:ridʒin]	몡 기원, 근원
alphabet [ǽlfəbet]	몡 알파벳
modern [mádərn]	혱 현대의
write ~ down	~을 적다
carved [kɑːrvd]	혱 조각된
mean [mi:n]	통 ~을 뜻하다
express [iksprés]	통 표현하다
basic [béisik]	혱 기본적인
hunt [hʌnt]	통 사냥하다
cave [keiv]	몡 동굴
common [kámən]	혱 흔한
site [sait]	몡 장소
trade [treid]	통 거래하다
spread [spred]	통 퍼지다

01 

□ **female** [fí:meil]	형 여성인 명 여성
□ **celebrate** [sélibreit]	동 축하하다
□ **creature** [krí:tʃər]	명 생물
□ **administration** [ədmìnistréiʃən]	명 행정국
□ **respect** [rispékt]	동 존중하다
□ **eco-friendly** [ì:kou-fréndli]	형 친환경적인
□ **marine** [mərí:n]	형 해양의
□ **know-how** [nóu-hàu]	명 비결, 노하우

02

□ **cashless** [kǽʃləs]	형 현금이 없는
□ **payment** [péimənt]	명 결제, 지불
□ **throw away**	처분하다
□ **cash register**	금전 등록기
□ **homeless people**	노숙자
□ **disappear** [dìsəpíər]	동 사라지다
□ **electronic** [ilektránik]	형 전자의
□ **customer** [kʌ́stəmər]	명 고객

03 

□ **teen** [ti:n]	명 청소년, 십 대
□ **treat** [tri:t]	동 대우하다, 취급하다
□ **workplace** [wɛ́:rkplèis]	명 일터, 직장
□ **injure** [índʒər]	동 부상을 입다

□ **prohibit** [prouhíbit]	동 금지하다
□ **high-risk** [háɪ-risk]	형 위험성이 큰
□ **right** [rait]	명 권리
□ **part-time job**	아르바이트
□ **allow** [əláu]	동 허락하다
□ **permit** [pə́:rmit]	명 허가(증)
□ **wage** [weidʒ]	명 임금
□ **sign** [sain]	동 서명하다
□ **contract** [kántrækt]	명 계약(서)
□ **unfair** [ʌnfɛ́r]	형 부당한

04 

□ **modified** [má:difaid]	형 수정된
□ **pressure** [préʃər]	명 압박, 압력
□ **extremely** [ikstrí:mli]	부 극단적으로
□ **skinny** [skíni]	형 마른
□ **comparison** [kəmpǽrisn]	명 비교
□ **in turn**	결국
□ **risk** [risk]	명 위험(성)
□ **impact** [ímpækt]	명 영향
□ **government** [gʌ́vərnmənt]	명 정부
□ **legislate** [lédʒisleit]	동 입법하다
□ **require** [rikwáiər]	동 요구하다
□ **minimum** [míniməm]	형 최소한의
□ **label** [léibəl]	동 라벨을 붙이다
□ **self-confidence** [sèlfká:nfɪdəns]	명 자신감
□ **occur** [əkɜ́:r]	동 발생하다, 일어나다
□ **worth** [wə:rθ]	형 ~할 가치가 있는

UNIT 08

□ **mental** [méntəl] — ⑲ 정신의

□ **collapse** [kəlǽps] — ⑲ 붕괴

□ **warn** [wɔːrn] — ⑧ 경고하다

□ **communication** [kəmjùːnɪkéiʃən] — ⑲ 의사소통

□ **bridge a gap** — 간극을 메우다

□ **accept** [əksépt] — ⑧ 받아들이다

□ **perspective** [pərspéktiv] — ⑲ 관점

□ **priority** [praiɔ́(ː)rəti] — ⑲ 우선 사항

□ **slave** [sleiv] — ⑲ 노예

□ **population** [pàpjuléiʃən] — ⑲ 인구

□ **countryside** [kʌ́ntrisaid] — ⑲ 시골

□ **produce** [prɑdjúːs] — ⑧ 생산하다

□ **physical** [fízikəl] — ⑲ 육체적인, 신체의

□ **account** [əkáunt] — ⑲ 회계, 거래

□ **paperwork** [péipərwɛ̀ːrk] — ⑲ 서류 작업

□ **economics** [ìːkənámiks] — ⑲ 경제학

□ **downside** [dáunsaid] — ⑲ 부정적인 면

□ **research** [rísəːrtʃ] — ⑲ 연구, 조사

□ **depressed** [diprést] — ⑲ 우울한

□ **satisfied** [sǽtisfaid] — ⑲ 만족하는

□ **envy** [énvi] — ⑲ 부러움, 질투, 시기

□ **compare A with B** — A와 B를 비교하다

□ **daily life** — 일상생활

□ **personal** [pə́rsənəl] — ⑲ 개인적인

□ **prevent** [privént] — ⑧ 막다

□ **negative** [négətiv] — ⑲ 부정적인

□ **draw** [drɔː] — ⑧ (결론 등을) 이끌어내다

□ **conclusion** [kənklúːʒən] — ⑲ 결론

□ **recognize** [rékəgnaiz] — ⑧ 깨닫다

□ **normal** [nɔ́ːrml] — ⑲ 평범한, 정상의

□ **dominate** [dámineit] — ⑧ 지배하다

□ **public** [pʌ́blik] — ⑲ 공공의

□ **vote** [vout] — ⑧ 투표하다

□ **western** [wéstərn] — ⑲ 서부의

□ **developing country** — 개발도상국

□ **equal** [íːkwəl] — ⑲ 동등한

□ **tribe** [traib] — ⑲ 부족, 종족

□ **highland** [háilənd] — ⑲ 고지대

□ **head** [hed] — ⑲ 우두머리

□ **household** [háushould] — ⑲ 가족, 식구

□ **control** [kəntróul] — ⑧ 통제하다

□ **possession** [pəzéʃən] — ⑲ 소유물

□ **opposite** [ápəzət] — ⑲ 반대의

□ **completely** [kəmplíːtli] — ⑨ 완전히, 전적으로

□ **religious** [rilídʒəs] — ⑲ 종교적인

□ **political** [pəlítikəl] — ⑲ 정치적인

UNIT 09

01

☐ **fit** [fit]	통 끼우다, 맞추다
☐ **form** [fɔːrm]	통 형성하다
☐ **perhaps** [pərhǽps]	부 아마
☐ **printer** [príntər]	명 인쇄공
☐ **stick** [stik]	통 붙이다
☐ **instructive** [instrʌ́ktiv]	형 유익한, 교훈적인
☐ **improve** [imprúːv]	통 향상하다
☐ **concentration** [kὰnsəntréiʃən]	명 집중(력)

02

☐ **visual** [víʒuəl]	형 시각적인
☐ **related to**	~에 관련된
☐ **arrange** [əréindʒ]	통 배열하다
☐ **brush** [brʌʃ]	명 붓
☐ **vertical** [və́ːrtikəl]	형 수직의
☐ **letter** [létər]	명 글자
☐ **curve** [kəːrv]	명 곡선
☐ **creative** [kriéitiv]	형 창의적인

03

☐ **spare time**	여가 시간
☐ **celebrity** [səlébrəti]	명 유명인
☐ **pirate** [páiərət]	명 해적
☐ **tough** [tʌf]	형 거친
☐ **award-winning** [əwɔ́ːrd-wìniŋ]	형 상을 받은

☐ **actress** [ǽktrəs]	명 여배우
☐ **knit** [nit]	통 뜨개질을 하다
☐ **shawl** [ʃɔːl]	명 숄
☐ **former** [fɔ́ːrmər]	형 이전의
☐ **beekeeping** [bíːkìːpiŋ]	명 양봉
☐ **whole** [houl]	형 전체의, 모든
☐ **hive** [haiv]	명 벌 떼; 벌집
☐ **fascinating** [fǽsineitiŋ]	형 매혹적인, 재미있는
☐ **hang out**	시간을 보내다
☐ **collect** [kəlékt]	통 수집하다
☐ **typewriter** [táipraitər]	명 타자기

04

☐ **beetle** [bíːtl]	명 딱정벌레
☐ **cruel** [krú(ː)əl]	형 잔인한
☐ **garden** [gáːrdən]	통 정원 가꾸기를 하다
☐ **chore** [tʃɔːr]	명 (정기적으로 하는) 일
☐ **shape** [ʃeip]	통 (모양을) 만들다
☐ **dinosaur** [dáinəsːr]	명 공룡
☐ **extreme** [ikstríːm]	형 극한, 극도의
☐ **iron** [áiərn]	통 다림질하다
☐ **surf** [sɜːrf]	통 파도타기를 하다
☐ **skip** [skip]	통 물 수제비를 뜨다
☐ **pond** [pɑnd]	명 연못
☐ **take place**	개최되다
☐ **compete** [kəmpíːt]	통 경쟁하다
☐ **sink** [siŋk]	통 가라앉다
☐ **precious** [préʃəs]	형 귀중한
☐ **high-tech** [hái-tèk]	형 최첨단의

01

advantageous [æ̀dvəntéidʒəs]	형 이로운, 유리한
individual [ìndivíʤuəl]	형 개인적인
attention [əténʃn]	명 관심
distracted [distrǽktid]	형 산만한
violence [váiələns]	명 폭력
disadvantage [dìsədvǽntiʤ]	명 단점
interact with	~와 교류하다
compare [kəmpér]	동 비교하다

02

step into	~에 발을 들여 놓다
pound [paund]	동 (심장이) 마구 뛰다
curiosity [kjùriásəti]	명 호기심
overseas [òuvərsíːz]	형 해외의
volunteering [vɑ̀ːləntíriŋ]	명 자원봉사
desire [dizáiər]	명 열망
custom [kʌ́stəm]	명 관습
worthy [wɝ́ːrði]	형 가치 있는

03

popularity [pɑ̀ːpjulǽrəti]	명 인기
language [lǽŋgwidʒ]	명 언어

pay attention to	~에 주목하다
demand [dimǽnd]	명 수요
soar [sɔːr]	동 (가치, 물가 등이) 치솟다
thanks to	~ 덕분에
introduce [ìntrədjúːs]	동 도입하다
apply [əplái]	동 지원하다
scale [skeil]	명 규모
private [práivət]	형 사설의, 사립의
academy [əkǽdəmi]	명 학원
improve [imprúːv]	동 향상시키다
skill [skil]	명 능력, 기술
greeting [gríːtiŋ]	명 인사

04

virtual [vɝ́ːrtʃuəl]	형 가상의
fiction [fíkʃən]	명 소설
fantasy [fǽntəsi]	명 공상, 상상
vividly [vívidli]	부 생생하게
presence [prézəns]	명 실재, 존재
simulation [sìmjuléiʃən]	명 시뮬레이션, 모의실험
drag [dræg]	동 끌다
position [pəzíʃən]	명 자리, 위치
biology [baiálədʒi]	명 생물학
separate [sépəreit]	동 분리하다
explore [iksplɔ́ːr]	동 탐험하다
supply [sʌplái]	동 공급하다
benefit [bénifit]	동 이익을 얻다
area [ériə]	명 영역

Memo

READING TAPA
WORKBOOK

LEVEL 2

CONTENTS

Word Test

A 영어 단어는 우리말 뜻으로, 우리말 단어는 영어로 쓰시오.

1 author _______________
2 tradition _______________
3 nowadays _______________
4 recognize _______________
5 artistic _______________
6 previous _______________
7 imagine _______________
8 invention _______________
9 mood _______________
10 attract _______________

11 감각 _______________
12 관심 _______________
13 보장하다 _______________
14 최근의 _______________
15 영향력 있는 _______________
16 안전한 _______________
17 대단히 _______________
18 그러므로 _______________
19 즉시, 곧바로 _______________
20 ~와 달리 _______________

B 우리말 뜻과 같도록 빈칸에 알맞은 말을 넣으시오.

1 그 서비스는 현재 사용할 수 없습니다.
⇨ The service is not __________ available.

2 설문 조사를 위해서 우리는 100명의 학생 표본을 무작위로 선발할 것이다.
⇨ For the survey, we will __________ a random sample of 100 students.

3 Brad는 많은 위대한 문학 작품들을 읽었다.
⇨ Brad has read many of the great works of __________.

4 Claire는 가장 친한 친구가 휴가를 가서 외로움을 느꼈다.
⇨ Claire felt __________ because her best friend went on vacation.

C 짝지어진 관계가 같도록 빈칸에 알맞은 단어를 넣으시오.

- produce : production = create : __________
- normal : normality = popular : __________

Writing Test

A   문장의 <u>틀린</u> 부분을 한 군데 찾아 바르게 고쳐 쓰시오.

1   How about go for a walk?
⇨ ____

2   Mary was too frightened speak.
⇨ ____

3   I felt like take a picture with the singer.
⇨ ____

4   Jordan is enough smart to answer all the questions.
⇨ ____

5   We can't stop anyone from leave here.
⇨ ____

B   우리말과 같도록 괄호 안의 말을 이용하여 문장을 완성하시오.

1   나는 2주 뒤에 당신을 만나기를 기대합니다. (look forward to, meet)
____

2   Jiho는 너무 어려서 스스로 결정할 수 없다. (young, decide)
____

3   당신은 성공하기 위해서 최선을 다해야 한다. (do your best, succeed)
____

4   그에게 도움을 요청하는 건 어때? (ask, help)
____

5   이 모형 비행기는 너무 복잡해서 조립할 수가 없다. (complicated, put together)
____

Translation Test

A

01

You might be too young to be familiar with the music of Bob Dylan.

However, you may have heard *Blowin' in the Wind* and *Like a Rolling Stone*.

Two of his most famous songs will surely take your parents back in time.

B

02

Third, you don't need to pay much in order to enjoy webtoons. In general,

webtoons are cheaper than printed comic books because production costs

are lower. Webtoons might be part of your daily routine. But don't get too

absorbed in them.

C

04

These days, many Koreans look forward to watching their favorite cooking

shows. Many celebrities and chefs appear on the TV shows and cook with

just a few ingredients. The ingredients are easy to find in our fridges, such

as leftover *jokbal*, gimchi, and vegetables.

Word Test

A 영어 단어는 우리말 뜻으로, 우리말 단어는 영어로 쓰시오.

1	indoors	__________	11	껍데기	__________
2	grace	__________	12	약한	__________
3	unexpected	__________	13	독특한	__________
4	wonder	__________	14	제공하다	__________
5	define	__________	15	고용하다	__________
6	overweight	__________	16	강건한	__________
7	fatty	__________	17	~할 여유가 있다	__________
8	tool	__________	18	차량, 운송 수단	__________
9	abroad	__________	19	잡다, 쥐다	__________
10	bridegroom	__________	20	신부	__________

B 우리말 뜻과 같도록 빈칸에 알맞은 말을 넣으시오.

1 당신의 발을 비누로 문지르세요.

⇨ __________ your feet with the soap.

2 나는 아침으로 신선한 과일과 빵을 먹었다.

⇨ I ate __________ fruit and bread for breakfast.

3 새로운 학교의 규칙들에 대해 토론해 보는 게 어떤가요?

⇨ Why don't we __________ the new school rules?

4 그 결과는 당신에게 무엇을 시사하나요?

⇨ What do the results __________ to you?

C 빈칸에 공통으로 들어갈 단어로 알맞은 것은?

> • Plants depend __________ sunlight and water.
> • Don't look down __________ me because I'm young.

① in   ② on   ③ to

④ with   ⑤ about

Writing **Test**

A 문장의 <u>틀린</u> 부분을 한 군데 찾아 바르게 고쳐 쓰시오.

1 Water vegetables in run water.

⇨ ____

2 The boy name Daniel won first prize.

⇨ ____

3 Ann found the gold hiding in the wall.

⇨ ____

4 We saw a big eagle flown above us.

⇨ ____

5 I was surprising to hear the news.

⇨ ____

B |보기|와 같이 분사를 이용하여 두 문장을 한 문장으로 연결하시오.

> ┤ 보기 ├
> Do you know the boy? He is sitting next to Mina.
> ⇨ Do you know the boy sitting next to Mina?

1 I threw away the vase. The vase was broken.

⇨ ____

2 Let's pick up those leaves. They have fallen.

⇨ ____

3 The man is my teacher. He is standing in front of the door.

⇨ ____

4 The boys are my brothers. They are dancing on the stage.

⇨ ____

» Answer p.32

Translation Test

A

01

Do you ever wonder what children are eating for lunch across the world? In

America where the number of overweight students has increased, parents are

more interested in school lunch than before.

B

02

One of the most unexpected tools is the human body. Finger painting is the

oldest way of using the body to paint. For example, look at the very old

paintings made by cavemen. They were probably done by using fingers.

C

04

Defining beauty is interesting because it is something seen differently in

different times and places. For example, in the 19th century England, most

women didn't like very strong men. Farming and factory work were hard

jobs requiring strong workers.

Word Test

A   영어 단어는 우리말 뜻으로, 우리말 단어는 영어로 쓰시오.

1	reply	____________	11	톱	____________
2	disease	____________	12	끝, 가장자리	____________
3	atmosphere	____________	13	흔들다	____________
4	branch	____________	14	목수	____________
5	follow	____________	15	노력	____________
6	ground	____________	16	층	____________
7	refuse	____________	17	기록	____________
8	travel	____________	18	발견하다	____________
9	repeat	____________	19	분야	____________
10	minister	____________	20	높이	____________

B   우리말 뜻과 같도록 빈칸에 알맞은 말을 넣으시오.

1   어떤 사람들은 특정 음식을 먹지 않는다.

⇨ Some people don't eat ___________ foods.

2   나는 대부분의 것들에 대해 그의 의견에 동의한다.

⇨ I ___________ with him on most things.

3   미래에는 로봇이 환자들을 치료할 수 있을 것이다.

⇨ Robots will be able to ___________ patients in the future.

4   나는 그가 그녀를 이해할 것이라고 예상하지 않았다.

⇨ I didn't ___________ him to understand her.

C |보기|에서 알맞은 단어를 골라 문장을 완성하시오.

보기
happen   raise   hesitate   discover

1   Don't ___________ to express your opinion.
2   What time did the accident ___________ ?
3   ___________ your arms over your shoulders.

» Answer p.33

Writing Test

A 화법을 바꿨을 때, <u>틀린</u> 부분을 찾아 바르게 고쳐 쓰시오.

1
> Mark said to me, "Are they going to help me?"
> ⇒ Mark asked me that they were going to help him.

⇒ ____

2
> Alice said to me, "I want to be a teacher."
> ⇒ Alice told me that I want to be a teacher.

⇒ ____

3
> The boss said to me, "Don't make the same mistake again."
> ⇒ The boss advised me to not make the same mistake again.

⇒ ____

B 직접화법 문장을 간접화법 문장으로 바꿔 쓰시오.

1 Wendy said to me, "I'll be home late tonight."
⇒ ____

2 The foreigner said to me, "Can you speak English?"
⇒ ____

3 My uncle said to me, "How is your family these days?"
⇒ ____

4 Eric said, "What do Koreans do on the Lunar New Year's Day?"
⇒ ____

5 I said to my sister, "Wait here for a minute."
⇒ ____

Translation **Test**

A

01

Smiling brightly, he hugged his children and gave his wife a kiss. I asked

him, "What does the tree mean to you?" He said, "Oh, it's my trouble tree.

I always hang my worries on that tree whenever I come home."

B

02

All of the doctors said, "Nothing can be done about ALD. Lorenzo will die

soon." But Augusto asked himself whether he could let Lorenzo die without

any effort. He answered, "No! He is only 5 years old. I'm his father."

C

04

He became the first human to travel faster than the speed of sound without

a vehicle. Now, do you know what Baumgartner said? He told us to go up

really high to understand how small we are. He also told us not to hesitate

in making your dreams come true.

Word Test

A 영어 단어는 우리말 뜻으로, 우리말 단어는 영어로 쓰시오.

1	similar	11	증가; 증가하다
2	crushed	12	성장률
3	combination	13	합리적인; 비싸지 않은
4	sesame oil	14	유기농의
5	trend	15	밑반찬
6	convenience store	16	출산하다
7	relatively	17	빠르게
8	triangular	18	다양한
9	sale	19	전통적으로
10	proportion	20	성장

B 우리말 뜻과 같도록 빈칸에 알맞은 말을 넣으시오.

1 우유를 작은 그릇에 부으세요.

⇒ ___________ the milk into a small bowl.

2 나는 Tim의 생일에 집에서 만든 케이크를 준비했다.

⇒ I prepared a(n) ___________ cake for Tim's birthday.

3 이번 시즌의 곡물 수확량은 2,000만 톤까지 증가할 것이다.

⇒ This season's ___________ harvest will increase by 20 million tons.

4 소기업들은 비용을 줄일 방책을 고안하고 있다.

⇒ Small businesses are making a plan to ___________ costs.

C 영영풀이에 해당하는 단어를 |보기|에서 찾아 쓰시오.

보기				
statue	beef	royalty	flour	statue

1 the meat from a cow ⇒ ___________

2 a powder that is made by crushing wheat or other grain ⇒ ___________

3 members of a royal family ⇒ ___________

Writing Test

A 괄호 안의 말을 바르게 배열하여 문장을 완성하시오.

1 Samuel은 무언가가 그의 머리를 건드리는 것을 느꼈다.
(felt / his head / touch / something / Samuel)
⇨ ____

2 나는 아이가 우는 것을 멈추게 할 수 없다.
(stop / the baby / can't / I / make / crying)
⇨ ____

3 나는 그녀가 그녀의 치마를 고르는 것을 도왔다.
(her / helped / I / her / choose / skirt / to)
⇨ ____

4 그들은 그들의 아이들이 열심히 공부하게 했다.
(children / let / study / hard / their / they)
⇨ ____

5 당신은 사람들이 길을 건너는 것을 보았나요?
(Did / see / crossing / the people / you / the street)
⇨ ____

B 문장의 **틀린** 부분을 찾아 바르게 고쳐 쓰시오.

1 The man helped his guests delivering their bags.
⇨ ____

2 Aron had me to come to clean the garage.
⇨ ____

3 Harry heard his dog to bark.
⇨ ____

4 This song made her missing her hometown.
⇨ ____

» Answer p.33

Translation Test

A 01

Cold desserts are perfect for hot summer days. They really make you feel

cool and refreshed. In Korea, we eat *patbingsu* on hot days. It's a dessert

made of crushed ice, red beans, chopped fruits, milk, and strawberry syrup.

B 03

Some *dosiraks* offer a taste of as many as 11 side dishes. Another secret of

their success is that they offer the feeling of having home-cooked meals. If

these trends continue, we can expect to see the growth rate of the *dosirak*

market speed up.

C 04

Have you seen someone making or eating *miyeokguk*? This soup has special

meaning for Koreans. In Korean culture, mothers traditionally eat this soup

for several days after they give birth. It is also usually the soup that Koreans

eat to celebrate birthdays.

Word **Test**

A 영어 단어는 우리말 뜻으로, 우리말 단어는 영어로 쓰시오.

1	barely		11	눕다
2	experience		12	요트 타기
3	deck		13	혼자의
4	offer		14	사촌
5	lake		15	편안한
6	adventure		16	대륙
7	volunteer		17	돌아오다
8	tropical		18	안정을 취하다, 쉬다
9	orphanage		19	낯선 사람
10	equipment		20	관광객

B 우리말 뜻과 같도록 빈칸에 알맞은 말을 넣으시오.

1 그 집은 공원을 내다보는 굉장히 멋진 전망을 갖고 있다.
⇒ The house has a wonderful ___________ over the park.

2 그는 그 결정에 대해 몹시 화가 났다.
⇒ He is very angry about the ___________.

3 Mark는 우리를 방문하고 싶다는 바람을 표현했다.
⇒ Mark expressed a(n) ___________ to visit us.

4 나는 외국에 가서 공부할 기회를 얻었다.
⇒ I had a(n) ___________ to go abroad to study.

C 밑줄 친 It이 가리키는 단어는?

> It is an object made out of stone, wood, clay etc by an artist.

① bean ② culture ③ landscape
④ market ⑤ sculpture

Writing **Test**

A 괄호 안의 말을 바르게 배열하여 문장을 완성하시오.

1   Jamie는 이미 회의를 준비했다.
(already / for / Jamie / has / the meeting / prepared)
➡ ______________________________________

2   그녀의 어머니는 방금 일본에서 도착하셨다.
(has / from / arrived / just / Japan / her mother)
➡ ______________________________________

3   최근에 날씨는 계속 매우 덥고 습했다.
(humid / hot / the weather / lately / very / has / and / been)
➡ ______________________________________

4   Susan은 전에 그 영화를 본 적이 있다.
(watched / the movie / Susan / has / before)
➡ ______________________________________

5   김 선생님은 서울로 이사 가기 전에는 종종 쇼핑하러 가곤 했었다.
(often / before / he / Mr. Kim / had / shopping / gone / moved / to Seoul)
➡ ______________________________________

B 우리말과 같도록 괄호 안의 말을 이용하여 현재완료 문장을 완성하시오.

1   Sam은 택시에 그의 지갑을 두고 내렸다. (leave, wallet)
➡ ______________________________________

2   나는 내 과학 리포트를 아직 끝내지 못했다. (finish, science report)
➡ ______________________________________

3   Julie는 도쿄에서 3년 동안 살았다. (live)
➡ ______________________________________

4   나의 아버지는 나에게 가방을 사 주셨다. (buy)
➡ ______________________________________

Translation **Test**

• 다음 주어진 문장을 끊어 읽고, 우리말로 해석하시오.

A　01

Have you had cold weather since last winter? Then you should call *Paradise*

Travel. We offer wonderful tours to beautiful areas. If you join our popular

tours, you can see lovely tropical islands like Bali, Phuket, and the Maldives.

It's a great way to relax.

B　03

Saturday was my second day in Chicago. I had to get up early even though

I was very tired. On the previous day, we had visited so many places. I

went to Northerly Island Park, the Willis Tower, etc. Willis Tower, the second

highest building in the U.S., was especially an exciting place to me.

C　04

I first got the idea from my cousin, Sarah. She had started to tour around

the world before she was 19. She visited many exciting places. She saw the

Taj Mahal in India, and enjoyed shopping in markets for tourists.

Word **Test**

A 영어 단어는 우리말 뜻으로, 우리말 단어는 영어로 쓰시오.

1	sign	__________	11	상징, 기호	__________
2	modern	__________	12	~을 뜻하다	__________
3	faint	__________	13	건축가	__________
4	following	__________	14	표현하다	__________
5	settler	__________	15	지역의, 현지의	__________
6	descend	__________	16	공식적인	__________
7	introduce	__________	17	조각하다	__________
8	trace	__________	18	장식품	__________
9	pop	__________	19	꼬리	__________
10	common	__________	20	거래하다	__________

B 우리말 뜻과 같도록 빈칸에 알맞은 말을 넣으시오.

1 전기 수요가 급격하게 증가하고 있다.
⇨ Demand for __________ power is increasing rapidly.

2 우주의 기원은 여전히 미스터리이다.
⇨ The __________ of the universe is still a mystery.

3 그 동굴 안에는 보물이 있다.
⇨ There is a treasure in the __________.

4 어떤 지역의 전설에 따르면, 옛날에 이 호수에는 용이 살았다고 한다.
⇨ According to a local __________, a dragon lived in this lake long ago.

C 우리말 뜻과 같도록 할 때, 빈칸에 공통으로 들어갈 단어를 쓰시오.

> • 유리잔에 뜨거운 물을 넣지 마라, 그렇지 않으면 금이 갈 것이다.
> ⇨ Don't put hot water in the glass, or it will __________.
> • 벽에 금 하나가 나타나기 시작했다.
> ⇨ A __________ began to appear in the walls.

Writing **Test**

A   우리말과 같도록 괄호 안의 말을 이용하여 비교의 문장을 완성하시오.

1   그녀의 집은 나의 집보다 네 배 더 크다. (four times, big)
⇒ ____

2   Brad는 클수록 점점 더 강해진다. (get stronger, grow up)
⇒ ____

3   가능한 자세하게 네 계획에 대해 말해 줘. (as, specifically)
⇒ ____

4   날씨가 더워지면 더워질수록, 더 많은 사람들이 차가운 음료를 마신다.
(get hot, drinks, the weather)
⇒ ____

B   괄호 안의 말을 바르게 배열하여 문장을 완성하시오.

1   안개가 점점 더 짙어진다. (getting / thicker / the fog / is / and / thicker)
⇒ ____

2   그 흰 드레스는 검정 드레스만큼 비싸지 않다.
(not / expensive / the black dress / is / so / as / the white dress)
⇒ ____

3   더 비가 거세게 올수록, 사람들은 더 빨리 걷는다.
(the faster / people / heavily / it / rains / the more / walk)
⇒ ____

4   내 TV는 너의 것보다 두 배 더 크다. (twice / large / yours / my / as / TV / as / is)
⇒ ____

5   너는 가능한 집에 빨리 돌아오는 편이 좋겠다.
(come back / as / you'd / you / early / as / can / better / home)
⇒ ____

» Answer p.34

Translation Test

A 

Seokguram is the 24th national treasure in Korea. There is an interesting

legend about Seokguram. The architect of Seokguram was carving the central

ceiling stone as carefully as he could. Suddenly, it cracked before his eyes

and he fell down.

B 

The @ symbol, before the introduction of e-mail, was not as popular as it is

these days. It was just used to show the cost or weight of something. For

example, if you bought 10 apples, you might write it as 10 apples @ $1.10 each.

C 

Making symbols for everything got harder and harder as time passed. So,

many people started to feel the need to invent a set of letters, an alphabet.

Egyptians tried to make one and did it. And it became common in Egypt.

Word Test

A   영어 단어는 우리말 뜻으로, 우리말 단어는 영어로 쓰시오.

1	modified	____________	11	부당한	____________
2	label	____________	12	대우하다, 취급하다	____________
3	disappear	____________	13	압박, 압력	____________
4	marine	____________	14	생물	____________
5	comparison	____________	15	금지하다	____________
6	cashless	____________	16	위험(성)	____________
7	legislate	____________	17	부상을 입다	____________
8	female	____________	18	자신감	____________
9	require	____________	19	발생하다, 일어나다	____________
10	electronic	____________	20	행정국	____________

B   우리말 뜻과 같도록 빈칸에 알맞은 말을 넣으시오.

1   팬들은 가수의 사생활을 존중하지 않았다.

⇒ The fans didn't ____________ the singer's privacy.

2   모든 사람들은 의견을 표현할 권리가 있다.

⇒ Everyone has the ____________ to express his or her opinion.

3   나의 부모님은 내가 새 가방을 사도록 허락하지 않으실 것이다.

⇒ My parents wouldn't ____________ me to buy a new bag.

4   그녀의 연설은 내 삶에 커다란 영향을 주었다.

⇒ Her speech had a big ____________ on my life.

C   밑줄 친 It이 가리키는 단어는?

> <u>It</u> is money you earn, which is paid according to the number of hours, days, or weeks that you work.

① wage   ② customer   ③ teen

④ workplace   ⑤ payment

          » Answer p.35

Writing Test

A　문장의 <u>틀린</u> 부분을 한 군데 찾아 바르게 고쳐 쓰시오.

1　We need a person which can fix the car.

⇒

2　This computer is which I want to buy.

⇒

3　Jenny, that is my best friend, lives next door.

⇒

4　David is the rude boy about that I talked.

⇒

5　The police officer what I asked for directions is my friend's dad.

⇒

B　관계대명사를 이용하여 두 문장을 한 문장으로 바꾸시오.

1　The volunteer work changed me a lot. I did the volunteer work during the vacation.

⇒

2　The bed was very comfortable. I slept in the bed last night.

⇒

3　A nurse was taking care of a patient. The nurse didn't wear a uniform.

⇒

4　Have you ever heard about the girl? Her name is Sophia.

⇒

5　We can't go to the birthday party. We were invited to it.

⇒

Translation Test

A

01

Haenyeo use a unique and eco-friendly way of harvesting, which protects the marine environment. Also, they have passed down diving know-how to younger generations. This helped *Haenyeo* to be listed as a UNESCO cultural heritage.

B

02

A cashless society is coming. Scandinavians use cash for no more than 6% of all payments they make. In Denmark, the government has proposed that stores throw their cash registers away. In Korea, you can even use a credit card to buy newspapers that homeless people sell.

C

04

We all have seen some typical images, in which models have been photoshopped to appear extremely skinny. One research shows that women compare themselves with those images. This comparison can lead them to develop a poor self-image.

» Answer p.35

Word Test

A 영어 단어는 우리말 뜻으로, 우리말 단어는 영어로 쓰시오.

1	account	____________	11	관점 ____________
2	developing country	____________	12	인구 ____________
3	economics	____________	13	동등한 ____________
4	slave	____________	14	부정적인 ____________
5	physical	____________	15	정신의 ____________
6	opposite	____________	16	투표하다 ____________
7	collapse	____________	17	우선 사항 ____________
8	political	____________	18	고지대 ____________
9	religious	____________	19	소유물 ____________
10	tribe	____________	20	시골 ____________

B | 보기 |에서 알맞은 단어를 골라 문장을 완성하시오.

> ┤ 보기 ├
>
> accept   control   warn   normal

1 Paul wanted to live a(n) __________ life.
2 You have to __________ your temper.
3 Mira decided to __________ the job offer.

C 짝지어진 단어의 관계가 같도록 빈칸에 알맞은 단어를 넣으시오.

> • separate : separately = complete : __________
> • dominate : domination = conclude : __________

Writing **Test**

A 두 문장이 같은 뜻이 되도록 밑줄 친 부분을 관계부사로 바꿔 문장을 완성하시오.

1 Tim won't tell anyone the reason for which he missed the test.

⇨ ____

2 Yoga teaches us the way in which we can relax our mind and body.

⇨ ____

3 The New Year's Day is known as the day on which people eat *tteokguk*.

⇨ ____

4 I want to visit a town in which the artist was born and raised.

⇨ ____

5 Would you recommend a restaurant in which we can have fresh seafood?

⇨ ____

B 우리말과 같도록 관계부사와 괄호 안의 말을 이용하여 문장을 완성하시오.

1 나는 학업에 집중할 수 있는 조용한 장소가 필요하다. (concentrate on)

⇨ I need a quiet place ____.

2 삼촌은 나에게 종이 접는 방법을 보여주셨다. (fold the paper)

⇨ My uncle showed me ____.

3 나는 우리가 처음으로 만난 그 날을 기억한다. (meet)

⇨ I remember the day ____.

4 왜 그런 결정을 했는지 물어봐도 될까요? (decision)

⇨ Can I ask you the reason ____?

5 학교는 학생들이 대부분의 시간을 보내는 장소이다. (spend)

⇨ School is the place ____.

≫ Answer p.35

Translation **Test**

A 

We have to accept that we live in a different world where we cannot

understand each other. You have to make the effort to understand and

accept your mother's perspectives and priorities.

B 

Now let's find out how you can prevent those negative feelings. First, don't

draw conclusions about other people from the web. Be sure to step away

from your computer and get the full story about the other person.

C 

There was a time when most societies were dominated by men. Men still

hold most of the power in family and public life. For example, it was only a

short time ago when women could not vote in most Western countries.

Word Test

A 영어 단어는 우리말 뜻으로, 우리말 단어는 영어로 쓰시오.

1	improve	___________	11 수직의	___________
2	curve	___________	12 거친	___________
3	celebrity	___________	13 수집하다	___________
4	beekeeping	___________	14 잔인한	___________
5	fit	___________	15 형성하다	___________
6	extreme	___________	16 경쟁하다	___________
7	stick	___________	17 유익한, 교훈적인	___________
8	chore	___________	18 해적	___________
9	precious	___________	19 이전의	___________
10	visual	___________	20 집중(력)	___________

B 우리말 뜻과 같도록 빈칸에 알맞은 말을 넣으시오.

1 작은 구멍이 큰 배를 가라앉힌다.

⇒ A small leak will ___________ a great ship.

2 여러분은 알파벳 카드를 올바른 순서로 배열해야 한다.

⇒ You should ___________ the alphabet cards in the correct order.

3 Daniel은 하루 종일 소설을 읽으며 보내곤 했다.

⇒ Daniel used to spend the ___________ day reading a novel.

4 대부분의 학부모들은 자신의 아이들이 창의력을 개발하기를 기대한다.

⇒ Most parents expect their children to develop their ___________ ability.

C 빈칸에 들어갈 말이 바르게 짝지어진 것은?

> • Many people suffer from problems related ___________ employment.
> • I hang ___________ with my friends every Friday night.

① for – to　　② for – out　　③ to – into

④ to – up　　⑤ to – out

Writing Test

A |보기|에서 접속사를 골라, 두 문장을 한 문장으로 연결하시오. (단, 두 번째 문장을 종속절로 넣을 것)

> 보기
>
> even though　　　because　　　unless　　　that　　　when

1   I couldn't arrive on time.　I missed the bus.

　⇨ --

2   Eric was listening to music.　His cellphone rang at that time.

　⇨ --

3   It is very important.　We must do something to help him.

　⇨ --

4   Mr. Brown enjoys eating gimchi.　He is not a Korean.

　⇨ --

5   You will get lost in a strange city.　You follow the directions.

　⇨ --

B   문장의 틀린 부분을 한 군데 찾아 바르게 고쳐 쓰시오.

1   Both my mother or my baby were found to be healthy.

　⇨ --

2   Where I was waiting for a bus, Paul saw me.

　⇨ --

3   Tom ate neither meat and fish.

　⇨ --

4   Because of he was injured badly, we decided to go home.

　⇨ --

Translation Test

A

Putting puzzle pieces together is a pleasant and instructive way of relaxing.

It is good for your brain. It's because both sides of your brain work when

you do jigsaw puzzles.

B

What do you usually do in your spare time? Do you play either the guitar

or the piano? Do you dance or draw? Celebrities also have some interesting

hobbies. Everyone knows Johnny Depp who stars in *Pirates of the Caribbean.*

He usually shows a tough image, but at home he sometimes plays with

dolls!

C

Geocaching is a compound word; "geo" means "earth," and "cache" means

"a hiding place" or "a precious thing." It is a high-tech treasure hunt game

because it is a game to find a hidden thing using GPS.

Word Test

A 영어 단어는 우리말 뜻으로, 우리말 단어는 영어로 쓰시오.

1	position	___________	11	도입하다	___________
2	drag	___________	12	관습	___________
3	soar	___________	13	능력, 기술	___________
4	worthy	___________	14	단점	___________
5	curiosity	___________	15	공상, 상상	___________
6	individual	___________	16	이로운, 유리한	___________
7	demand	___________	17	사설의, 사립의	___________
8	area	___________	18	실재, 존재	___________
9	volunteering	___________	19	분리하다	___________
10	simulation	___________	20	산만한	___________

B 우리말 뜻과 같도록 빈칸에 알맞은 말을 넣으시오.

1 그 게임에는 폭력이 너무 많다.

⇒ There is too much ___________ in the game.

2 그 연설자는 사람들의 관심을 이끌었다.

⇒ The speaker attracted public ___________.

3 나는 그 대학교에 지원할 계획이다.

⇒ I'm planning to ___________ for the university.

4 Dean 선생님은 생물학 분야에서 인정받는 지도자이다.

⇒ Ms. Dean is the acknowledged leader in her field of ___________.

C 영영풀이에 해당하는 단어를 | 보기 | 에서 찾아 쓰시오.

보기				
virtual	fiction	desire	skill	scale

1 a strong hope or wish   ⇒ ___________

2 stories about imaginary people and events   ⇒ ___________

3 the size or extent of something big   ⇒ ___________

Writing Test

A   밑줄 친 부분이 문장의 주어가 되도록 다시 고쳐 쓰시오.

1   Brian laughed at <u>my sister</u> so loud.

   ⇨ --

2   Minji's exam results satisfied <u>her teacher</u>.

   ⇨ --

3   The manager may accept <u>my proposal</u>.

   ⇨ --

4   My mom is washing <u>the dirty plates and bowls</u>.

   ⇨ --

5   The staff cleaned <u>the meeting room</u> last night.

   ⇨ --

B   문장의 틀린 부분을 찾아 바르게 고쳐 쓰시오.

1   Food waste should taken out separately.

   ⇨ --

2   I don't like asked to hold a party.

   ⇨ --

3   The thief was arresting by the police officer.

   ⇨ --

4   The girl is take care of by his grandparents.

   ⇨ --

5   I expected the project be finished soon.

   ⇨ --

Translation Test

• 다음 주어진 문장을 끊어 읽고, 우리말로 해석하시오.

A 02

I met the group of children I was going to help. I was impressed by their interest and desire to learn. While they were being taught, we helped them with various subjects.

B 03

We often hear about lots of non-Koreans to be taught Korean in Korea or in other foreign countries. For example, the Korean classes in universities are filled with the students who want to learn Korean as exchange students.

C 04

VR hardware will become cheaper, so it can be supplied to the developing countries. This will allow students around the world to benefit from the same level of experience. VR technologies can also be made use of in many areas other than education.

Answer

unit 01   pp.02~04

Word Test

A 1 작가 2 전통 3 요즈음 4 인정하다 5 예술적인 6 이전의 7 상상하다 8 발명(품) 9 분위기 10 끌다 11 sense 12 attention 13 guarantee 14 recent 15 influential 16 safe 17 greatly 18 therefore 19 instantly 20 unlike **B** 1 currently 2 select 3 literature 4 lonely

C creation, popularity

Writing Test

A 1 How about going for a walk? 2 Mary was too frightened to speak. 3 I felt like taking a picture with the singer. 4 Jordan is smart enough to answer all the questions. 5 We can't stop anyone from leaving here. **B** 1 I look forward to meeting you in two weeks. 2 Jiho is too young to decide for himself. 3 You have to do your best (in order) to succeed. 4 How about asking him for help? 5 This model plane is too complicated to put together.

Translation Test

A 여러분은 너무 어려서 밥 딜런의 음악에 친숙하지 않을지도 모른다. 하지만 여러분은 〈Blowin' in the Wind〉와 〈Like a Rolling Stone〉을 들어본 적은 있을지도 모른다. 그의 가장 유명한 노래들 중 두 곡은 틀림없이 여러분들의 부모님의 시간을 과거로 되돌아가게 해 줄 것이다.

B 셋째, 여러분은 웹툰을 즐기기 위해서 (돈을) 많이 지불 할 필요가 없다. 보통, 웹툰은 제작 비용이 더 낮기 때문에 인쇄 된 만화책보다 더 저렴하다. 웹툰은 여러분 일상의 일부가 될 수도 있다. 하지만 그것에 지나치게 빠지지는 마라.

C 요즈음 많은 한국인들은 자신이 가장 좋아하는 요리 프로그램을 시청하기를 기대한다. 많은 유명인들과 셰프들이 TV 쇼에 등장하여 단지 몇 가지의 재료로 요리를 한다. 재료들은 우리의 냉장고에서 찾아보기 쉬운 남은 족발, 김치 그리고 채소와 같은 것들이다.

unit 02   pp.05~07

Word Test

A 1 실내에서 2 품위 3 예상치 못한 4 궁금해하다 5 정의하다 6 과체중의 7 기름진 8 도구 9 해외에서 10 신랑 11 shell 12 weak 13 unique 14 provide 15 hire 16 athletic 17 afford 18 vehicle 19 hold 20 bride **B** 1 Rub 2 fresh 3 discuss 4 suggest

C ②

Writing Test

A 1 Water vegetables in running water. 2 The boy named Daniel won first prize. 3 Ann found the gold hidden in the wall. 4 We saw a big eagle flying above us. 5 I was surprised to hear the news. **B** 1 I threw away the broken vase. 2 Let's pick up those fallen leaves. 3 The man standing in front of the door is my teacher. 4 The boys dancing on the stage are my brothers.

Translation Test

A 여러분은 전 세계의 아이들이 점심으로 무엇을 먹는지 궁금해한 적이 있나요? 과체중인 학생 수가 증가해 온 미국에서는, 부모들이 예전보다 학교 급식에 관심이 더 많습니다.

B 가장 예상치 못한 도구들 중의 하나가 사람의 몸이다. 손가락으로 그림을 그리는 것은 그림을 그리기 위해 신체를 이용하는 가장 오래된 방법이다. 예를 들어, 원시인에 의해 그려진 매우 오래된 그림들을 봐라. 그것들은 아마도 손가락을 사용하여 완성된 것이다.

C 아름다움을 정의하는 것은 흥미로운데, 그것은 다른 시대와 장소에서 다르게 보여지는 것이기 때문이다. 예를 들어, 19세기 영국에서 대부분의 여성들은 매우 강한 남성을 좋아하지 않았다. 농사와 공장의 일은 강한 일꾼을 요구하는 힘든 직업들이었다.

Word Test

A 1 대답하다 2 질병 3 대기 4 나뭇가지 5 따라가다 6 땅, 지면 7 거부하다 8 이동하다 9 반복하다 10 목사 11 saw 12 edge 13 shake 14 carpenter 15 effort 16 layer 17 record 18 discover 19 field 20 height **B** 1 certain 2 agree 3 cure 4 expect **C** 1 hesitate 2 happen 3 Raise

Writing Test

A 1 Mark asked me if (whether) they were going to help him. 2 Alice told me that she wanted to be a teacher. 3 The boss advised me not to make the same mistake again.
B 1 Wendy told me that she would be home late that night. 2 The foreigner asked me whether (if) I could speak English. 3 My uncle asked me how my family was those days. 4 Eric asked what Koreans did on the Lunar New Year's Day. 5 I asked (told) my sister to wait there for a minute.

Translation Test

A 그는 밝게 웃으면서 자신의 아이들을 안아 주었고 아내에게 키스를 했다. 나는 그에게 물었다. "그 나무는 당신에게 무엇을 의미하나요?" 그는 말했다. "오, 그것은 나의 걱정 나무입니다. 나는 집에 올 때마다 항상 걱정거리들을 저 나무 위에 걸어 두죠."
B 모든 의사들은 말했다. "ALD에 관해서 할 수 있는 것은 아무것도 없습니다. Lorenzo는 곧 사망할 것입니다." 그러나 Augusto는 아무 노력도 하지 않고 Lorenzo를 죽게 놔둘 수 있는지 스스로에게 물었다. 그는 "안 돼! 그 아이는 겨우 5살이야. 나는 그 아이의 아빠다."라고 답했다.
C 그는 이동수단 없이 음속보다 더 빨리 이동한 최초의 인간이 되었다. 이제 당신은 Baumgartner가 뭐라고 말을 했는지 알겠는가? 그는 우리에게 우리가 얼마나 작은지 알기 위해서 정말 높이 올라가라고 말했다. 그는 또한 당신의 꿈을 실현하는 데 주저하지 말라고 말했다.

Word Test

A 1 유사한, 비슷한 2 분쇄된 3 조합, 결합 4 참기름 5 동향, 추세 6 편의점 7 비교적 8 삼각형의 9 판매 10 비율 11 increase 12 growth rate 13 reasonable 14 organic 15 side dish 16 give birth 17 rapidly 18 diverse 19 traditionally 20 growth **B** 1 Pour 2 homemade 3 grain 4 reduce **C** 1 beef 2 flour 3 royalty

Writing Test

A 1 Samuel felt something touch his head. 2 I can't make the baby stop crying. 3 I helped her to choose her skirt. 4 They let their children study hard. 5 Did you see the people crossing the street? **B** 1 The man helped his guests (to) deliver their bags. 2 Aron had me come to clean the garage. 3 Harry heard his dog barking. 4 This song made her miss her hometown.

Translation Test

A 차가운 디저트는 더운 여름날에 완벽하다. 그것들은 정말로 여러분이 시원하고 상쾌한 느낌을 느끼도록 만든다. 한국에서 우리는 더운 날에 팥빙수를 먹는다. 그것은 분쇄된 얼음, 팥, 잘게 썬 과일, 우유, 그리고 딸기 시럽으로 만들어진 디저트이다.
B 어떤 도시락은 무려 11가지나 되는 반찬으로 이루어진 맛을 선사한다. 그들의 성공의 또 다른 비결은 집에서 조리된 식사를 하는 것 같은 느낌을 제공하는 것이다. 만약 이러한 추세가 계속된다면, 우리는 도시락 시장의 성장률이 빠르게 올라가는 것을 볼 것을 기대할 수 있다.
C 여러분은 누군가가 미역국을 만들고 있거나 먹고 있는 것을 본 적이 있습니까? 이 국은 한국인들에게는 특별한 의미가 있습니다. 한국 문화에서 어머니들은 전통적으로 출산을 한 후에 며칠 동안 이 국을 먹습니다. 그것은 또한 한국인들이 보통 생일을 축하하기 위해 먹는 국이기도 합니다.

Word Test

A 1 거의 ~ 아닌 2 경험; 경험하다 3 갑판 4 제공하다 5 호수 6 모험 7 자원 봉사하다 8 열대의 9 고아원 10 장비 11 lie 12 sailing 13 solo 14 cousin 15 comfortable 16 continent 17 return 18 relax 19 stranger 20 tourist **B** 1 view 2 decision 3 desire 4 opportunity **C** ⑤

Writing Test

A 1 Jamie has already prepared for the meeting. 2 Her mother has just arrived from Japan. 3 The weather has been very hot and humid lately. 4 Susan has watched the movie before. 5 Mr. Kim had often gone shopping before he moved to Seoul. **B** 1 Sam has left his wallet on the taxi. 2 I haven't finished my science report yet. 3 Julie has lived in Tokyo for 3 years. 4 My father has bought a bag for me.

Translation Test

A 당신은 지난겨울부터 추운 날씨를 겪고 있나요? 그렇다면 당신은 *Paradise Travel*에 전화해야 합니다. 우리는 아름다운 지역으로 멋진 여행을 제공합니다. 만약 당신이 우리의 인기 있는 여행에 참여한다면, 당신은 발리, 푸껫, 그리고 몰디브와 같은 매력적인 열대 섬들을 볼 수 있습니다. 그것은 휴식을 취하는 멋진 방법입니다.

B 토요일은 시카고에서의 둘째 날이었다. 나는 몹시 피곤했지만 일찍 일어나야 했다. 그 전날, 우리는 너무나 많은 곳을 방문했었다. 나는 Northerly Island Park와 Willis Tower 등에 갔었다. 미국에서 두 번째로 높은 빌딩인 Willis Tower는 특히 내게 가장 신나는 장소였다.

C 나는 처음에 그 아이디어를 나의 사촌인 Sarah로부터 얻었다. 그녀는 19살 이전에 세계 여행을 시작했었다. 그녀는 많은 흥미로운 장소들을 방문했다. 그녀는 인도에서 타지마할을 보았고, 관광객들을 위한 시장에서 쇼핑하는 것을 즐겼다.

Word Test

A 1 기호 2 현대의 3 희미한 4 다음에 언급되는 것 5 정착인, 이주자 6 내려오다 7 소개하다 8 흔적 9 튀기다 10 흔한 11 symbol 12 mean 13 architect 14 express 15 local 16 official 17 carve 18 decoration 19 tail 20 trade **B** 1 electric 2 origin 3 cave 4 legend **C** crack

Writing Test

A 1 Her house is four times as big as my house. 2 Brad is getting stronger and stronger as he grows up. 3 Tell me about your plan as specifically as you can. 4 The hotter the weather gets, the more people have cold drinks. **B** 1 The fog is getting thicker and thicker. 2 The white dress is not so expensive as the black dress. 3 The more heavily it rains, the faster people walk. 4 My TV is twice as large as yours. 5 You'd better come back home as early as you can.

Translation Test

A 석굴암은 한국의 국보 제24호이다. 석굴암에 관한 흥미로운 전설이 있다. 석굴암의 건축가는 중앙 석조 천장을 가능한 조심스럽게 조각하고 있는 중이었다. 갑자기, 그것은 그의 눈앞에서 깨져버렸고 그는 쓰러졌다.

B 전자우편이 도입되기 전에 @ 기호는 오늘날만큼 유명하지 않았다. 그것은 단지 어떤 것의 가격이나 무게를 보여주는 데 사용되었다. 예를 들어, 당신이 10개의 사과를 샀다면 각각 1달러 10센트 가격의 사과 10개라고 썼을지도 모른다.

C 시간이 흐를수록 모든 것들에 대한 기호를 만드는 것은 점점 더 어려워졌다. 그래서 많은 사람들은 문자 체계 즉, 알파벳을 만들어야 할 필요성을 느끼기 시작했다. 이집트 사람들은 그것을 만들기 위해 노력했고 만들어냈다. 그리고 그것은 이집트에서 흔해졌다.

Word Test

A 1 수정된 2 라벨을 붙이다 3 사라지다 4 해양의 5 비교 6 현금이 없는 7 입법하다 8 여성인;
여성 9 요구하다 10 전자의 11 unfair 12 treat 13 pressure 14 creature 15 prohibit
16 risk 17 injure 18 self-confidence 19 occur 20 administration **B** 1 respect 2 right
3 allow 4 impact **C** ①

Writing Test

A 1 We need a person who can fix the car. 2 This computer is what I want to buy.
3 Jenny, who is my best friend, lives next door. 4 David is the rude boy that I talked about.
5 The police officer whom I asked for directions is my friend's dad. **B** 1 The volunteer
work which(that) I did during the vacation changed me a lot. 2 The bed in which I slept last
night was very comfortable. / The bed which I slept in last night was very comfortable. 3 A
nurse, who didn't wear a uniform, was taking care of a patient. 4 Have you ever heard about
the girl whose name is Sophia? 5 We can't go to the birthday party to which we were
invited. / We can't go to the birthday party which(that) we were invited to.

Translation Test

A 해녀는 채취를 위한 독특하고 친환경적인 방식을 사용하는데, 그것은 해양 환경을 보호한다. 또한 그들은 젊은
세대들에게 잠수 비결을 전수해 왔다. 이것은 해녀가 유네스코 문화유산으로 등재되는 것을 도왔다.

B 현금 없는 사회가 도래하고 있다. 북유럽인들은 그들이 하는 모든 지불 중 단지 6%에 지나지 않는 만큼만
현금을 사용한다. 덴마크에서 정부는 상점들이 그들의 현금등록기를 처분하도록 제안해 왔다. 한국에서 여러분은
심지어 노숙자들이 판매하는 신문을 사기 위해서 신용카드를 사용할 수도 있다.

C 우리 모두는 전형적인 이미지들을 보아 왔는데 모델들은 그 안에서 극단적으로 말라 보이도록 포토샵 처리가
되었다. 어느 연구에서는 여성들이 스스로를 이러한 이미지와 비교한다는 것을 보여주고 있다. 이러한 비교는
그들이 자신에 대한 나쁜 이미지를 만들어 나가게 할 수 있다.

Word Test

A 1 회계, 거래 2 개발도상국 3 경제학 4 노예 5 육체적인, 신체의 6 반대의 7 붕괴 8 정치적인
9 종교적인 10 부족, 종족 11 perspective 12 population 13 equal 14 negative 15 mental
16 vote 17 priority 18 highland 19 possession 20 countryside **B** 1 normal 2 control
3 accept **C** completely, conclusion

Writing Test

A 1 Tim won't tell anyone why he missed the test. 2 Yoga teaches us how we can relax
our mind and body. 3 The New Year's Day is known as the day when people eat *tteokguk*.
4 I want to visit a town where the artist was born and raised. 5 Would you recommend a
restaurant where we can have fresh seafood? **B** 1 where I can concentrate on my study
2 how I could fold the paper 3 when we meet at the first time 4 why you made that
decision 5 where students spend most of their time

Translation Test

A 우리는 우리가 서로 이해할 수 없는 다른 세계에 살고 있다는 것을 받아들여야만 합니다. 당신은 엄마의
관점과 우선순위를 이해하려고 노력을 해야만 해요.

B 이제 당신이 그러한 부정적인 감정들을 막을 수 있는 방법을 찾아보자. 먼저, 웹사이트로부터 다른 사람들에
대한 결론을 이끌어내지 마라. 반드시 컴퓨터에서 떨어져서 다른 사람에 대한 충분한 이야기를 입수하라.

C 대부분의 사회가 남성에 의해 지배되던 때가 있었습니다. 여전히 남성들은 가정생활이나 공적 생활에서
대부분의 힘을 가지고 있습니다. 예를 들어, 대부분의 서구 나라에서 여성들이 투표를 할 수 없었던 때가 불과 얼마
전이었습니다.

Word Test

A 1 향상하다 2 곡선 3 유명인 4 양봉 5 끼우다, 맞추다 6 극한, 극도의 7 붙이다 8 (정기적으로 하는) 일 9 귀중한 10 시각적인 11 vertical 12 tough 13 collect 14 cruel 15 form 16 compete 17 instructive 18 pirate 19 former 20 concentration **B** 1 sink 2 arrange 3 whole 4 creative **C** ⑤

Writing Test

A 1 I couldn't arrive on time because I missed the bus. 2 Eric was listening to music when his cellphone rang. 3 It is very important that we must do something to help him. 4 Mr. Brown enjoys eating gimchi even though he is not a Korean. 5 Unless you follow the directions, you will get lost in a strange city. **B** 1 Both my mother and my baby were found to be healthy. 2 When I was waiting for a bus, Paul saw me. 3 Tom ate neither meat nor fish. 4 Because he was injured badly, we decided to go home.

Translation Test

A 함께 조각 그림을 맞추는 것은 휴식을 취하는 즐겁고 유익한 방법이다. 그것은 당신의 두뇌에도 좋다. 당신이 조각 그림 퍼즐 맞추기를 할 때 양쪽 두뇌가 활동하기 때문이다.

B 여러분은 여가 시간에 주로 무엇을 하는가? 기타를 치거나 피아노를 연주하는가? 춤을 추거나 그림을 그리는가? 유명인들 또한 몇 가지 흥미로운 취미를 가지고 있다. 조니뎁이 〈캐리비안의 해적〉에서 주연을 맡은 것은 누구나 알고 있다. 그는 주로 거친 인상을 보여 주지만, 때때로 집에서는 인형을 가지고 논다!

C Geocaching은 합성어이다. geo는 '땅'을 의미하고 cache는 '숨을 곳', 혹은 '귀중품'을 의미한다. 그것은 GPS를 이용하여 숨겨진 물건을 찾는 놀이이기 때문에 첨단 보물찾기이다.

Word Test

A 1 자리, 위치 2 끌다 3 (가치, 물가 등이) 치솟다 4 가치 있는 5 호기심 6 개인적인 7 수요 8 영역 9 자원봉사 10 시뮬레이션, 모의실험 11 introduce 12 custom 13 skill 14 disadvantage 15 fantasy 16 advantageous 17 private 18 presence 19 separate 20 distracted **B** 1 violence 2 attention 3 apply 4 biology **C** 1 desire 2 fiction 3 scale

Writing Test

A 1 My sister was laughed at so loud by Brian. 2 Her teacher was satisfied with Minji's exam results. 3 My proposal may be accepted by the manager. 4 The dirty plates and bowls are being washed by my mom. 5 The meeting room was cleaned by the staff last night. **B** 1 Food waste should be taken out separately. 2 I don't like being asked to hold a party. 3 The thief was being arrested by the police officer. 4 The girl is taken care of by his grandparents. 5 I expected the project to be finished soon.

Translation Test

A 나는 내가 도움을 줄 한 무리의 어린이들을 만났다. 나는 배우려는 그들의 관심과 열망에 감명을 받았다. 그들이 배우는 동안 우리는 다양한 주제로 그들을 도왔다.

B 우리는 한국이나 다른 외국에서 한국어를 가르침 받는 많은 비 한국인들에 대해 자주 듣고 있다. 예를 들어 대학에서의 한국어 수업은 교환학생으로 한국어를 배우기를 원하는 학생들로 가득 찬다.

C VR(가상현실) 장비는 더 저렴해질 것이므로, 개발도상국에 제공될 수 있다. 이것은 전 세계 학생들이 똑같은 수준의 경험으로 혜택을 받도록 해 줄 것이다. VR(가상현실) 기술은 또한 교육 외에 많은 영역에서 사용될 수 있다.

구문으로 격파하는

READING TAPA

정답과 해설

LEVEL 2

책 속의 가접 별책 (특허 제 0557442호)

'정답과 해설'은 본책에서 쉽게 분리할 수 있도록 제작되었으므로
유통 과정에서 분리될 수 있으나 파본이 아닌 정상제품입니다.

visang

ABOVE IMAGINATION

우리는 남다른 상상과 혁신으로
교육 문화의 새로운 전형을 만들어
모든 이의 행복한 경험과 성장에 기여한다

READING TAPA

정답과 해설

LEVEL 2

01 2016년에 누가 노벨 문학상을 받았나요?　02 '웹툰'이라는 단어는 어떻게 생겨났는지 추측해 봅시다.　03 여러분은 슈퍼영웅 영화를 본 적 있나요?　04 TV 요리 프로그램(쇼)은 어떻게 변화해왔나요?

Before Reading　pp.10~11

1 너는 충분히 정직하다 / 진실을 이야기할 만큼　2 Sue는 TV를 켰다 / 그 프로그램(쇼)을 보기 위해서　3 나는 집에 가고 싶다 / 지금　4 우리는 일할 것을 기대한다 / 그녀와 함께

Basic Test

1 to apply　2 to invite　3 closing　4 joining　5 to winning　6 to keep

Preview Test

01 You might be too young to be familiar / with the music of Bob Dylan. 여러분은 너무 어려서 친숙하지 않을지도 모른다 / 밥 딜런의 음악에　02 You don't need to pay much / in order to enjoy / webtoons. 당신은 (돈을) 많이 지불할 필요가 없다 / 즐기기 위해서 / 웹툰을　03 Especially, I feel like trying on / his suits. 특히, 나는 입어 보고 싶다 / 그의 옷을　04 These days / many Koreans look forward to watching / their favorite cooking shows. 요즈음 / 많은 한국인들은 시청하는 것을 기대한다 / 자신이 가장 좋아하는 요리 프로그램(쇼)들을

Real-Life Reading　pp.12~17

01 1 ③　2 밥 딜런은 노벨 문학상을 받은 최초의 작가가 아닌 사람이었기 때문이다.　**Words** familiar with ~에 친숙한　select 선발하다　author 작가　tradition 전통　02 1 ④　2 ⑤　**Words** greatly 대단히　guarantee 보장하다　publisher 출판업자　03 1 ④　2 ②　3 ⑤　4 ①　**Words** nowadays 요즈음　safe 안전한　alone 혼자　impress 깊은 인상을 주다　04 1 ④　2 ⓒ is → are　3 ③　4 셰프들이 그것들을 멋진 요리로 바꾸는 것을 보고 모두가 놀라워한다.　**Words** ingredient 재료　prior to ~이전에　previous 이전의　recent 최근의　mood 분위기　popularity 인기

01　노벨상 수상자, 밥 딜런　p.12

❶▼**You might be** too young to be **familiar / with the music of Bob Dylan.** ❷However, / you may have heard *Blowin' in the Wind* and
　　　　　　　　　may have p.p.: ~이었을지도 모른다
Like a Rolling Stone. ❸Two of his most famous songs will surely take your parents / back in time. ❹Bob Dylan is one of the most
　　　　　　　　　　　　　　　　　　　　　　　　　　　　　最상급
influential singer-songwriters / of the 20th century. ❺In 2016, / he was selected / as the winner of the Nobel Prize / in Literature.
　　수동태　　　로서(자격)
❻This was a total surprise / to the public. ❼Bob Dylan is the first non-author / to receive the prize. ❽The Swedish Academy recognized
　　　　　　　　　형용사적 용법

❶여러분은 너무 어려서 친숙하지 않을지도 모른다 / 밥 딜런의 음악에 ❷그러나 / 여러분은 〈Blowin' in the Wind〉와 〈Like a Rolling Stone〉을 들어본 적이 있을지도 모른다 ❸그의 가장 유명한 노래들 중 두 곡은 여러분들의 부모님을 되돌아가게 해 줄 것이다 / 과거로 ❹밥 딜런은 가장 영향력 있는 가수 겸 작곡가들 중 한 명이다 / 20세기의 ❺2016년에 / 그는 선정되었다 / 노벨상 수상자로 / 문학상에 ❻이것은 완전히 놀라운 일이었다 / 대중들에게 ❼밥 딜런은 최초의 작가가 아닌 사람이다 / 그 상을 받은 ❽스웨덴 아카데미는 그의 시적 표현 창

his creation of poetic expressions/within the American song tradition. ❾His songs deal with social issues/such as war and civil rights. ❿However,/not everyone was happy/to see him win. ⓫Some authors complained/about the award/going to a musician. ⓬What's your opinion/on this? ⓭Can song lyrics be literature? ⓮Please listen to some of his songs/before you decide.

작을 인정했다 / 미국의 음악 전통 안에서 ❾그의 노래는 사회적 문제를 다룬다 / 전쟁과 시민권과 같은 ❿하지만 / 모두가 기뻐한 것은 아니었다 / 그가 수상하는 것을 보고 ⓫일부 작가들은 불평하기도 했다 / 그 상에 대해 / 음악가에게 수여되는 ⓬여러분의 견해는 어떤가 / 이것에 대한 ⓭노래 가사가 문학이 될 수 있을까? ⓮그의 노래 중 몇 곡을 들어보길 바란다 / 여러분이 (그 답을) 결정하기 전에

---

1 이 글의 주요 내용은 밥 딜런의 노벨 문학상 수상이 갖는 의미에 관한 것이므로 제목으로 가장 적절한 것은 ③ '문학의 경계를 바꾼 밥 딜런'이다.

2 7행에서 사람들이 놀란 이유로 '밥 딜런은 그 상을 받은 최초의 작가가 아닌 사람이었음'을 밝히고 있다.

 02 웹툰: 오늘날의 만화책

p.13

❶Webtoon is a combination of the words "web" and "cartoon." ❷These days, the number of people enjoying webtoons has greatly increased. ❸Why are webtoons gaining popularity? ❹First, webtoons guarantee more artistic freedom. ❺Webtoon artists have more control over their work than comic book artists. ❻They are their own editors and publishers. ❼They are free to express what they imagine. ❽Second, webtoons can be viewed instantly. ❾Anyone with an Internet connection has easy access to webtoons. ❿▼Third, you don't need to pay much in order to enjoy webtoons. ⓫In general, webtoons are cheaper than printed comic books because production costs are lower. ⓬Webtoons might be part of your daily routine. ⓭But don't get too absorbed in them.

❶웹툰은 'web(웹)'과 'cartoon(만화)'이라는 단어의 결합이다. ❷요즈음 웹툰을 즐기는 사람들의 수가 크게 증가해 왔다. ❸왜 웹툰이 인기를 얻고 있을까? ❹첫째, 웹툰은 더 많은 예술적 자유를 보장한다. ❺웹툰 작가들은 그들의 작품에 대해 만화책 작가들보다 더 많은 지배력을 갖고 있다. ❻그들은 스스로의 편집자이자 출판업자이다. ❼그들은 자신이 상상하는 것을 표현하는 것이 자유롭다. ❽둘째, 웹툰은 즉시 보여질 수 있다. ❾인터넷 접속을 할 수 있는 사람이면 누구나 웹툰에 쉽게 접근할 수 있다. ❿셋째, 여러분은 웹툰을 즐기기 위해서 (돈을) 많이 지불할 필요가 없다. ⓫보통, 웹툰은 제작 비용이 더 낮기 때문에 인쇄된 만화책보다 더 저렴하다. ⓬웹툰은 여러분 일상의 일부가 될 수도 있다. ⓭하지만 그것에 지나치게 빠지지는 마라.

---

1 이 글의 주요 내용은 웹툰이 인기를 얻고 있는 이유에 관한 것이므로 주제로 가장 적절한 것은 ④ '웹툰이 인기를 얻고 있는 이유'이다.

2 웹툰은 일상의 일부가 될 수도 있지만 지나치게 빠지지는 말라고 조언하며 글을 마무리 하는 것이 자연스럽다.

❶ Nowadays, we often see many superheroes in Hollywood movies.
빈도부사는 일반동사 앞에 위치
❷ Who is your favorite superhero and why? ❸ Here are some answers from around the world.

❹ **Tom** Batman is my hero. ❺ He saved his hometown in the dark. ❻▼Especially, I feel like trying on his suits. ❼ And I
feel like -ing: ~하고 싶다
want to drive his Batmobile, too. ❽ They're cool!
→ *his suits and Batmobile*

❾ **Jihun** My favorite superhero changes often. ❿ Currently, my favorite is Iron Man. ⓫ In fact, he wasn't a superhero, but a
not A but B: A가 아니라 B
mad scientist. ⓬ However, he tried to keep the world safe, so
keep+명사+형용사: ~를 …하게 유지하다
he became a real hero to me. ⓭ Besides, I love his high-tech inventions, and the actor Robert Downey Jr. is so funny.

⓮ **Sarah** Spider-Man is wonderful. ⓯ He is super strong, super fast, and has super senses like a spider. ⓰ He climbs up high
~와 같은
buildings to defeat bad men. ⓱ But, unlike other heroes,
부사적 용법
Spider-Man lives a lonely life, because he is an orphan. ⓲ So,
he had to learn how to use his great powers alone, which
how+to부정사: ~하는 방법   *관계대명사의 계속적 용법(= and it)*
impresses me a lot.

⓳ Now, it's your turn. ⓴ Who is your superhero?

---

❶ 요즘, 우리는 종종 할리우드 영화에서 많은 슈퍼영웅들을 봅니다. ❷ 여러분이 가장 좋아하는 슈퍼영웅은 누구이고 그 이유는 무엇입니까? ❸ 여기 전 세계로부터 온 몇 가지 대답이 있습니다.

❹ Tom: 배트맨이 나의 영웅입니다. ❺ 그는 어둠 속에서 자신의 고향을 지켰죠. ❻ 특히, 저는 그의 옷을 입어 보고 싶어요. ❼ 그리고 배트맨 전용 자동차도 운전하고 싶어요. ❽ 그것들은 멋져요!

❾ 지훈: 내가 가장 좋아하는 슈퍼영웅은 자주 바뀌어요. ❿ 현재 내가 가장 좋아하는 슈퍼영웅은 아이언맨이에요. ⓫ 사실, 그는 슈퍼영웅이라기보다는 미친 과학자였어요. ⓬ 하지만 그는 세계를 안전하게 지키기 위해 노력했고, 그래서 그가 나에게는 진정한 영웅이 되었죠. ⓭ 그 이외에도, 나는 그의 첨단 발명품들이 너무 마음에 들고, 배우인 Robert Downey Jr.가 너무 재미있어요.

⓮ Sarah: 스파이더맨은 정말 멋져요. ⓯ 그는 굉장히 힘이 세고, 엄청 빠르고, 거미처럼 탁월한 감각을 가지고 있어요. ⓰ 그는 악당들을 무찌르기 위해 고층 건물들을 기어오르죠. ⓱ 그러나 다른 영웅들과는 달리, 스파이더맨은 고아이기 때문에 외로운 삶을 살아요. ⓲ 그래서 그는 혼자서 자신의 초능력을 사용하는 법을 배워야만 했는데, 그 점이 나에게 깊은 인상을 주었답니다.

⓳ 자, 여러분의 차례입니다. ⓴ 여러분의 슈퍼영웅은 누구인가요?

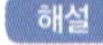 **해설**

1 자신이 가장 좋아하는 슈퍼영웅에 대해 이야기하고 있으므로 ④가 알맞다.
　① 내가 가장 좋아하는 액션 스타 　　　　　　② 슈퍼영웅이 되는 방법
　③ 가장 인기 있는 슈퍼영웅 　　　　　　　　④ 내가 가장 좋아하는 슈퍼영웅
　⑤ 슈퍼영웅의 믿을 수 없는 의상들

2 ⓐ는 내가 가장 좋아하는 영웅은 아이언맨이지만, '사실' 그는 슈퍼영웅이 아니었다는 흐름이 자연스러우므로 In fact가 알맞다.
　ⓑ는 좋아하는 이유를 추가하고 있으므로 Besides 또는 In addition이 알맞다.

3 ① Tom은 배트맨의 의상을 입어 보고 싶다고 했다. ② 지훈이의 현재 슈퍼영웅은 아이언맨이다. ③ 지훈이는 아이언맨이 지구를 지키려고 노력했기 때문에 좋아한다. ④ Robert Downey Jr.는 아이언맨을 연기했다.

4 defeat은 '~를 무찌르다, 패배시키다'의 뜻으로 beat과 같은 뜻이다.
　① 이기다 　　　　　　② 당황스럽게 만들다 　　　　　　③ 양보하다
　④ 놀라게 하다 　　　　⑤ 피하다

04 먹고 요리하고 시청하세요

❶ ▼These days, many Koreans look forward to watching their favorite cooking shows. ❷ Many celebrities and chefs appear on the TV shows and cook with just a few ingredients. ❸ The ingredients are easy to find in our fridges, such as leftover *jokbal*, gimchi, and vegetables. ❹ Everyone is surprised to watch the chefs turn them into great dishes. ❺ Cooking shows have become an important part of TV programming in Korea. ❻ Of course, prior to these shows, there were other shows dealing with food. ❼ Cooking shows in the mornings targeted housewives and other shows introduced famous restaurants. ❽ The main differences between the previous and the latest cooking shows are people and ingredients. ❾ The new shows feature celebrities and chefs cooking with ingredients which can be obtained easily. ❿ Also, recent cooking shows focus on storytelling, creating a light-hearted mood. ⓫ Therefore, anyone can watch and enjoy these shows. ⓬ This is why food-related shows are attracting attention and are gaining more and more popularity.

❶ 요즈음 많은 한국인들은 자신이 가장 좋아하는 요리 프로그램을 시청하기를 기대한다. ❷ 많은 유명인들과 셰프들이 TV 쇼에 등장하여 단지 몇 가지의 재료로 요리를 한다. ❸ 재료들은 우리의 냉장고에서 찾아보기 쉬운 남은 족발, 김치 그리고 채소와 같은 것들이다. ❹ 셰프들이 그것들을 멋진 요리로 바꾸는 것을 보고 모두가 놀라워한다. ❺ 요리 프로그램들은 한국의 TV 프로그램의 중요한 부분이 되었다. ❻ 물론 이 프로그램들 이전에 음식을 (주제로) 다루는 다른 프로그램(쇼)들이 있었다. ❼ 아침 요리 프로그램들은 주부들을 대상으로 했고 다른 프로그램(쇼)들은 유명한 식당들을 소개했다. ❽ 이전 프로그램들과 최근 요리 프로그램들 사이의 주요 차이점은 사람과 재료이다. ❾ 새로운 쇼들은 쉽게 얻을 수 있는 재료를 가지고 요리를 하는 유명인과 셰프들을 출연시킨다. ❿ 또한 최근 요리 프로그램들은 이야기에 주력하여 편한 분위기를 만들어낸다. ⓫ 그러므로 누구든지 이러한 프로그램들을 보고 즐길 수 있다. ⓬ 이것이 바로 음식 관련 프로그램들이 관심을 끌고 더욱더 많은 인기를 얻고 있는 이유이다.

문제 해석

1 이 글의 중심 소재로 알맞은 것은?
① 음식물 쓰레기를 줄이는 효과적인 방법
② 남은 음식을 멋진 요리로 바꾸는 비결
③ 요리 쇼를 더 성공적이게 만드는 방법
④ 한국에서 증가하는 요리 프로그램들의 인기
⑤ 더욱더 많은 유명인들이 요리 쇼에 출연하는 이유

2 이 글의 ⓐ~ⓔ 중 알맞지 않은 것은? 그 단어를 고치시오.

3 이 글의 내용과 일치하지 않는 것은?
① 최근 요리 프로그램에서는 유명인들이 요리를 한다.
② 요리 프로그램은 한국의 TV 프로그램에서 중요한 부분이다.
③ 이전의 요리 프로그램은 유명인들을 대상으로 했다.
④ 요리 프로그램은 변화해왔다.
⑤ 누구든지 최근의 요리 프로그램을 즐길 수 있다.

4 이 글의 밑줄 친 문장이 의미하는 것은 무엇인가? 우리말로 쓰시오.

해설

1 글의 주요한 내용은 최근 요리 프로그램이 인기를 끌고 있다는 점에 관한 것이므로 중심 소재로 가장 적절한 것은 ④이다.
2 ⓒ는 주어 The main differences의 동사 자리로 주어가 복수이므로 수 일치를 시켜 복수형 are로 고쳐야 한다.
3 9행에서 이전의 요리 프로그램은 주로 주부를 대상으로 유명한 식당을 소개했다고 했으므로 일치하지 않는 것은 ③이다.
4 감정의 원인을 나타내는 부사적 용법의 to부정사와 〈지각동사＋목적어＋목적격보어〉의 구조에 유의하여 해석해야 한다.

01 전 세계의 학생들은 점심으로 주로 무엇을 먹나요?   **02** 여러분이 가장 좋아하는 그림 도구는 무엇인가요?   **03** 특이한 교통수단을 이용해 본 적 있나요?   **04** 아름다움의 기준은 항상 변한다!

Before Reading   pp.20~21

1 타고 있는 촛불들이 / 케이크 위에서 / 매우 아름답다   **2** 그들은 유일한 손님들이다 / 머무르고 있는 / 호텔에서   **3** 엄마는 사주셨다 / 나에게 / 새 지갑을 / 이탈리아에서 만들어진   **4** 당신은 나를 도와줄 수 있나요 / 찾는 것을 / 나의 잃어버린 강아지를   **5** 그 코미디 영화는 ~이었다 / 매우 흥미로운   **6** Robert는 신이 났다 / 파티에서

Basic Test

1 sleeping   **2** barking   **3** made   **4** written   **5** climbing   **6** frightened

Preview Test

01 Do you ever wonder / what children are eating for lunch?   여러분은 궁금해한 적이 있나요 / 아이들이 점심으로 무엇을 먹는지   **02** One of the most unexpected tools / is the human body.   가장 예상치 못한 도구들 중의 하나가 / 사람의 몸이다   **03** In Cambodia, / you'll find an interesting train / called the bamboo train.   캄보디아에서 / 여러분은 흥미로운 기차를 발견할 것이다 / 대나무 기차라고 불리는   **04** Defining beauty is interesting / because it is something / seen differently / in different times and places.   아름다움을 정의하는 것은 흥미롭다 / 그것은 무언가 때문이다 / 다르게 보이는 / 다른 시대와 장소에서

Real-Life Reading   pp.22~27

01 1 ②   2 ②   **Words** wonder 궁금해하다   provide 제공하다   fresh 신선한   **02** 1 ④   2 ④   **Words** tool 도구   hold 잡다, 쥐다   hire 고용하다   rub 문지르다   **03** 1 ①   2 ⓐ traveling ⓑ named   3 ②   4 It is a dragon-shaped boat (made of reed).   **Words** unique 독특한   transportation 교통수단   bamboo 대나무   shell 껍데기   noisy 시끄러운   recommend 추천하다   **04** 1 ④   2 ③   3 ④   4 ⑤   **Words** discuss 토론하다   indoors 실내에서   weak 약한   afford ~할 여유가 있다   bridegroom 신랑   bride 신부

01   전 세계의 학교 급식   p.22

❶▼Do you ever wonder/what children are eating for lunch/across the world? ❷In America/where the number of overweight students has increased,/parents are more interested in school lunch/than before. ❸They don't want/their kids to eat fast food,/such as hamburgers, chips, or soda/for lunch. ❹The Chinese school lunches are usually provided by the school,/but some children go home for lunch. ❺In India,/a food service worker called a *dabbawalla*/brings

❶여러분은 궁금해한 적이 있나요 / 아이들이 점심으로 무엇을 먹는지 / 전 세계의 ❷미국에서는 / 과체중인 학생 수가 증가해 온 / 부모들이 학교 급식에 관심이 더 많습니다 / 예전보다 ❸그들은 원하지 않습니다 / 그들의 자녀들이 패스트푸드를 먹는 것을 / 햄버거, 감자튀김 또는 탄산음료와 같은 / 점심으로 ❹중국 학교의 급식은 보통 학교에서 제공됩니다 / 하지만 일부 아이들은 점심을 먹기 위해 집에 갑니다 ❺인도에서는 / *dabbawalla*(다바왈라)라고 불리는 음식 배달부가 / 음식을 학교로 가지고 옵니다 ❻그

food to school. ❻ The workers pick up fresh meals/from students' homes/and <u>deliver</u> them to school. ❼ School lunches in West Africa/<u>depend on</u> foreign aid. ❽ The UN World Food Program provides meals/for most school children.

provide A for B: B에게 A를 제공하다

<table>
<tr><td>일꾼들은 신선한 음식을 수거합니다 / 학생들의 집에서 / 그리고 그것들을 학교로 배달합니다 ❼ 서아프리카의 학교 급식은 / 외국의 원조에 의존합니다 ❽ UN 세계식량계획은 식사를 제공합니다 / 대부분의 학생들에게</td></tr>
</table>

1 4행에서 미국의 부모들은 자녀들이 점심으로 패스트푸드를 먹는 것을 원하지 않는다고 했으므로 ②는 일치하지 않는다.

2 (A)는 미국 부모들이 전보다 학교 급식에 더 많은 관심을 갖게 되었다고 했으므로 비만 학생이 '증가하다'의 의미인 increased, (B)는 일부 학생만이 집에서 점심을 먹는다고 했으므로 '보통은' 학교에서 급식을 한다는 의미인 usually, (C)는 인도는 음식 배달부가 학생의 집에서 점심을 가져온다고 했으므로 '배달하다'의 의미인 deliver가 알맞다.

02 독특한 그림 도구들을 시도해 보세요

p.23

❶ Think about painting. ❷ You're probably imagining an artist holding a brush. ❸ But there are actually more interesting ways of painting a picture. ❹ Creative artists use all kinds of different painting tools. ❺▼One of the most unexpected tools is the human body. ❻ Finger painting is the oldest way of using the body to paint. ❼ For example, look at the very old paintings made by cavemen. ❽ They were probably done by using fingers. ❾ These days, some famous artists also paint with their fingers. ❿ A French artist named Yves Klein decided to use more than just his fingers. ⓫ He hired models to be his "human paintbrushes". ⓬ He had these models covered in blue and gold paint. ⓭ Then he asked them to rub themselves against the white canvas. ⓮ Surprisingly, the paintings made in this way became very famous and expensive.

❶ 그림을 그리는 것에 대해 생각해 보아라. ❷ 당신은 아마도 붓을 쥐고 있는 화가를 상상하고 있을 것이다. ❸ 그러나 사실 그림을 그리는 더욱 흥미로운 방법들이 있다. ❹ 창의적인 예술가들은 모든 종류의 다양한 그림 도구들을 사용한다. ❺ 가장 예상치 못한 도구들 중의 하나가 사람의 몸이다. ❻ 손가락으로 그림을 그리는 것은 그림을 그리기 위해 신체를 이용하는 가장 오래된 방법이다. ❼ 예를 들어, 원시인에 의해 그려진 매우 오래된 그림들을 봐라. ❽ 그것들은 아마도 손가락을 사용하여 완성된 것이다. ❾ 요즘에는 몇몇 유명한 예술가들도 그들의 손가락으로 그림을 그린다. ❿ Yves Klein이란 이름의 프랑스 화가는 단지 그의 손가락보다 더 많은 것들을 사용하기로 결심했다. ⓫ 그는 그의 '인간 붓'이 될 모델들을 고용했다. ⓬ 그는 이 모델들이 파란색과 금색의 페인트에 덮이도록 했다. ⓭ 그 다음에 그는 그들에게 하얀 캔버스에 그들 스스로 문지를 것을 요청했다. ⓮ 놀랍게도, 이 방법으로 만들어진 그림들은 매우 유명하고 값비싸졌다.

1 이어지는 내용에서 Yves Klein이 페인트를 덮어 쓴 모델들을 이용하여 그림을 그렸다고 했으므로, ④ '단지 그의 손가락보다 더 많은 것들을 사용하기로 결심했다'는 내용이 알맞다.

① 나이 때문에 은퇴할 것을　　　　　　② 그의 작품들 중 하나를 팔 것을
③ 그의 손가락을 이용하여 그림을 그릴 것을　　④ 단지 그의 손가락보다 더 많은 것들을 사용할 것을
⑤ 가장 좋은 물감과 캔버스를 구입할 것을

2 모델들이 파란색과 금색 페인트에 덮인 것이므로 ⓓ의 covering은 수동의 의미를 나타내는 과거분사 covered가 알맞다.

❶ I'm Chris Kim and a world traveler. ❷ When you travel, what kinds of transportation do you use? ❸ Buses, subways, trains, and taxies are the most popular forms of transportation. ❹ How about going from place to place in a unique way while abroad?

❺ ▼In Cambodia, you'll find an interesting train called the bamboo train. ❻ As its name suggests, it is made of bamboo. ❼ Although slow, it is one of the cheapest rides in the country. ❽ While traveling Peru, I explored Lake Titicaca on a boat named *Barco de Totora*. ❾ It is a dragon-shaped boat made of reed. ❿ It was an amazing experience. ⓫ In Thailand, taking a ride in a *tuk-tuk* is a must. ⓬ It is a kind of a small three-wheeled taxi. ⓭ You can find them moving quickly around the streets of many cities in Thailand. ⓮ Moreover, I remember a different kind of taxi that can be found in Cuba. ⓯ Its name is *Coco Taxi* because the vehicle looks like the shell of a coconut. ⓰ It is a bit noisy but cheaper than a regular taxi. ⓱ Next time you visit Havana in Cuba, I recommend traveling the city in a *Coco Taxi*.

❶ 저는 Chris Kim이고 세계 여행가입니다. ❷ 여러분은 여행을 할 때, 어떤 종류의 교통수단을 이용하시나요? ❸ 버스, 지하철, 기차, 그리고 택시는 가장 인기 있는 교통수단의 형태입니다. ❹ 해외에 있는 동안 독특한 방식으로 이곳 저곳을 가보는 것은 어떨까요?

❺ 캄보디아에서 여러분은 대나무 기차라고 불리는 흥미로운 기차를 발견할 것입니다. ❻ 그것의 이름이 시사하듯이, 그것은 대나무로 만들어졌습니다. ❼ 느리기는 하지만 그것은 그 나라에서 가장 저렴한 운송 수단 중 하나입니다. ❽ 페루를 여행하는 동안, 저는 *Barco de Totora*라는 이름이 붙여진 보트를 타고 티티카카 호를 탐험했습니다. ❾ 그것은 갈대로 만들어진 용 모양의 보트입니다. ❿ 그것은 놀라운 경험이었습니다. ⓫ 태국에서 툭툭을 타는 것은 필수입니다. ⓬ 그것은 일종의 작은 바퀴가 세 개 달린 택시입니다. ⓭ 여러분은 그것들이 태국의 많은 도시의 도로에서 빠르게 이동하는 것을 찾아볼 수 있습니다. ⓮ 게다가 저는 쿠바에서 찾아볼 수 있는 다른 종류의 택시를 기억합니다. ⓯ 그 차량은 코코넛 껍질처럼 생겼기 때문에 그것의 이름은 코코 택시입니다. ⓰ 그것은 약간 시끄럽긴 하지만 일반 택시보다 더 저렴합니다. ⓱ 다음에 여러분이 쿠바에 있는 하바나를 방문할 때, 코코 택시를 타고 그 도시를 여행하시길 추천합니다.

해설

1 글의 주요 내용은 세계 각국의 이색적인 교통수단에 관해 이야기하는 글이므로 ①이 알맞다.

2 ⓐ 접속사가 남아 있는 분사구문으로 While I was traveling Peru, ~의 문장에서 분사구문으로 만들기 위해 주절의 주어와 동일한 주어인 I는 생략하여 While being traveling Peru로 변형하고, being을 생략하고 나면 While traveling Peru가 된다. ⓑ name은 '이름을 붙이다'라는 뜻이고 수식을 받는 a boat는 행위의 대상이 되므로 과거분사 named가 적절하다.

3 페루의 *Barco de Totora*는 갈대로 만들어졌다고 했으므로 일치하지 않는 것은 ②이다.

4 본문의 9행에 언급된 It is a dragon-shaped boat made of reed.를 이용하여 답한다.

 **04 아름다움에 대한 다양한 생각들** pp.26~27

❶ ▼Defining beauty is interesting because it is something seen

❶ 아름다움을 정의하는 것은 흥미로운데,

differently in different times and places. ❷ For example, in the 19th
century England, most women didn't like very strong men.
❸ Farming and factory work were hard jobs requiring strong
workers. ❹ Rich people looked down on the strong men doing
these jobs. ❺ Rich men didn't do physical work. ❻ They read books
and discussed business indoors. ❼ So, women usually thought strong
and athletic men lacked style and grace. ❽ That's why weak and
thin men were preferred and they were satisfied with their figure.

❾ In some cultures, fat women are considered beautiful. ❿ One
example is the Annang tribe of Nigeria. ⓫ The women from rich
families are fat because they can afford a lot of food. ⓬ So, Annang
men prefer big women. ⓭ Rich Annang parents actually send their
daughters to special fattening rooms. ⓮ The girls in these places are
fed a very fatty diet. ⓯ They live there for about six months.
⓰ Once they are big enough, they are ready to get married. ⓱ The
bridegroom hopes his bride is as big as possible!

그것은 다른 시대와 장소에서 다르게 보여지는 것이기 때문이다. ❷예를 들어, 19세기 영국에서 대부분의 여성들은 매우 강한 남성을 좋아하지 않았다. ❸농사와 공장의 일은 강한 일꾼을 필요로 하는 힘든 직업들이었다. ❹부유한 사람들은 이런 일을 하는 강한 남성들을 무시했다. ❺부유한 남성들은 육체적인 일을 하지 않았다. ❻그들은 실내에서 책을 읽고 사업에 대해 논했다. ❼그래서 여성들은 보통 튼튼하고 강건한 남성들은 스타일과 품위가 결여되었다고 생각했다. ❽그것이 바로 약하고 마른 남자들이 선호되었고 그들이 자신의 몸매에 만족했던 이유였다.

❾몇몇 문화에서, 뚱뚱한 여성들은 아름답다고 여겨진다. ❿한 가지 예가 나이지리아의 Annang 부족이다. ⓫부유한 가정의 여성들은 많은 음식을 먹을 여유가 있기 때문에 뚱뚱하다. ⓬그래서 Annang의 남성들은 뚱뚱한 여성들을 선호한다. ⓭부유한 Annang의 부모들은 실제로 그들의 딸을 특별한 살찌우는 방으로 보낸다. ⓮이러한 곳의 소녀들은 매우 기름진 음식물을 먹게 된다. ⓯그들은 그곳에서 약 6개월 동안 산다. ⓰그들이 일단 충분히 뚱뚱해지면, 그들은 결혼할 준비가 된 것이다. ⓱신랑은 그의 신부가 가능한 한 뚱뚱하기를 바란다!

---

 1 이 글의 요지로 알맞은 것은?
　① 여성이 남성보다 더 강해야 한다.
　② 강건한 남자들은 미의 기준에 맞지 않다.
　③ 몇몇 문화에서는 뚱뚱한 여성들이 아름답다고 여겨진다.
　④ 아름다움은 다른 시대와 장소에서 다르게 보여진다.
　⑤ 19세기 영국에서 노동자 계층의 남자가 인기 있었다.

2 이 글의 빈칸 ⓐ에 알맞은 것은?
　① 단순한　　② 자유로운　　③ 힘든　　④ 빠른　　⑤ 신나는

3 이 글을 읽고 Annang 부족에 관해 유추할 수 있는 것은?
　① 뚱뚱한 여성들은 보통 결혼을 하지 않는다.
　② 대부분의 여성들이 살을 빼기 위해 노력한다.
　③ 여성들은 약하고 마른 남성을 선호한다.
　④ 가난한 집의 여성들은 뚱뚱하지 않을 것이다.
　⑤ 모든 여성들은 6개월 동안 특별한 살찌우는 방에서 산다.

4 이 글의 빈칸 ⓑ에 알맞은 것은?
　① 점점 마르기를　　② 그보다 키가 더 크기를　　③ 다이어트를 하기를
　④ 채식주의자가 되기를　　⑤ 가능한 한 뚱뚱하기를

 1 이 글의 첫 번째에서 아름다움은 다른 시대와 장소에서 다르게 보여진다고 요지를 말하고 있으므로 ④가 알맞다.
2 농사와 공장 일은 강한 일꾼들을 필요로 하는 일이라는 것으로 보아 '힘든(hard)' 일이었음을 알 수 있다.
3 Annang 부족 중 부유한 가정의 여성들은 음식을 충분히 먹어 살이 쪘다고 했으므로 가난한 집의 여성들은 대부분 살이 찌지 않았을 것이라고 유추할 수 있다.
4 신부가 뚱뚱해지면 결혼할 준비가 된 것이라고 했으므로, 신랑은 신부가 가능한 한 뚱뚱하기를 바랄 것이다.

01 걱정 나무가 무엇인지 추측할 수 있겠니?   **02** 로렌조 오일에 대해 들어본 적 있니?   **03** "신은 어디에 계신가요?"라는 문장의 뜻은 무엇일까?   **04** 네가 우주 끝에서 뛰어내린다고 상상해봐!

Before Reading   pp.30~31

1 Tom은 나에게 말했다 / 그는 학교에 가야 한다고   **2** Kate는 나에게 물었다 / 내가 자전거를 탈 수 있는지   **3** Brown 선생님은 Maria에게 물었다 / 그녀가 어디에 사는지   **4** 나는 Erica에게 말했다 / 창문을 열라고

Basic Test

1 John said to me, "Can you give me a hand?"   **2** Peter said that he was watching a movie with Mina.   **3** I told (ordered / asked / advised ...) Lisa to clean her room.   **4** Ronald said to me, "Where do you buy your clothes?"   **5** Linda asked Jinho when he wanted to leave.

Preview Test

01 I asked him, / "What does the tree mean / to you?" 나는 그에게 물었다 / 그 나무는 무엇을 의미하나요 / 당신에게   **02** Augusto asked himself / whether he could let Lorenzo die / without any effort. Augusto는 자기 자신에게 물었다 / 그가 Lorenzo를 죽게 놔둘 수 있는지를 / 어떤 노력도 없이   **03** The parents asked a minister / in town / what they should do. 그 부모들은 목사에게 물었다 / 마을에 사는 / 그들이 무엇을 해야 하는지를   **04** He told us / to go up really high / to understand / how small we are. 그는 우리에게 말했다 / 정말 높이 올라가라고 / 이해하기 위해서 / 얼마나 우리가 작은지를

Real-Life Reading   pp.32~37

01 1 ②   2 ④   Words carpenter 목수   saw 톱   refuse 거부하다   **02** 1 ④   2 if(whether) they could cure his son   Words cure 치료하다   effort 노력   expect 예상하다   **03** 1 ④   2 ④   3 ③   4 ② Words minister 목사   voice 목소리   shake 흔들다   follow 따라가다   missing 사라진   **04** 1 ④   2 ③   3 ③   4 Don't hesitate   Words field 분야   height 높이   atmosphere 대기   hesitate 망설이다

01   걱정 나무   p.32

❶ On Monday, / the carpenter finished / a rough first day. ❷ First, / he got a flat tire / while driving to my farm. ❸ Then / his electric saw stopped working / and his old truck refused to start. ❹ So, / I offered / to drive him home. ❺ He seemed to be in a bad mood. ❻ As he walked up to his house, / he stopped briefly / in front of a small tree. ❼ He touched the tips of the branches / with his hands / and then opened the door. ❽ Surprisingly, / he became a totally different

❶월요일에 / 목수는 마무리했다 / 힘든 첫 날을 ❷먼저 / 그가 탄 차의 타이어에 바람이 빠졌다 / 내 농장으로 운전해 오는 중에 ❸그 다음에 / 그의 전기톱이 작동을 멈추었다 / 그리고 그의 오래된 트럭은 시동이 걸리지 않았다 ❹그래서 / 나는 제안한다 / 그를 집까지 차로 데려다 주기로 ❺그는 기분이 좋지 않아 보였다 ❻그가 집까지 걸어갈 때 / 그는 잠시 멈춰 섰다 / 작은 나무 앞에서 ❼그는 나뭇가지의 끝을 만졌다 / 그의 손으로 / 그리고 나서 문을 열었다

person. ❾ Smiling brightly,/he hugged his children/and gave his
분사구문(= While he was smiling brightly)

wife a kiss. ❿ ▼I asked him,/"What does the tree mean/to you?"

⓫ He said,/"Oh, it's my trouble tree. ⓬ I always hang my worries/
빈도부사(일반동사 앞에 위치)

on that tree/whenever I come home. ⓭ In the morning/I pick them
~할 때마다   동사＋대명사＋부사

up again."

❽놀랍게도 / 그는 완전히 다른 사람이 되었다 ❾밝게 웃으면서 / 그는 자신의 아이들을 안아 주었다 / 그리고 아내에게 키스를 했다 ❿나는 그에게 물었다 / 그 나무는 무엇을 의미하나요 / 당신에게 ⓫그는 말했다 / 오, 그것은 나의 걱정 나무입니다. ⓬나는 항상 나의 걱정거리들을 걸어 두죠 / 저 나무 위에 / 집에 올 때마다 ⓭아침이 되면 / 저는 그것들을 다시 집어 간답니다.

 **1** 목수는 집에 들어가기 전에 자신의 일터에서 생긴 걱정거리들을 입구의 작은 나무에 걸어 둔다고 했다.
2 목수(carpenter)는 일터에서 모든 것들이 마음대로 되지 않아 화가 났다가(angry), 나무에 걱정거리들을 걸어 두고 집에 와서는 밝게 웃으며 아이들과 아내를 대하고 있으므로 긍정적으로(positive) 변했음을 알 수 있다.

 **로렌조 오일**

❶ Augusto had a 5-year-old son, Lorenzo. ❷ One day, Lorenzo got
cf. 5-years-old(×)

sick with a disease called ALD. ❸ Augusto said to doctors, "Can
과거분사   의문사 없는 의문문의 직접화법

you cure my son?" ❹ All of the doctors said, "Nothing can be done
수동태

about ALD. Lorenzo will die soon." ❺ ▼But Augusto asked himself
재귀용법

whether he could let Lorenzo die without any effort. ❻ He
의문사 없는 의문문의 간접화법

answered, "No! He is only 5 years old. I'm his father." ❼ To find a
부사적 용법(목적)

medicine, Augusto started to study ALD. ❽ Finally, he discovered a

certain kind of oil and Lorenzo took it. ❾ It worked on him!
→ A certain kind of oil

❿ Lorenzo was able to live much longer than everyone expected.
비교급 강조 부사(= still, far)

⓫ He died at 30 years old in 2008 and Augusto died in 2013.

⓬ The medicine has been named "Lorenzo's Oil" to remember a
현재완료 수동태   부사적 용법(목적)

father's great love. ⓭ Lorenzo's Oil is helpful for all ALD patients

now.

❶Augusto에게는 Lorenzo라는 5살짜리 아들이 있었다. ❷어느 날, Lorenzo는 ALD라고 불리는 병에 걸렸다. ❸"당신들은 제 아들을 치료할 수 있나요?" Augusto가 의사들에게 말했다. ❹모든 의사들은 답했다. "ALD에 관해서 할 수 있는 것은 아무것도 없습니다. Lorenzo는 곧 사망할 것입니다." ❺그러나 Augusto는 아무 노력도 하지 않고 Lorenzo를 죽게 놔둘 수 있는지 스스로에게 물었다. ❻그는 "안 돼! 그 아이는 겨우 5살이야. 나는 그 아이의 아빠다."라고 답했다. ❼약을 찾기 위해 Augusto는 ALD에 대해 공부하기 시작했다. ❽마침내 그는 어떤 오일을 발견했고 Lorenzo는 그것을 복용했다. ❾그것은 그에게 효력이 있었다! ❿Lorenzo는 모두가 예상했던 것보다 훨씬 더 오래 살 수 있었다. ⓫그는 2008년에 30살의 나이로 죽음을 맞이했고, Augusto는 2013년에 사망했다. ⓬그 약은 한 아버지의 위대한 사랑을 기억하기 위해 '로렌조 오일'이라는 이름이 붙여졌다. ⓭로렌조 오일은 지금도 모든 ALD 환자들에게 도움을 주고 있다.

 **1** Augusto의 사망 연도는 알려졌으나 그 당시 그의 나이는 알 수 없다.
2 의문사가 없는 의문문의 직접화법을 간접화법으로 바꾸는 문제로, 〈if(whether)＋주어＋동사〉 어순을 이용하여 문장을 완성한다. 이때, 인용문의 you는 doctors를 나타내는 they가 되고, my son은 his son으로 바뀜에 유의한다.

❶A couple had two bad little boys. ❷They were 8 and 10 years old, and they got into trouble a lot. ❸If there was any trouble in their town, the two young boys were always there. ❹▼The parents asked a minister in town what they should do. ❺They asked him for help because he helped bad children become good. ❻The minister agreed to speak with the boys, but he asked to see them one by one. ❼The 8-year-old boy went to meet with him first. ❽The minister sat the boy down and asked him sincerely, "Where is God?" ❾The boy did not answer. ❿So, the minister repeated the question in a louder voice, "Where is God?" ⓫Again, the boy was quiet. ⓬So the minister raised his voice even more and shook his finger in front of the boy's face, "WHERE IS GOD?" ⓭The boy jumped up and ran directly home. ⓮His older brother followed him and asked what happened. ⓯The younger brother replied, "We are in BIG trouble this time. ⓰God is missing and people think we did it."

1 이 글은 두 소년에 관한 재미있는 이야기를 하고 있으므로 ④ humorous(재미있는)이 알맞다.

2 소년이 질문에 대답하지 않아서 목사님이 더 큰 목소리로 물었지만, 또다시 대답하지 않아 더욱더 큰 목소리로 물었다는 흐름이 자연스러우므로 (D)가 알맞다.

3 목사님을 만나고 온 동생은 신이 사라졌는데 사람들이 그들이 한 일인 줄 안다며 큰일이 났다고 했다. 이것으로 보아 아이들을 교화시키려고 한 목사님의 질문(Where is God?)을 아이들이 오해하고 있음을 알 수 있다.

4 목사님이 말썽꾸러기 아이를 앉혀 놓고 진지하게 질문을 했다는 맥락이므로 sincerely는 seriously(진지하게)의 뜻으로 쓰였음을 알 수 있다.

❶Have you ever dreamed of skydiving from the edge of space?

번역 (우측)

❶한 부부에게 두 명의 버릇없는 어린 소년들이 있었다. ❷그들은 8살과 10살이었고, 문제를 많이 일으켰다. ❸만약 그들의 마을에 어떤 문제가 생기면, 그 두 소년들이 항상 그곳에 있었다. ❹그 부모들은 마을에 사는 목사에게 무엇을 해야 할지를 물었다. ❺그는 못된 아이들이 착해지도록 도왔기 때문에 부모들은 그에게 도움을 요청했다. ❻목사님은 그 소년들과 이야기를 해보겠다고 했는데, 그들을 한 명씩 볼 것을 요청했다. ❼8살짜리 소년이 먼저 그를 만나기 위해 갔다. ❽목사님은 소년을 앉히고 진지하게 물었다. "신은 어디 계시니?" ❾소년은 대답하지 않았다. ❿그래서 목사님은 더 큰 목소리로 질문을 반복했다. "신은 어디 계시니?" ⓫소년은 또 다시 조용했다. ⓬그래서 목사님은 더욱더 목소리를 높였고 소년의 얼굴 앞에서 손가락을 흔들었다. "신은 어디 계시니?" ⓭그 소년은 뛰어 일어나서 곧바로 집으로 달려갔다. ⓮그의 형은 그를 따라가서 무슨 일이 일어났는지 물었다. ⓯남동생은 대답했다. "이번에 우리는 진짜 큰 문제에 처했어. ⓰신이 사라졌는데 사람들은 우리가 그랬다고 생각하고 있어."

❶당신은 우주 끝에서 스카이다이빙 하는

❷ Felix Baumgartner has. ❸ He finally made his dream come true.
❹ Born in Austria, Baumgartner imagined flying through the air when he was a child. ❺ He began skydiving at the age of 16. ❻ And he has set many records in the field of skydiving. ❼ Baumgartner set his most significant record on October 14, 2012. ❽ He jumped down from a small space capsule at the height of about 38.6 km. ❾ It was the highest skydiving ever. ❿ On that day, Baumgartner was pulled up to the second layer of Earth's atmosphere in a small space capsule carried by a large helium balloon. ⓫ Finally, he jumped down from the capsule wearing a spacesuit and helmet. ⓬ After nine minutes, he touched down safely on the ground. ⓭ He became the first human to travel faster than the speed of sound without a vehicle. ⓮ Now, do you know what Baumgartner said? ⓯ ▼He told us to go up really high to understand how small we are. ⓰ He also told us not to hesitate in making your dreams come true.

것을 꿈꿔 본 적이 있는가? ❷ Felix Baumgartner는 꿈꿔 왔다. ❸ 그는 마침내 자신의 꿈을 실현시켰다. ❹ 오스트리아에서 태어난 Baumgartner는 어렸을 때 공중을 나는 것을 상상했다. ❺ 그는 16세에 스카이다이빙을 시작했다. ❻ 그리고 스카이다이빙 분야에서 많은 기록을 세웠다. ❼ Baumgartner는 2012년 10월 14일에 그의 가장 중대한 기록을 세웠다. ❽ 그는 약 38.6 km의 높이에 있는 작은 우주 캡슐에서 뛰어내렸다. ❾ 그것은 지금까지 가장 높은 스카이다이빙이었다. ❿ 그날 Baumgartner는 커다란 헬륨 기구로 운반된 작은 우주 캡슐을 타고 지구 대기의 두 번째 층(성층권)까지 끌어 올려졌다. ⓫ 마침내, 그는 우주복과 헬멧을 착용하고 캡슐에서 뛰어내렸다. ⓬ 9분 뒤에 그는 무사히 땅에 닿았다. ⓭ 그는 이동수단 없이 음속보다 더 빨리 이동한 최초의 인간이 되었다. ⓮ 이제 당신은 Baumgartner가 뭐라고 말을 했는지 알겠는가? ⓯ 그는 우리에게 우리가 얼마나 작은지 알기 위해서 정말 높이 올라가라고 말했다. ⓰ 그는 또한 당신의 꿈을 실현하는 데 주저하지 말라고 말했다.

 **문제 해석**

1 이 글의 중심 소재로 알맞은 것은?
① 소리의 속도
② 우주인의 도전
③ 우주 다이버가 되는 방법
④ 우주에서 뛰어내린 첫 번째 인간
⑤ 우리의 꿈을 실현시키는 방법

2 이 글에서 Baumgartner와 우주에서의 그의 점프에 대한 내용과 일치하지 <u>않는</u> 것은?
① 그는 매우 중요한 기록을 세웠다.
② 그는 9분 뒤에 땅에 착륙했다.
③ 그는 우주복과 헬멧 없이 뛰어내렸다.
④ 그는 지구 대기의 두 번째 층에서 뛰어내렸다.
⑤ 그는 음속보다 더 빠르게 이동했다.

3 이 글의 밑줄 친 significant와 의미가 가장 가까운 것은?
① 심각한
② 독특한
③ 중요한
④ 긴급한
⑤ 보통의

4 이 글의 밑줄 친 ⓐ를 다시 쓰시오.
그는 우리에게 "당신의 꿈을 실현하는 데 <u>주저하지 마세요.</u>"라고 말했다.

해설

1 이 글은 우주에서 다이빙한 최초의 인간인 Felix Baumgartner에 대해 이야기 하고 있으므로 ④가 알맞다.
2 우주복과 헬멧을 착용하고 뛰어내렸다고 했으므로 ③은 알맞지 않다.
3 significant는 '의미 있는, 중요한'의 의미를 지니는 표현으로 ③ important와 의미가 가장 가깝다.
4 명령문의 간접화법에서 쓰인 〈not to+동사원형〉은 직접화법에서는 〈Don't+동사원형〉이 된다.

01 더운 날 여러분이 가장 좋아하는 디저트는 무엇입니까?　**02** 아침은 든든하게 먹어야 해요.　**03** 여러분은 도시락에 무슨 반찬이 있길 바라나요?　**04** 미역으로 무엇을 만들 수 있을까요?

Before Reading　pp.40~41

1 엄마는 (~하도록) 만들었다 / 내가 / 설거지를 하도록　**2** Holly는 (~하도록) 허락하지 않을 것이다 / 내가 / 그녀의 남동생을 돌보도록　**3** 팀 지도자들은 (~하도록) 시켰다 / 팀원들이 / 그 일을 끝내도록　**4** 나는 보았다 / Jack이 기타를 치는 것을 / 그의 방에서　**5** Emily는 들었다 / 새가 지저귀고 있는 것을 / 나무에서　**6** 나는 냄새를 맡았다 / 무언가 타고 있는 / 주방에서　**7** 김 선생님은 (~하는 것을) 도와주었다 / 내가 / 상자를 옮기는 것을

Basic Test

1 pay　**2** to wash　**3** clean　**4** crying　**5** be　**6** cook

Preview Test

01 They really make / you / feel cool and refreshed.　그들은 정말로 만들다 / 네가 / 시원하고 상쾌하게 느끼도록
02 Only one *gimbap* / can help / them / to feel full.　단 하나의 김밥은 / 도울 수 있다 / 그들이 / 포만감을 느끼는 것을
03 If these trends continue, / we can expect / to see the growth rate of the *dosirak* market speed up.　만약 이러한 추세가 계속된다면 / 우리는 기대할 수 있다 / 도시락 시장의 성장률이 빠르게 올라가는 것을 볼 것을　**04** Have you seen / someone making or eating *miyeokguk*?　너는 본 적 있니 / 누군가가 만들거나 먹는 것을 / 미역국을

Real-Life Reading　pp.42~47

01 1 ①　2 ⓔ that → which　Words similar 유사한, 비슷한　flour 밀가루　statue 조각상, 동상　**02** 1 ②　2 ③　Words organic 유기농의　grain 곡물; 알갱이　**03** 1 ⑤　2 ⓐ carries → carry　3 diverse, low-quality　4 ①, ②　Words increase 증가하다; 증가　a variety of 다양한　relatively 비교적　reasonable 합리적인; 비싸지 않은　trend 동향, 추세　**04** 1 ④　2 ②　3 ④　4 전통적으로 어머니들이 출산하고 나서 며칠 동안 미역국을 먹는다. / 미역국은 한국 사람들이 보통 생일날에 먹는 국이다.　Words traditionally 전통적으로　beef 소고기　pour 붓다　reduce 줄이다

01　더운 날 시원하게 보내세요
p.42

---

❶ Cold desserts are perfect / for hot summer days.　❷ ▼They really make / you / feel cool and refreshed.　❸ In Korea, / we eat *patbingsu* / on hot days.　❹ It's a dessert / made of crushed ice, red beans, chopped fruits, milk, and strawberry syrup.　❺ Koreans are not the only ones / who love cold desserts.　❻ In Malaysia and Singapore, / you can find people / eating a similar cold dessert / named *Ais*

(주격관계대명사)
(which is)

❶ 차가운 디저트는 완벽하다 / 더운 여름 날에 ❷ 그들은 정말로 만들다 / 여러분이 / 시원하고 상쾌하게 느끼도록 ❸ 한국에서 / 우리는 팥빙수를 먹는다 / 더운 날에 ❹ 그 것은 디저트이다 / 분쇄된 얼음, 팥, 잘게 썬 과일, 우유, 그리고 딸기 시럽으로 만들어진 ❺ 한국인들은 유일한 사람들이 아니다 / 차가운 디저트를 좋아하는 ❻ 말레이시아와 싱가포르에서 / 여러분은 사람들을 찾을 수 있다 / 비슷한 차가운 디저트를 먹고

Kacang. ❼It means "bean ice"/in English. ❽In India,/people eat *Kulfi*,/which is made with milk, nuts, flour, and dried fruits. ❾In the old days,/it was made with ice/from the mountains in the Himalayas. ❿At that time,/it was enjoyed only/by royalty. ⓫In Mexico,/people enjoy eating *Paletas*,/which are made with fresh fruits. ⓬They are similar/to popsicles. ⓭If you visit the city of Tocumbo in Mexico,/look for a statue of a huge *Paleta*. ⓮It greets visitors/there.

있는 / *Ais Kacang*이라는 이름의 ❼그것은 '콩 얼음'을 의미한다 / 영어로 ❽인도에서 / 사람들은 *Kulfi*를 먹는다 / 그런데 그것은 우유, 견과류, 밀가루, 그리고 말린 과일로 만들어진다 ❾옛날에 / 그것은 얼음으로 만들어졌다 / 히말라야 산맥에서 나온 ❿그때는 / 그것은 오직 즐겨졌다 / 왕족들에게만 ⓫멕시코에서 / 사람들은 *Paleta*를 즐겨 먹는다 / 그것은 신선한 과일로 만들어진다 ⓬그것은 비슷하다 / 아이스캔디와 ⓭만약 여러분이 Tocumbo라는 도시를 방문한다면 / 멕시코의 / 거대한 *Paleta* 조각상을 찾아보아라 ⓮그것은 방문객들을 맞이하고 있다 / 거기에서

 **해설**

1 세계 여러 나라의 차가운 디저트를 소개하는 글이므로 주제로 알맞은 것은 ① '세계의 다양한 차가운 디저트'이다.

2 ⓔ 계속적 용법의 관계대명사는 that을 쓸 수 없으므로 which로 고쳐 쓰는 것이 알맞다.

02 아침 식사, 거르지 마세요! p.43

❶Today, a busy life makes more people eat out for breakfast than before. ❷As a result, the number of new breakfast options is increasing rapidly.

❸**At fast food restaurants** In 2013, a new morning combination set menu came out. ❹This is very popular for two reasons: it is a hot meal for early birds and is sold at a low price for young people.

❺**At major supermarkets** Lately, the number of "home meal replacements" has been growing! ❻They are not exactly homemade foods, but working moms and office workers welcome them. ❼As for healthy food, several sorts of organic cereals and powder made of mixed grains are found at many supermarkets.

❽**At convenience stores** Super triangular *gimbaps* catch consumers' eyes. ❾They are larger than the earlier version by 36%. ❿▼Only one *gimbap* can help them to feel full.

❶오늘날, 바쁜 생활은 전보다 더 많은 사람들이 아침 식사로 외식을 하게 한다. ❷그 결과, 새로운 아침 식사 선택권의 개수가 빠르게 증가하고 있다.

❸[패스트푸드점] 2013년에 새로운 모닝 콤비네이션 세트 메뉴가 출시되었다. ❹이것은 두 가지 이유로 매우 인기가 있는데, 아침에 일찍 일어나 활동하는 사람들을 위한 따뜻한 식사라는 점과 젊은 사람들을 위하여 저렴한 가격으로 판매된다는 점이다. ❺[대형 슈퍼마켓] 최근에 '가정식 대체식품'의 수가 늘어나고 있다! ❻그것들은 정확히 집에서 만든 것은 아니지만 직장에 다니는 엄마들과 회사원들은 그것들을 환영한다. ❼건강식품으로는 몇몇 종류의 유기농 시리얼과 혼합 곡물로 만든 선식을 많은 슈퍼마켓에서 찾을 수 있다.

❽[편의점] 슈퍼 삼각 김밥이 소비자들의 눈길을 사로잡는다. ❾그것들은 그 이전의 것보다 36% 정도 더 크다. ❿단 하나의 김밥으로도 그들은 포만감을 느낄 수 있다.

1 이 글은 최근의 아침 식사 대용식에 대한 인기를 소개하는 기사이다.
2 슈퍼마켓에서 파는 가정식 대체식품은 정확히 집에서 만든 음식이 아니라고 했다.

03 도시락 시장의 성장

❶ In Korea, the *dosirak* market is growing rapidly. ❷ Recently, the sales of *dosirak* at convenience stores increased by over 50 percent on average, as compared to the previous year. ❸ A dosirak is a box lunch, and you can easily find it for sale. ❹ Convenience stores on every street corner carry a variety of box lunches. ❺ The growth of the *dosirak* market is directly related to the increase of single-person households. ❻ The proportion of single-person households is now over 26 percent and still growing. ❼ Especially, customers in their 20s and 30s show a high satisfaction with the cheap price of *dosirak*. ❽ A *dosirak* is not a new concept in Korea. ❾ *Dosiraks* have taken up space in convenience stores for a long time. ❿ But they have recently changed. ⓫ They used to be relatively low-quality meals for quick lunches. ⓬ However, today's *dosisaks* are healthy and diverse options are offered at reasonable prices. ⓭ Some *dosiraks* offer a taste of as many as 11 side dishes. ⓮ Another secret of their success is that they offer the feeling of having home-cooked meals. ⓯ ▼If these trends continue, we can expect to see the growth rate of the *dosirak* market speed up.

❶한국에서 도시락 시장은 빠르게 성장하고 있다. ❷최근, 편의점에서의 도시락 판매량은 지난해와 비교하여 평균 50% 이상 상승했다. ❸도시락은 용기에 든 점심인데, 여러분은 판매 중인 그것을 쉽게 찾아볼 수 있다. ❹길모퉁이마다 있는 편의점은 다양한 도시락을 취급한다. ❺도시락 시장의 성장은 1인 가구의 증가와 직접적으로 관련되어 있다. ❻1인 가구의 비율은 현재 26%를 넘었고 여전히 증가하고 있다. ❼특히, 20대와 30대 소비자들은 도시락의 저렴한 가격에 대해 높은 만족도를 보인다. ❽도시락은 한국에서 새로운 개념이 아니다. ❾도시락은 오랫동안 편의점에서 자리를 잡아 왔다. ❿그런데 그것들이 최근에 변화했다. ⓫그것들은 빠른 점심 식사를 위한 비교적 품질이 낮은 식사였다. ⓬하지만 오늘날의 도시락은 건강에 좋고, 다양한 (음식의) 선택권이 합리적인 가격으로 제공된다. ⓭어떤 도시락은 무려 11가지나 되는 반찬으로 이루어진 맛을 선사한다. ⓮그들의 성공의 또 다른 비결은 집에서 조리된 식사를 하는 것 같은 느낌을 제공하는 것이다. ⓯만약 이러한 추세가 계속된다면, 우리는 도시락 시장의 성장률이 빠르게 올라가는 것을 볼 것을 기대할 수 있다.

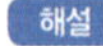

1 글의 내용은 한국에서 요즘 도시락이 인기를 얻고 있는 비결에 관한 것이므로 알맞은 것은 ⑤ '한국에서 도시락 시장의 성장 원인이다.
2 주어가 on every street corner의 수식을 받는 Convenience stores로 복수이므로 복수동사를 써야 한다.
3 오늘날의 도시락과 예전의 도시락의 주요 차이는 오늘날 도시락은 건강하고 '다양한' 선택권이 제공되는 반면 예전의 도시락은 빠른 점심을 위한 비교적 '품질이 낮은' 식사라고 했으므로 빈칸에는 차례로 diverse, low-quality가 알맞다.
4 글에서 편의점의 다양화와 건강에 대한 인식 변화에 대한 내용은 언급되지 않았다.

[A] ❶▼Have you seen someone making or eating *miyeokguk*? ❷ This soup has special meaning for Koreans. ❸In the Korean culture, mothers traditionally eat this soup for several days after they give birth. ❹It is also usually the soup that Koreans eat to celebrate birthdays.

[B] ❺Now you know what *miyeokguk* is. ❻Then how about making it yourself? ❼Let me tell you about how to make it. ❽First, put the *miyeok* in water to soften it. ❾When it becomes soft, take it out and cut it into pieces. ❿After that, it's time to heat up a pot. ⓫Add some chopped beef with a little bit of sesame oil, soy sauce, and salt, and cook it for 1 minute. ⓬Next put the *miyeok* and 1 spoon of soy sauce into the pot and cook it for 1 more minute. ⓭Remember to stir it often. ⓮After that, pour in 6 cups of water and boil it. ⓯Then you can reduce the heat. ⓰Lastly, cook it for 20 minutes, and add some salt. ⓱That's all. ⓲Isn't it simple? ⓳Now serve it to your family or friends. ⓴I'm sure you'll see them enjoy it very much.

[A] ❶여러분은 누군가가 미역국을 만들고 있거나 먹고 있는 것을 본 적이 있습니까? ❷이 국은 한국인들에게는 특별한 의미가 있습니다. ❸한국 문화에서 어머니들은 전통적으로 출산을 한 후에 며칠 동안 이 국을 먹습니다. ❹그것은 또한 한국인들이 보통 생일을 축하하기 위해 먹는 국이기도 합니다.

[B] ❺이제 당신은 미역국이 무엇인지 알고 있습니다. ❻그렇다면 그것을 직접 만들어 보는 것은 어떨까요? ❼그것을 만드는 방법에 대해 알려주겠습니다. ❽먼저, 미역을 부드럽게 하기 위해서 그것을 물에 담그세요. ❾미역이 부드러워지면 꺼내서 잘게 자르세요. ❿그다음, 냄비를 뜨겁게 데울 시간입니다. ⓫약간의 참기름, 간장, 그리고 소금과 함께 다진 소고기를 넣고 1분 동안 요리하세요. ⓬다음으로 미역과 간장 1스푼을 냄비에 넣고 1분간 더 요리하세요. ⓭그것을 자주 저어야 한다는 것을 기억하세요. ⓮그런 다음, 물 6컵을 붓고 끓이세요. ⓯그리고 나서 불을 줄이세요. ⓰마지막으로 20분 동안 조리하고 약간의 소금을 넣으세요. ⓱다 됐습니다. ⓲간단하지 않나요? ⓳이제 그것을 여러분의 가족이나 친구들에게 대접하세요. ⓴틀림없이 여러분은 그들이 그것을 맛있게 먹는 것을 보게 될 것입니다.

문제 해석

1 글 [B]의 중심 소재로 알맞은 것은?
① 건강에 좋은 몇 가지 종류의 음식   ② 미역국의 기원   ③ 한국 전통 음식의 좋은 점
④ 미역국을 만드는 방법   ⑤ 한국인들에게 미역국의 의미

2 이 글에서 미역국에 대한 내용으로 일치하지 <u>않는</u> 것은?
① 한국인들은 그것이 그들에게 특별한 음식이라고 생각한다.   ② 미역을 부드럽게 하기 전에 잘게 잘라야 한다.
③ 그것에는 약간의 참기름이 필요하다.   ④ 마지막 단계에서 약간의 소금을 넣을 필요가 있다.
⑤ 그것은 만들기가 어렵지 않다.

3 ①~⑤ 중 미역국을 가리키는 것이 <u>아닌</u> 것은?

4 이 글의 밑줄 친 ⓐ가 의미하는 것은 무엇인가? 두 가지를 우리말로 쓰시오.

해설

1 [B]에는 미역국을 만드는 방법이 차례대로 제시되어 있으므로 주제로 가장 알맞은 것은 ④이다.

2 미역을 물에 담근 다음 부드러워지면 꺼내서 자르고 끓여야 한다고 했으므로 ②는 알맞지 않다.

3 ④는 불린 미역을 의미하고, 나머지는 모두 미역국을 의미한다.

4 한국인들에게 미역국은 특별한 의미를 가지는데, 그 특별한 의미는 바로 다음 문장에 나오는 것으로 어머니들이 출산 후 며칠간 먹는다는 것과 한국 사람들이 보통 생일날에 먹는 국이라는 것이다.

01 열대 섬으로 여행가보는 게 어때?　02 당신은 혼자 여행하는 사람들을 위해 어떤 조언을 해줄 수 있나요?　03 우리는 시카고에서 무엇을 볼 수 있나요?　04 꿈을 가지는 것은 중요해요.

Before Reading　pp.50~51

1 Susan은 살아오고 있다 / 캐나다에서 / 2015년부터　2 Jack은 (지금 막) 끝마쳤다 / 그의 숙제를　3 내 남동생은 가본 적이 있다 / 유럽에　4 나는 잃어버렸다 / 나의 가방을　5 Mark는 먹어본 적이 없었다 / 햄버거를 / 그가 10살이었을 때까지　6 그들은 이미 가 버렸다 / Tom이 도착했을 때

Basic Test

1 have learned　2 has cooked　3 has known　4 have been　5 had never seen　6 had lived

Preview Test

01 Have you had cold weather / since last winter? 당신은 추운 날씨를 겪고 있나요 / 지난겨울부터　**02** I have heard / from a tour guide / that he had barely seen / so many solo travelers / before. 나는 들은 적이 있다 / 여행 가이드로부터 / 그는 거의 본 적이 없었다는 말을 / 그렇게 많은 혼자 여행하는 사람들을 / 전에는　**03** On the previous day, / we had visited / so many places. 그 전날 / 우리는 방문했었다 / 매우 많은 장소들을　**04** She had started / to tour around the world / before she was 19. 그녀는 시작했다 / 세계 여행하는 것을 / 그녀가 19살 전에

Real-Life Reading　pp.52~57

01 1 ④　2 ③　Words offer 제공하다　comfortable 편안한　equipment 장비　**02** 1 ④　2 ①　Words solo 혼자의　unknown 알려지지 않은　desire 바람　stranger 낯선 사람　**03** 1 ③　2 ④　3 ⑤　4 It was the best pizza I had ever eaten.　Words huge 거대한　lake 호수　aquarium 수족관　view 풍경, 전망　**04** 1 ⑤　2 ③　3 ②　4 ②　Words return 돌아오다　opportunity 기회　continent 대륙　landscape 풍경　volunteer 자원 봉사하다

01　열대 섬 관광　p.52

❶▼**Have you had** cold weather/since last winter? ❷Then you should call *Paradise Travel*. ❸We offer wonderful tours/to beautiful areas. ❹If you join our popular tours,/you can see lovely tropical islands/like Bali, Phuket, and the Maldives. ❺It's a great way/to relax. ❻You can lie on the beach/and enjoy the sun.

현재완료(계속)
조건의 접속사
~와 같은
형용사적 용법　　lie – lay – lain

❼•**Duration:** 4 days 3 nights
　　3박 4일
❽•**Hotel:** five-star hotels/with great swimming pools and
　　~이 있는(소지, 소유)
　　comfortable rooms

❶당신은 추운 날씨를 겪고 있나요 / 지난 겨울부터 ❷그렇다면 당신은 *Paradise Travel*에 전화해야 합니다 ❸우리는 멋진 여행을 제공합니다 / 아름다운 지역으로 ❹만약 당신이 우리의 인기 있는 여행에 참여한다면 / 당신은 매력적인 열대 섬들을 볼 수 있습니다 / 발리, 푸껫, 그리고 몰디브와 같은 ❺그것은 멋진 방법입니다 / 휴식을 취하는 ❻당신은 해변에 누울 수 있습니다 / 그리고 햇빛을 즐길 수 있습니다 ❼기간: 3박 4일 ❽호텔: 5성급 호텔 / 근사한 수영장과 편안한 방이 있는

⑨ •**Activities:** scuba diving, sailing, and nature walking

⑩ •**Price:** $500 (including a hotel bill for 3 nights, American breakfast, equipment fee)

⑪ Call us at 636-0000 / to reserve a *Paradise Travel* tour. ⑫ If you want to know more information, / please visit *www.paradisetravel. com.* ⑬ It will be a great decision!

1 이 글에서 ④ 항공권 가격은 언급되지 않았다.

2 *Paradise Travel* 관광을 예약하기 위해 전화하라는 말이므로 ③ book(예약하다)이 알맞다.

혼자 여행하는 사람들을 위한 조언

❶ I have heard from a tour guide that he had barely seen so many solo travelers before. ❷ But not now. ❸ Why? ❹ With the help of Internet, people can easily get information about the parts of the unknown world to them. ❺ Here are some tips for solo travelers. ❻ First, keep in touch with your friends and family by e-mail, text, social media or phone so they can lend a hand if needed. ❼ Second, don't be afraid to let plans change. ❽ Solo travelers don't have to worry about someone else's desires. ❾ Some of the best travel stories come from unexpected adventures and last-minute decisions to go somewhere new. ❿ Be brave! ⓫ Third, keep your most important things in one place. ⓬ Then you can find them easily when you need them. ⓭ Last but not least, open up to others. ⓮ If you smile and talk to others first, you will learn a lot from these strangers in a strange land.

⑨ 활동: 스쿠버 다이빙, 요트 타기, 그리고 자연 산책

⑩ 가격: 500$ (3박의 호텔 숙박비, 미국식 아침 식사, 장비 비용 포함)

⑪ 636-0000으로 전화 주세요. *Paradise Travel* 관광을 예약하시려면 **⑫** 만약 더 많은 정보를 알고 싶다면 / www.paradisetravel. com으로 방문해 주세요. **⑬** 그것은 훌륭한 결정일 것입니다!

❶ 나는 여행 가이드에게 전에는 그렇게 많은 혼자 여행하는 사람들을 거의 본 적이 없었다는 말을 들은 적이 있다. **❷** 하지만 지금은 아니다. **❸** 왜일까? **❹** 인터넷의 도움으로 사람들은 그들에게 알려지지 않은 세계에 대한 정보를 쉽게 얻을 수 있다. **❺** 여기 혼자 여행하는 사람들을 위한 몇 가지 조언이 있다. **❻** 먼저, 여러분의 친구와 가족들과 전자 우편, 문자 메시지, 소셜 미디어 또는 휴대 전화를 이용하여 연락을 하면서 지내라 그래야 당신이 도움이 필요할 때 그들이 도울 수 있다. **❼** 둘째, 일정을 변경하는 것을 두려워하지 마라. **❽** 혼자 여행하는 사람들은 다른 사람(여행 동행자)의 바람을 신경 쓸 필요가 없다. **❾** 가장 좋은 여행 이야기의 몇 가지는 예상치 못한 모험에서 나오고, 새로운 어떤 장소로 가기로 한 마지막 결정의 순간에 찾아온다. **❿** 용기를 가져라! **⓫** 셋째, 가장 중요한 물건들을 한 곳에 보관하라. **⓬** 그러면 당신은 그것들이 필요할 때 쉽게 찾을 수 있다. **⓭** 마지막이지만 중요한 것은, 다른 사람들에게 마음을 열어라. **⓮** 당신이 먼저 다른 사람들에게 미소 짓고 말을 걸면, 당신은 낯선 땅의 이런 낯선 사람들로부터 많은 것을 배울 것이다.

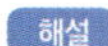

1 이 글에서 물과 간식을 가지고 다니라는 말은 언급되지 않았다.

2 이 글은 혼자 여행하는 사람들을 위해 조언을 하는 글이다.

❶ Saturday was my second day in Chicago. ❷ I had to get up early even though I was very tired. ❸▼ **On the previous day, we had**
= although, even if   과거완료(대과거)
visited so many places. ❹ I went to Northerly Island Park, the Willis Tower, etc. ❺ Willis Tower, the second highest building in the U.S.,
기타 등등(= and so on)   동격
was especially an exciting place to me. ❻ I was so scared <u>but</u> excited while walking on the sky deck.
분사구문(= while I was walking ~)

❼ This morning I went to Millennium Park after finishing my breakfast. ❽ I saw 'The Bean' there. ❾ It was a huge bean-shaped
–shaped는 '~ 모양의'의 의미가 있음
sculpture. ❿ After that, I went to the Navy Pier. ⓫ <u>It</u> is a large pier
→ Navy Pier
on Lake Michigan. ⓬ There were so many <u>must-see</u> places, such as
꼭 봐야 할
the Ferris Wheel, Shedd Aquarium, the Michigan Museum, <u>and so</u>
= etc.
on. ⓭ <u>When leaving</u> the Navy Pier, I felt hungry. ⓮ <u>Thanks to</u> my
= When I left   ~ 덕분에(= Owing to)
smartphone, I was able to find a popular restaurant. ⓯ I tried a
Chicago deep-dish pizza for lunch. ⓰ It was the best pizza I had
that
최상급 + (that) + 주어 + 완료시제: ~한 것 중 가장 …한
ever eaten. ⓱ After lunch, I enjoyed the boat tour of the Chicago River. ⓲ On the boat, I could <u>not only</u> enjoy the view of Chicago
not only A but also B: A뿐만 아니라 B도
<u>but also</u> learn about the city itself.
강조용법

❶ 토요일은 시카고에서의 둘째 날이었다. ❷ 나는 몹시 피곤했지만 일찍 일어나야 했다. ❸ 그 전날, 우리는 너무나 많은 곳을 방문했었다. ❹ 나는 Northerly Island Park와 Willis Tower 등에 갔었다. ❺ 미국에서 두 번째로 높은 빌딩인 Willis Tower는 특히 내게 가장 신나는 장소였다. ❻ 하늘 갑판에서 걸어 다니는 동안 나는 무척 겁이 났지만 신이 났다.

❼ 오늘 오전에는 아침 식사를 끝내고 나서 Millennium Park로 갔다. ❽ 나는 그곳에서 'The Bean'을 보았다. ❾ 그것은 거대한 콩 모양의 조형물이었다. ❿ 그리고 나서, 나는 Navy Pier로 갔다. ⓫ 그것은 미시간 호에 있는 커다란 부두이다. ⓬ 그곳에는 페리스 관람차, Shedd 수족관, 미시간 박물관 등과 같이 꼭 방문해야 할 곳들이 많이 있었다. ⓭ Navy Pier를 떠날 때 나는 배가 고팠다. ⓮ 스마트폰 덕분에 나는 유명한 식당을 찾을 수 있었다. ⓯ 나는 점심으로 시카고 두꺼운(딥디쉬) 피자를 먹어 보았다. ⓰ 그것은 내가 먹어본 것 중 최고의 피자였다. ⓱ 점심 식사 후, 나는 시카고 강의 보트 투어를 즐겼다. ⓲ 보트에서 나는 시카고의 풍경을 즐길 수 있었을 뿐만 아니라 도시 그 자체에 대해서도 배울 수 있었다.

해설

1. 시카고 여행 둘째 날에 있었던 일을 시간 순서대로 기록하면서 간략한 느낌을 쓴 기행문이다.
2. 콩 모양의 조형물은 Millennium Park에 있다고 했다.
3. 첫 번째 빈칸에는 두려웠지만 신이 났다는 흐름이 알맞고, 두 번째 빈칸에는 'A 뿐만 아니라 B도'의 뜻을 가지는 not only A but also B의 구문이므로 공통으로 들어갈 말은 but이다.
4. pizza 다음에 목적격 관계대명사 that이 생략된 구문이며, that 이하는 과거 시점 이전의 일이 과거까지 영향을 미치는 과거완료 문장이 되어야 한다.

04 나의 꿈   pp.56~57

(B) ❶ I have a dream. ❷ After I finish high school, I want to travel
명사적 용법

(B) ❶ 내게는 꿈이 있다. ❷ 고등학교를 졸업

around the world for a year. ❸I will buy a "round-the-world"
ticket. ❹It's a special ticket that lets me visit many places. ❺By the
end of the trip, I will have visited 5 continents. ❻I will have stayed
in over 20 different countries.

(C) ❼I first got the idea from my cousin, Sarah. ❽▼She had started
to tour around the world before she was 19. ❾She visited many
exciting places. ❿She saw the *Taj Mahal* in India, and enjoyed
shopping in markets for tourists. ⓫She traveled through Europe by
train, so she could take pictures of lots of beautiful landscapes. ⓬
She stayed in guest houses around the world and spent some time
with new people. ⓭She also volunteered to teach children at an
orphanage in Kenya. ⓮Through these experiences, she told me that
she could learn a lot.

(A) ⓯Like my cousin, I want to learn a lot from the experience. ⓰
By the time I return, I will have seen many different cultures. ⓱I
think the experience will have changed me. ⓲It will be a great
opportunity for me.

한 후에 나는 일 년 동안 세계를 여행하고 싶다. ❸나는 '세계 일주' 표를 살 것이다. ❹그것은 내가 많은 곳을 방문하게 해줄 특별한 표이다. ❺여행이 끝날 때쯤에 나는 5개 대륙을 방문하게 될 것이다. ❻나는 20개 이상의 다른 나라들에서 머물게 될 것이다.

(C) ❼나는 처음에 그 아이디어를 나의 사촌인 Sarah로부터 얻었다. ❽그녀는 19살 이전에 세계 여행을 시작했었다. ❾그녀는 많은 흥미로운 장소들을 방문했다. ❿그녀는 인도에서 타지마할을 보았고, 관광객들을 위한 시장에서 쇼핑하는 것을 즐겼다. ⓫그녀는 기차를 타고 유럽을 여행해서 많은 아름다운 풍경 사진들을 찍을 수 있었다. ⓬그녀는 전 세계의 게스트 하우스에서 머물렀고 새로운 사람들과 시간을 보냈다. ⓭그녀는 또한 케냐의 한 고아원에서 자원봉사로 아이들을 가르쳤다. ⓮그러한 경험들을 통해서 그녀는 많이 배울 수 있었다고 내게 말했다.

(A) ⓯나의 사촌처럼 나는 경험으로부터 많은 것을 배우기를 바란다. ⓰내가 돌아올 무렵에 나는 많은 다양한 문화들을 보게 될 것이다. ⓱나는 그 경험이 나를 바꿔 놓을 것이라고 생각한다. ⓲그것은 나에게 엄청난 기회가 될 것이다.

---

 1 이 글의 중심 소재로 알맞은 것은?
   ① 여행 경비   ② 사촌의 유럽 여행   ③ 다양한 학교 활동
   ④ 자원봉사 경험   ⑤ 세계 여행

2 이 글의 (A) ~ (C)를 순서대로 바르게 배열한 것은?

3 이 글의 내용과 일치하지 <u>않는</u> 것은?
   ① 글쓴이는 특별한 여행 표를 살 계획이다.   ② Sarah는 20개 이상의 다른 나라들을 여행했다.
   ③ Sarah는 여러 나라를 여행했다.   ④ Sarah는 케냐에서 자원봉사자로 일했다.
   ⑤ 글쓴이는 외국의 문화를 경험하고 싶다.

4 이 글의 밑줄 친 opportunity와 의미가 가장 가까운 것은?
   ① 문제   ② 기회   ③ 비용
   ④ 변화   ⑤ 어려움

 1 글쓴이는 세계 여행을 한 사촌의 예를 들며 자신도 경험을 쌓기 위해 세계 여행을 하고 싶다고 말하고 있다.
2 세계를 여행하고 싶은 글쓴이의 소망이 나오고 (B) → 글쓴이에게 이런 생각을 가지게 한 사촌의 이야기가 언급된 다음에 (C) → 사촌처럼 경험을 넓히고 싶은 글쓴이의 바람 (A)의 흐름이 자연스럽다.
3 ② 글쓴이가 20개 이상의 다른 나라들을 여행하길 원한다고 했다.
4 문맥상 '그것은 나에게 엄청난 기회'라는 뜻이므로 opportunity가 chance(기회)의 뜻으로 쓰였음을 알 수 있다.

01 한국의 국보 제24호는 무엇인가?　02 '@'의 의미는 무엇인가?　03 네가 가장 좋아하는 음식의 역사를 생각해 보아라.
04 알파벳은 어떻게 발명되었는가?

Before Reading　pp.60~61

1 Jack은 그의 부모님 댁을 방문했다 / 그가 가능한 자주　2 Mina는 달린다 / 가능한 빨리　3 Katie는 ~만큼 키가 크지 않다 /
그녀의 오빠 (만큼)　4 그의 가방은 ~이다 / 내 가방보다 세 배 더 큰　5 네가 빨리 떠나면 떠날수록 / 너는 더 일찍 도착할 것이다
6 날씨가 ~되다 / 점점 더 따뜻하게

Basic Test

1 Throw the ball as far as you can.　2 Aron is not as heavy as Tim.　3 The more you give, the more you get
back.　4 The daytime grows longer and longer.

Preview Test

01 The architect of Seokguram was carving / the central ceiling stone / as carefully as he could. 석굴암의
건축가는 조각하고 있는 중이었다 / 중앙 석조 천장을 / 그가 가능한 조심스럽게　02 The @ symbol, / before the
introduction of e-mail, / was not as popular as it is these days. @ 기호는 / 전자우편의 도입 이전에 / 오늘날만큼
유명하지 않았다　03 It led popcorn / to become / more and more popular. 그것은 팝콘을 이끌었다 / ~가 되도록 /
점점 더 인기 있게　04 Making symbols / for everything / got harder and harder / as time passed. 기호를 만드는
것은 / 모든 것들에 대한 / 점점 더 어려워졌다 / 시간이 흐를수록

Real-Life Reading　pp.62~67

01 1 ④　2 ①　Words architect 건축가　descend 내려오다　trace 흔적　02 1 ④　2 하지만 놀랍게도 그 기호의
이름은 우리가 생각하는 것만큼 공식적이지는 않다.　Words official 공식적인　tail 꼬리　03 1 ⑤　2 ③　3 ③　4 ②
Words decoration 장식품　introduce 소개하다　settler 정착인, 이주자　machine 기계　electric 전기의　04 1 ④
2 ①　3 ②　4 ④　Words origin 기원, 근원　mean ~을 뜻하다　express 표현하다　site 장소　trade 거래하다

01　국보 석굴암

p.62

❶ Seokguram is the 24th national treasure / in Korea. （national treasure = 국보）❷ There is an
interesting legend / about Seokguram. ❸▼ The architect of Seokguram
was carving / the central ceiling stone / as carefully as he could. （과거진행형）（as ... as possible = 가능한）
❹ Suddenly, it cracked / before his eyes / and he fell down. （fell down = 쓰러졌다）❺ In a
dream, / he saw gods / descending from heaven / and they repaired the （descending = 현재분사）
ceiling stone. ❻ When he awoke, / he found the ceiling surface fixed / （awake – awoke – awaken）（find + 목적어 + 목적격보어(과거분사)）
but for the faint traces of cracks. ❼ Small cracks / on the ceiling

❶석굴암은 국보 제24호이다 / 한국에서
❷흥미로운 전설이 있다 / 석굴암에 관한
❸석굴암의 건축가는 조각하고 있는 중이
었다 / 중앙 석조 천장을 / 가능한 조심스
럽게 ❹갑자기, 그것은 깨져버렸다 / 그의
눈앞에서 / 그리고 그는 쓰러졌다 ❺꿈에서
/ 그는 신들을 보았다 / 천국에서 내려온 /
그리고 그들은 석조 천장을 수리해주었다
❻그가 깨어났을 때 / 그는 천장 표면이 수
리되어 있는 것을 발견했다 / 균열한 부분
의 희미한 자국을 제외하고 ❼작은 균열은

stone/can still be seen today. ❽Whether the legend is true or not,/
Seokguram had been abandoned/for centuries/until it was
rediscovered/in 1909. ❾A local postman was/in a rainstorm,/so he
found shelter/in the nearest cave. ❿He lit a candle/in the dark/
and found a large stone Buddha! ⓫Later,/he brought others/to
show the cave/and it became famous.

/ 석조 천장에 / 오늘날까지 여전히 볼 수 있다 ❽이 전설이 사실인지 아닌지 간에 / 석굴암은 방치되어 있었다 / 수 세기 동안 / 그것이 다시 발견되기까지 / 1909년에 ❾현지의 집배원이 ~에 있었다 / 폭풍우에 / 그래서 그는 피신처를 찾았다 / 가장 가까운 동굴에서 ❿그는 초에 불을 밝혔다 / 어둠 속에서 / 그리고 커다란 석조 불상을 발견했다! ⓫이후에 / 그는 다른 사람들을 데려왔다 / 그 동굴을 보여주기 위해 / 그리고 그것은 유명해졌다.

1 ④ 석굴암이 여러 번의 재건 작업을 거쳤다는 내용은 이 글에 언급되어 있지 않다.

2 빈칸이 포함된 문장은 석굴암이 유명해지게 된 계기를 언급하고 있으므로 ① famous(유명한)가 알맞다.
① 유명한
② 호화스러운
③ 일상의
④ 보통의
⑤ 비싼

02  @ 기호

❶▼The @ symbol, before the introduction of e-mail, was not as
popular as it is these days. ❷It was just used to show the cost or
weight of something. ❸For example, if you bought 10 apples, you
might write it as 10 apples @ $1.10 each. ❹But that changed when
Ray Tomlinson created the world's first e-mail system. ❺Since then,
the @ symbol has been used more than ever. ❻Surprisingly,
however, the symbol's name is not as official as we think. ❼
Actually, there is no official name for the sign. ❽There are dozens
of strange names for it. ❾For instance, it is called a monkey's tail
by Germans. ❿In China, they call it a mouse. ⓫In France, people
see a snail. ⓬It is called the "meow" in Finland, for they think of it
as a cat that curls up.

❶전자우편이 도입되기 전에 @ 기호는 오늘날만큼 유명하지 않았다. ❷그것은 단지 어떤 것의 가격이나 무게를 보여주는 데 사용되었다. ❸예를 들어, 당신이 10개의 사과를 샀다면 각각 1달러 10센트 가격의 사과 10개라고 썼을지도 모른다. ❹그러나 그것(기존의 사용법)은 Ray Tomlinson이 세계 최초의 전자우편 체계를 창조하면서 바뀌었다. ❺그때 이후로 @ 기호는 어느 때보다도 더 많이 사용되어졌다. ❻하지만 놀랍게도 그 기호의 이름은 우리가 생각하는 것만큼 공식적이지는 않다. ❼사실 그 기호에 대한 공식적인 이름은 없다. ❽그것에는 수많은 낯선 이름들이 있다. ❾예를 들어, 독일인들은 그것을 '원숭이의 꼬리'라고 부른다. ❿중국에서는 사람들이 그것을 '생쥐'라고 부른다. ⓫프랑스에서 사람들은 '달팽이'로 본다. ⓬핀란드에서는 "야옹"이라고 불리는데 그들이 그것을 웅크린 고양이라고 생각하기 때문이다.

---

1 원숭이 꼬리(a monkey's tail), 쥐(mouse), 달팽이(snail), 웅크린 고양이(meow: a cat that curls up)는 나와 있지만 코끼리 코는 언급되지 않았다.

2 〈not as+원급+as〉은 '~만큼 …하지 않은(않게)'이라는 뜻이므로 이에 유의하여 해석하도록 한다.

03 팝콘은 어디에서 왔을까?

(A) ❶ Do you know the history of popcorn? ❷ Popcorn was Native Americans' local food and used for decoration. ❸ They made it a long time ago. ❹ Native Americans knew there were three kinds of corn. ❺ These were sweet corn for eating, corn for animal feed, and corn for popping. ❻ The following is how Native Americans introduced corn to the first settlers, Pilgrims who came to America in 1620.

(C) ❼ One year after they came to America, the Pilgrims had a Thanksgiving dinner. ❽ They invited some Native Americans to the dinner. ❾ The Native Americans brought food with them and one of them brought popcorn. ❿ The Pilgrims liked the taste of popcorn, so they learned how to make popcorn from the Native Americans.

(D) ⓫ Since then, Americans have continued to make popcorn at home. ⓬ But, in 1945, there was a new machine that changed the history of popcorn. ⓭ This electric machine enabled people to make popcorn outside the home.

(B) ⓮ Soon movie theaters started to sell popcorn to make more money. ⓯ It led popcorn to become more and more popular. ⓰ Today Americans still enjoy popcorn at the movies.

(A) ❶ 당신은 팝콘의 역사를 알고 있는가? ❷ 팝콘은 아메리카 원주민들의 토속 음식이었고 장식품으로 사용되었다. ❸ 그들은 오래 전에 그것을 만들었다. ❹ 아메리카 원주민들은 세 종류의 옥수수가 있다는 것을 알고 있었다. ❺ 이것들은 먹기 위한 달콤한 옥수수, 동물 사료용 옥수수, 그리고 튀기기 위한 옥수수였다. ❻ 다음은 아메리카 원주민들이 첫 정착인들, 즉 1620년에 아메리카에 온 청교도들에게 옥수수를 알려준 방법이다.

(C) ❼ 청교도들이 아메리카로 온 지 일 년 후, 그들은 추수감사 만찬을 열었다. ❽ 그들은 몇몇 원주민들을 만찬에 초대했다. ❾ 그 아메리카 원주민들은 음식을 가지고 왔고, 그들 중 한 명이 팝콘을 가져왔다. ❿ 청교도들은 팝콘의 맛을 좋아해서 아메리카 원주민들에게 팝콘을 만드는 방법을 배웠다.

(D) ⓫ 그때부터 미국인들은 줄곧 집에서 팝콘을 만들었다. ⓬ 그러나 1945년에 팝콘의 역사를 바꾼 새 기계가 있었다. ⓭ 이 전기 기계는 사람들이 집 밖에서 팝콘을 만드는 것을 가능하게 했다.

(B) ⓮ 곧 영화관들은 돈을 더 벌기 위해 팝콘을 팔기 시작했다. ⓯ 그것은 팝콘을 점점 더 인기 있게 만들었다. ⓰ 오늘날 미국인들은 여전히 영화관에서 팝콘을 즐겨 먹는다.

1 팝콘의 역사에 대해 소개하는 내용이므로 정보 전달의 성격이 강하다.
① 재미있는
② 시적인
③ 과학적인
④ 낭만적인
⑤ 정보를 제공하는

2 단락 (A) 마지막에 아메리카 원주민들이 미국 초기 정착민들에게 어떻게 팝콘을 소개하였는지에 대한 내용이 나올 것을 예고하고 있으므로, 그 다음에는 원주민들이 팝콘을 추수감사절 만찬에 가져온 내용이 나오는 (C), 그 다음에 팝콘을 만드는 기계가 나오면서 팝콘을 집 밖에서 만들게 된다는 내용의 (D), 마지막으로 영화관에서 팝콘이 판매되고 오늘날까지 미국인들이 즐기고 있다는 내용의 (B)가 이어지는 것이 적절하다.

3 팝콘 만드는 기계가 나옴으로써 팝콘이 집 밖에서도 만들어지고 영화관에도 보급되는 등 팝콘 역사에 변화가 생겼다고 하였다.
① 튀기기 위한 옥수수
② 아메리카의 정착민들
③ 전기 팝콘 기계
④ 많은 극장들
⑤ 세 종류의 옥수수

4 청교도들이 옥수수로 만든 음식을 즐겨 먹었다거나 오늘날 더 인기 있는 간식에 대해서는 본문에 언급되지 않았다.

 **알파벳의 기원**

❶How did we get the modern alphabet? ❷It took thousands of years, and as much effort as any other invention. ❸The first people to write things down carved symbols onto rocks or shells. ❹These symbols usually represented people or things. ❺For instance, a drawing of a person might mean a person. ❻People who lived a long time ago led simple lives. ❼They used very easy symbols because they used them only to express their simple needs. ❽One of the most basic needs was food. ❾To tell each other about how to hunt animals or where to find food, people drew on cave walls. ❿Soon, people could grow their own food. ⓫So, they needed to use more symbols for more than just people, places, and things. ⓬▼Making symbols for everything got harder and harder as time passed.

❶우리가 어떻게 현대 알파벳을 갖게 됐을까? ❷그것은 수천 년이 걸렸고, 다른 어떤 발명품만큼 많은 노력이 들어갔다. ❸무언가 써 내려간 최초의 사람들은 바위나 껍데기에 기호들을 새겼다. ❹이러한 기호들은 대개 사람이나 물건을 나타냈다. ❺예를 들어, 사람 그림은 사람을 뜻하는 것이었을지도 모른다. ❻오래 전에 살았던 사람들은 단순한 삶을 살았다. ❼그들은 간단한 요구를 표현하는 데에만 기호들을 사용했기 때문에 굉장히 쉬운 기호들을 사용했다. ❽가장 기본적인 요구 중 하나는 음식이었다. ❾동물을 사냥하는 법이나 음식을 찾을 장소에 대해서 서로에게 이야기하기 위해 사람들은 동굴 벽에 그림을 그렸다. ❿곧, 사람들은 그들 자신의 식량을 기를 수 있었다. ⓫그래서 그들은 그저 사람, 장소 그리고 물건들보다 더 많은 것들에 대한 기호를 사용할 필요가 있었다. ⓬시간이 흐를수록 모든 것들에 대한 기호를 만드는 것은 점점 더 어려워졌다.

⓭So, many people started to feel the need to invent a set of letters, an alphabet. ⓮Egyptians tried to make one and did it. ⓯And it became common in Egypt. ⓰(There are many historical sites in Egypt.) ⓱Other countries that traded with or fought against Egypt knew this alphabet, and it was spread.

⓭그래서 많은 사람들은 문자 체계 즉, 알파벳을 만들어야 할 필요성을 느끼기 시작했다. ⓮이집트 사람들은 그것을 만들기 위해 노력했고 만들어냈다. ⓯그리고 그것은 이집트에서 흔해졌다. ⓰(이집트에는 유적지가 많다.) ⓱이집트와 거래를 하거나 대항하여 싸웠던 다른 나라들은 이 알파벳을 알게 되었고, 그것은 퍼지게 되었다.

---

1 이 글의 종류로 알맞은 것은?
① 여행 계획
② 여행 일기
③ 호텔 예약을 위한 조언
④ 역사 관련 기사
⑤ 이집트 여행안내

2 이 글의 밑줄 친 represented와 의미가 가장 가까운 것은?
① 표현했다
② 변화시켰다
③ 소개했다
④ 발견했다
⑤ 생각했다

3 이 글의 빈칸에 알맞은 것은?
① 그럼에도 불구하고
② 예를 들어
③ 그렇지만
④ 게다가
⑤ 이에 반해서

4 이 글의 흐름상 어색한 것은?

1 이 글은 알파벳의 시초와 역사에 대한 글로 historical article(역사 관련 기사)에 속한다.
2 기호가 사람이나 사물들을 표현한다는 문맥이므로 represent는 express(표현하다)의 의미로 쓰였음을 알 수 있다.
3 뒤 문장이 앞 문장에 대한 예시이므로 For instance(예를 들어)가 와야 한다.
4 이집트에서 알파벳이 흔해졌다는 내용 다음에 '이집트에는 유적지가 많이 있다.'는 문장이 오는 것은 어색하다.

UNIT 07 News

01 제주도를 대표하는 세 가지는 무엇인가? 02 모바일 결제 시스템의 어떤 점이 좋나요? 03 아르바이트를 위한 조언을 드립니다. 04 당신은 지금 모습 그대로 아름다워요.

Before Reading pp.70~71

1 저 남자를 봐 / 축구를 하고 있는 2 나는 한 소년을 만났다 / 그의 이름이 Robert인 3 이것은 그 자전거이다 / 내가 어제 구입한 4 누리는 남동생이 있다 / 중학생인 (누리는 중학생인 남동생이 있다) 5 누리는 남동생이 있다 / 중학생인 (누리는 남동생이 한 명 있는데, 그는 중학생이다) 6 내게 말해줘 / 네가 하고 싶은 것을 7 서울은 도시이다 / 내가 태어난

Basic Test

1 who 2 whose 3 what 4 of whom 5 in which 6 who

Preview Test

01 *Haenyeo* use / a unique and eco-friendly way of harvesting/, which protects the marine environment. 해녀는 이용한다 / 채취를 위한 독특하고 친환경적인 방식을 / 해양 환경을 보호하는 02 In Korea, / you can even use a credit card / to buy newspapers / that homeless people sell. 한국에서 / 여러분은 심지어 신용카드를 사용할 수 있다 / 신문을 사기 위해서 / 노숙자들이 판매하는 03 Here's what teens have to remember / before getting a part-time job. 여기에 청소년들이 기억해야 할 것들이 있다 / 아르바이트를 구하기 전에 04 We all have seen some images /, in which models have been photoshopped, / to appear extremely skinny. 우리 모두는 어떤 이미지들을 보아왔다 / (그 안에서) 모델들이 포토샵된 / 극단적으로 말라 보이도록

Real-Life Reading pp.72~77

01 1 ⑤ 2 ⑤ Words celebrate 축하하다 creature 생물 respect 존중하다 marine 해양의 02 1 ② 2 that Words payment 결제, 지불 disappear 사라지다 customer 고객 03 1 ① 2 ⑤ 3 ① 4 ② Words workplace 일터, 직장 injure 부상을 입다 right 권리 wage 임금 sign 서명하다 04 1 ⑤ 2 ③ 3 수정된 이미지가 여성들과 어린이들에게 엄청난 부정적인 영향을 미칠 수 있다는 것 4 ⓐ to have ⓑ to occur Words skinny 마른 comparison 비교 risk 위험(성) government 정부 require 요구하다 worth ~할 가치가 있는

01 무형 문화유산 '해녀'

p.72

❶ In 2016,/*Haenyeo*,/female divers on Jejudo,/had a reason to celebrate. ❷ They were listed/as Korea's 19th intangible cultural heritage of humanity by UNESCO. ❸ *Haenyeo* are women/who dive deep into the sea/with no scuba gear. ❹ They can hold their breath for two or three minutes,/and sometimes even ten. ❺ Their job is/to collect various sea creatures. ❻ They once were supporting

❶ 2016년에 / 해녀는 / 제주도의 여성 잠수부들인 / 축하할 이유가 생겼다 ❷ 그들은 등재되었다 / 한국의 19번째 유네스코 인류 무형 문화유산으로 ❸ 해녀는 여성들이다 / 바닷속 깊이 잠수하는 / 스쿠버 장비 없이 ❹ 그들은 2~3분 동안 숨을 참을 수 있다 / 그리고 때로는 10분간 ❺ 그들의 일은 / 다양한 바다 생물을 채집하는 것이다 ❻ 그들은 한때 가족을 부양했다 / 그리고 생명의 위협을 무릅썼다 / 생계를 유지하기 위해서

the family/and risked their lives/to make ends meet. ❼ According
to the Cultural Heritage Administration,/the *Haenyeo* culture
respects the ocean and represents the cultural identity of the
island/where people in the past/heavily relied on the sea/to survive.
❽▼*Haenyeo* uses/a unique and eco-friendly way of harvesting/
, which protects the marine environment. ❾ Also, they have passed
down diving know-how/to younger generations. ❿ This helped
Haenyeo to be listed/as a UNESCO cultural heritage.

❼문화유산 관리국에 따르면 / 해녀 문화는 바다를 존중하고 섬의 문화적 정체성을 나타낸다 / 과거 사람들이 / 바다에 크게 의존했던 / 생존을 위해 ❽해녀는 이용한다 / 채취를 위한 독특하고 친환경적인 방식을 / 그리고 그것은 해양 환경을 보호한다 ❾또한 그들은 잠수 비결을 전수해 왔다 / 젊은 세대들에게 ❿이것은 해녀가 등재되는 것은 도왔다 / 유네스코 문화유산으로

1 본문은 해녀가 유네스코 인류 무형 문화유산으로 등재되었다는 것과 그 이유를 설명하고 있으므로 제목으로 가장 적절한 것은 ⑤ '유네스코 문화유산 목록에 추가된 제주 해녀'가 알맞다.
① 제주도 해녀의 기원 　　　　② 한국에서 방문해야 할 세계 문화유산
③ 해녀가 되기 위한 조언 　　　④ 유네스코 문화유산에 추가되는 방법
2 make ends meet은 '생활하는 데 기본적으로 필요한 돈을 지불할 수 있을 정도로 돈을 갖고 있다'는 뜻이므로 가장 적절한 것은 ⑤ '살아갈만한 돈을 벌다'이다.
① 돈을 절약하다 　　　　　　② 뜻하지 않게 발견하다
③ 주제를 피하다 　　　　　　④ 밤늦게까지 일하다

02 현금이 필요 없는 미래 p.73

❶A cashless society is coming. ❷Scandinavians use cash for no
more than 6% of all payments they make. ❸In Denmark, the
government has proposed that stores throw their cash registers away.
❹▼In Korea, you can even use a credit card to buy newspapers that
homeless people sell. ❺One of the reasons why cash is disappearing
is the wide use of credit cards, but there's another. ❻These days,
many people carry digital wallets. ❼A digital wallet turns
smartphones into electronic wallets by using a mobile payment
system. ❽Customers can make payments at stores or online with
their smartphones. ❾A Bank of Korea report said that 41.8% of
Koreans in their 30s use a mobile payment method.

❶현금 없는 사회가 도래하고 있다. ❷북유럽인들은 그들이 하는 모든 지불 중 단지 6%에 지나지 않는 만큼만 현금을 사용한다. ❸덴마크에서 정부는 상점들이 그들의 금전 등록기를 처분하도록 제안해 왔다. ❹한국에서 여러분은 심지어 노숙자들이 판매하는 신문을 사기 위해서 신용카드를 사용할 수도 있다. ❺현금이 사라지고 있는 이유 중 하나는 신용카드의 폭넓은 사용때문이지만, 또 다른 이유가 있다. ❻요즈음 많은 사람들이 디지털 지갑을 가지고 다닌다. ❼디지털 지갑은 모바일 결제 시스템을 사용함으로써 스마트폰을 전자 지갑으로 바꾼다. ❽고객들은 그들의 스마트폰으로 상점에서 또는 온라인으로 결제를 할 수 있다. ❾한국은행의 보고서에서는 30대 한국인들의 41.8%가 모바일 결제 방식을 사용한다고 했다.

❿Koreans are also welcoming a cashless society. ⓫Do you still use cash? ⓬Then <u>how about buying</u> something with your smartphone?
how about+-ing: ~하는 게 어때? (권유)
⓭Cash is quickly becoming a thing of the past.

❿한국인들은 또한 현금이 없는 사회를 환영하고 있다. ⓫여러분은 여전히 현금을 사용하는가? ⓬그렇다면 여러분의 스마트폰으로 무언가를 구입해 보는 것은 어떨까? ⓭현금은 빠르게 과거의 것이 되고 있다.

---

1 현금이 없는 사회가 오고 있다는 내용을 디지털 지갑 등을 예로 들어 설명하는 글이므로 ② '현금은 모바일 결제 시스템으로 대체될 것이다.'가 알맞다.
① 한국인들은 돈을 현명하게 쓰는 방법을 배워야 한다.　　② 현금은 모바일 결제로 대체될 것이다.
③ 디지털 보안에 주의하는 것은 중요하다.　　④ 모바일 결제는 사용이 편리하다.
⑤ 우리는 소비를 줄여야 한다.

2 has proposed와 said의 목적어 역할을 하는 명사절을 이끄는 접속사가 각각 필요하므로 that을 써야 한다.

 부당한 대우를 받는 청소년 근로자들

❶It is said that about 80% of Korean teens have work experience.
~라고 한다(= They say that ~)
❷But <u>unfortunately</u>, many teens <u>are treated</u> unfairly at their
수동태
workplace. ❸In addition, they are far more likely than adults to <u>be
비교급 강조
injured</u> at work, even though they work fewer hours and <u>are
수동태　　　　비록 ~일지라도
prohibited by law from</u> working in high-risk jobs. ❹What's worse
be prohibited by law from -ing: 법으로 ~하는 것을 금지하다　　관계대명사
is <u>that</u> too many teens don't even know about their <u>rights</u> in the
접속사　　　　　　　　　　　　　　　　명 권리
workplace. ❺▾Here's what teens have to remember <u>before getting</u> a
관계대명사(= the thing which)　　　　= before they get ~
part-time job. ❻In Korea, teens <u>who</u> are 15 years old or over are
주격 관계대명사
allowed to work. ❼If you are younger, you have to get a permit
~하도록 허락되다
from the Ministry of Labor. ❽If you're <u>paid</u> <u>less than</u> the minimum
수동태　　열등 비교
wage, <u>ask the employer to pay</u> you more. ❾Also, teens' working
5형식 구문(동사+목적어+목적격보어)
hours are seven hours a day. ❿However, if you wish to work more,
<u>it</u> is possible <u>to work</u> one more hour per day. ⓫When you do, you
가주어　　　　진주어
should be paid for any overtime work. ⓬And <u>be sure to sign</u> a
반드시 ~하다
contract <u>before starting</u> a new job. ⓭If <u>anything unfair</u> happens at
= before you start ~　　　　-thing+형용사
your workplace, just call the Ministry of Labor and get some help.

❶한국의 청소년들 중 약 80%가 일을 한 경험이 있다고 한다. ❷하지만 불행히도 많은 청소년들은 일터에서 부당하게 대우를 받는다. ❸게다가 그들은 성인들 보다 더 적은 시간을 일하고 위험성이 큰 일을 하는 것이 법으로 금지될지라도 직장에서 성인들 보다 훨씬 더 많이 다치는 경향이 있다. ❹설상가상인 것은 너무나 많은 청소년들이 일터에서의 자신의 권리에 대해서조차 모르고 있다는 것이다. ❺여기 청소년들이 아르바이트 구하기 전에 기억해야 할 것이 있다. ❻한국에서는 15세 이상의 청소년들이 일을 하도록 허용되어 있다. ❼만약 당신이 더 어리다면, 노동부로부터 허가를 받아야 한다. ❽만약 최저 임금보다 더 적게 받는다면, 고용주에게 더 많이 지불하라고 요구하라. ❾또한 청소년들의 노동 시간은 하루 7시간이다. ❿하지만 여러분이 더 많이 일하기를 바란다면 하루에 한 시간씩 더 일하는 것은 가능하다. ⓫초과 근무를 할 때, 여러분은 초과업무에 대해 돈을 받아야 한다. ⓬그리고 새로운 일을 시작하기 전에 반드시 계약서에 서명하라. ⓭만약 일터에서 어떤 부당한 일이 일어난다면, 노동부에 전화를 해서 도움을 받아라.

1 이 글은 청소년들이 일터에서 부당하게 대우를 받는 실정에 대해 설명하고 그들이 가질 수 있는 권리에 대해 이야기하고 있으므로 ①이 알맞다.

2 연령(15 years old or over), 최저 임금(the minimum wage), 초과근무(the overtime work), 계약서(sign a contract)에 대해서는 언급되었으나, 보험에 대해서는 언급되지 않았다.

3 문맥상 많은 청소년들이 일터에서 부당하게 대우를 받는다는 내용이 들어가야 하므로 부사어는 fortunately가 아니라 unfortunately(불행히도)가 적절하다.

4 본문의 What은 주어 역할을 하는 선행사를 포함하는 관계대명사이고, ②는 '무엇'이란 뜻의 의문사이다. 나머지는 모두 관계대명사로 쓰여 '~한 것'의 의미를 나타낸다.

① 나는 그가 말한 것을 믿을 수 없다.　　　② James는 내게 그것이 무엇인지 물었다.

③ 오늘 그녀가 한 일은 나를 기쁘게 했다.　　④ 이 펜은 내가 정말 사고 싶었던 것이다.

⑤ 네가 가게에서 구입한 것을 내게 보여 줘.

04 수정된 모델의 이미지

❶ For a long time, there has been a lot of pressure on women to be thin. (= lots of, plenty of) ❷ ▼We all have seen some typical images, in which models have been photoshopped to appear extremely skinny. 현재완료의 수동태 ❸ One research shows that women compare themselves with those images. compare A with B: A와 B를 비교하다 ❹ This comparison can lead them to develop a poor self-image. ❺ In turn, this can increase their risk of developing an eating disorder. ❻ Modified images can have a huge negative impact on women and ~에 영향을 주다 even children. ❼ For this reason, some governments have legislated 현재완료 laws on modified images. ❽ For example, laws are being passed, like the "Photoshop Law" which requires models to have a require+목적어+목적격보어(to부정사) minimum BMI and advertisers to label retouched images. requires = modified ❾ When a model's image is modified to make her smaller, that fact must be 수동태 부사적 용법 조동사+수동태 stated. ❿ Governments and industries must work together to help 부사적 용법(목적) protect women's self-confidence and health. ⓫ The fashion media and advertising industries need to show healthy images of women. ⓬ It will take a long time for this change occur, but the effort is It takes+시간+for 의미상 주어+to부정사: ~가 …하는 데 시간이 −만큼 걸리다 surely worth it.

❶오랫동안 여성들은 날씬해야 한다는 많은 압박이 존재해 왔다. ❷우리 모두는 어떤 전형적인 이미지들을 보아 왔는데, 그 안에서 모델들은 극단적으로 말라 보이도록 포토샵 처리가 되었다. ❸어느 연구에서는 여성들이 스스로를 이러한 이미지와 비교한다는 것을 보여 주고 있다. ❹이러한 비교는 그들이 자신에 대한 나쁜 이미지를 만들어 나가게 할 수 있다. ❺결국 이것은 그들의 섭식 장애 발생의 위험을 증가시킬 수 있다. ❻수정된 이미지들은 여성들과 심지어 어린이들에게 엄청난 부정적인 영향을 미칠 수 있다. ❼이러한 이유로, 몇몇 정부는 수정된 이미지에 대한 법률을 제정했다. ❽예를 들어, 모델들이 최소한의 BMI(체질량 지수)를 가지는 것과 광고주들이 수정된 이미지라는 라벨을 붙이는 것을 요구하는 "포토샵 (금지) 법"과 같은 법안들이 통과되었다. ❾어떤 모델을 더 작아 보이도록 하기 위해 이미지가 수정될 때, 그 사실은 분명히 언급되어야 한다. ❿정부와 산업계는 여성들의 자신감과 건강을 보호하는 것을 돕기 위해 서로 협력해야 한다. ⓫패션매체와 광고 산업들은 여성의 건강한 이미지를 보여줘야 한다. ⓬이러한 변화가 일어나는 데는 오랜 시간이 걸릴 것이지만, 그 노력은 틀림없이 그만한 가치가 있다.

1 이 글의 요지로 알맞은 것은?

① 섭식 장애는 심각한 질병이다.

② 여성들은 날씬해야한다는 압박을 받는다.

③ 극한의 다이어트는 여성들에게 위험할 수 있다.

④ '포토샵 (금지) 법'은 건강 문제의 중요한 해결책이다.

⑤ 정부와 산업계는 여성들의 건강한 이미지를 보여주기 위해 노력해야 한다.

2 이 글의 빈칸에 알맞은 것은?

① 정반대로

② 그러므로

③ 예를 들어

④ 게다가

⑤ 반면에

3 이 글의 밑줄 친 this reason이 가리키는 것은? 그 의미를 우리말로 쓰시오.

4 이 글의 밑줄 친 ⓐ와 ⓑ를 알맞은 형태로 고쳐 쓰시오.

1 이 글은 정부와 산업계에서 왜곡된 여성의 이미지가 아니라 건강한 이미지를 보여주어야 한다는 내용이므로 필자의 의견과 가장 유사한 것은 ⑤ '정부와 산업계는 여성들의 건강한 이미지를 보여주기 위해 노력해야 한다'이다.

2 빈칸의 바로 앞 문장에서 '어떤 정부에서는 수정된 이미지에 대해 법률을 제정했다'라고 했고, 이어서 '포토샵 (금지) 법'의 예를 제시하고 있으므로 예시를 나타내는 연결어인 ③ For example(예를 들어)이 가장 적절하다.

3 밑줄 친 this reason이 가리키는 내용은 바로 앞 문장에 제시되어 있다.

4 ⓐ require는 목적격보어로 to부정사를 쓰는 동사이므로 to have가 알맞다. ⓑ It은 가주어이고 진주어로 to부정사가 필요하므로 to occur로 써야 한다.

01 세대 차이를 극복해 봅시다! **02** 고대 로마의 노예들은 무엇이든 할 수 있었습니다! **03** 여러분은 다른 사람들의 누리소통망 (SNS)의 게시물을 보고 '부러움'을 느끼나요? **04** 미낭카바우 사회는 무엇이 특별한가요?

Before **Reading** pp.80~81

1 이곳은 은행이다 / 내가 어제 방문했던 **2** 나는 시간을 모른다 / 야구 경기가 시작하는 **3** 내게 말해줘 / 그 이유를 / 왜 그가 화가 났는지 **4** 이것은 ~이다 / Susan이 수학 문제를 해결한 방법

Basic Test

1 where **2** why **3** when **4** when **5** how[the way]

Preview Test

01 We live in a different world / where we cannot understand each other. 우리는 다른 세상에 살고 있다 / 우리가 서로를 이해할 수 없는 **02** Do you know the reason / why slaves were such an important part of ancient Rome? 당신은 이유를 알고 있나요 / 왜 노예들은 고대 로마의 무척이나 중요했던 구성원이었는지를 **03** Now let's find out / how you can prevent those negative feelings. 지금 찾아보자 / 당신이 그러한 부정적인 감정들을 막을 수 있는 방법을 **04** There was a time / when most societies were dominated / by men. ~한 때가 있었다 / 대부분의 사회가 지배되던 / 남성에 의해

Real-Life **Reading** pp.82~87

01 1 ③ 2 ⑤ **Words** warn 경고하다 communication 의사소통 accept 받아들이다 **02** 1 ② 2 ④ **Words** slave 노예 produce 생산하다 paperwork 서류 작업 **03** 1 ③ 2 ② 3 ⑤ 4 그렇다면 그들이 우울함을 느끼는 이유는 무엇일까? **Words** depressed 우울한 satisfied 만족하는 personal 개인적인 negative 부정적인 **04** 1 ① 2 ④ 3 her daughter 4 ② **Words** public 공공의 western 서부의 equal 동등한 head 우두머리 religious 종교적인

01 세대 차이

p.82

❶ **Min** Today, / I said Mom, / "Mom, / I was so *men-boong* / today." ❷ But, my mom didn't understand / the word "*men-boong*." ❸ It means / the feeling shocked / to the point of mental collapse. ❹ Even she warned me / that I should not use that kind of words. ❺ I have no idea / why my mom keeps me from saying those words. ❻ Most of my friends use the words / such as *men-boong*, *no-jem*, and so on. ❼ I think / we are facing a generation gap.

❶ 민이: 오늘, / 저는 엄마에게 ~을 말했어요 / "엄마 / 나 너무 멘붕이었어요 / 오늘" ❷ 그러나 엄마는 이해하지 못하셨어요 / '멘붕'이라는 단어 ❸ 이것은 의미해요 / 충격을 받은 기분을 / 정신이 무너진다고 할 정도로 ❹ 심지어 엄마는 제게 경고하셨어요 / 제가 그런 종류의 단어를 쓰면 안 된다고 ❺ 저는 모르겠어요 / 왜 엄마가 그런 말을 못 쓰도록 막으시는지를 ❻ 제 친구들의 대부분은 그 단어를 사용하거든요 / 멘붕, 노잼 등과 같은 ❼ 저는 생각해요 / 우리는 세대 차이에 직면해 있다고

❽Please let me know/how I can solve this problem.
= the way

❾**Teacher** Communication plays an important role/in bridging
~에서 중요한 역할을 하다
gaps/not only between parents and children but also in every
not only A but also B: A뿐만 아니라 B도
relationship. ❿In addition,/we should try to understand each
other's world. ⓫▼We have to accept/that we live in a different
= must
world/where we cannot understand each other. ⓬You have to
make the effort/to understand and accept/your mother's
부사적 용법   to
perspectives and priorities.

1 앞의 문장에 추가하는 내용이 뒤에 나오고 있으므로 In addition이 자연스럽다.
① 그럼에도 불구하고
② 예를 들어
③ 또한, 게다가
④ 그러므로
⑤ 결과적으로
2 '어른들이 먼저 아이들의 세상을 이해하기 위해 노력해야 한다.'는 내용은 본문에 언급되지 않았다.

02 고대 로마의 노예들

❶▼Do you know the reason <u>why</u> slaves were such an important
선행사   이유를 나타내는 관계부사   such+a(an)+형용사+명사
part of ancient Rome? ❷They were around 25% of the population
of them
of ancient Rome. ❸Most had to do a lot of hard and tiring work
대명사   현재분사
because Rome was a slave-based society. ❹In the countryside, for
-based: ~에 기반을 둔
instance, slaves did most of the work on farms. ❺They produced
= for example
the food for everyone in the cities. ❻Some slaves worked on big
public projects, too. ❼They helped build roads and big public
help+(to) 동사원형
buildings. ❽But slaves didn't just do hard physical work. ❾Some
slaves
also did business and government work. ❿They ran shops, kept
did   run - ran - run
accounts, and did paperwork.

❶당신은 노예들이 고대 로마의 무척이나 중요한 구성원이었던 이유를 알고 있나요? ❷그들은 고대 로마 인구의 약 25%였습니다. ❸(고대) 로마는 노예에 기반을 둔 사회였기 때문에 대부분 노예들은 많은 어렵고 힘든 일을 해야만 했습니다. ❹예를 들어, 시골 지역에서 노예들은 농장 일의 대부분을 했습니다. ❺그들은 도시의 모든 사람들을 위한 식량을 생산했습니다. ❻몇몇 노예들은 또한 큰 공공사업에서도 일했습니다. ❼그들은 길과 큰 공공건물을 짓는 것을 도왔습니다. ❽그러나 노예들은 단지 힘든 육체노동만 하지는 않았습니다. ❾어떤 노예들은 또한 장사를 하고 정부의 일을 했습니다. ❿그들은 상점을 운영하고, 회계를 맡고 (장부에 기재하고), 서류 작업을 했습니다.

⓫ Some slaves even studied very hard and knew a lot about history, economics, math and science. ⓬ Slave owners usually treated these educated slaves very well.

과거분사

---

1 이 글은 고대 로마에서 노예들의 다양한 역할에 대해 설명하고 있으므로 ②가 가장 적절하다.
    ① 노예를 거느리는 것이 옳은지 논의하기 위해서
    ② 고대 로마에서 노예들의 역할을 설명하기 위해서
    ③ 노예를 거느린 것에 대해 로마인들을 비판하기 위해서
    ④ 노예 제도의 역사를 연구하기 위해서
    ⑤ 고대 로마에서 유명한 몇몇 노예들에 대해 이야기하기 위해서
2 농장 일, 건물 짓기, 가게 운영, 서류 작업 등은 노예의 일로 언급이 되었으나 ④ '다른 노예들을 교육시키기'는 본문에 언급되지 않았다.

 03 온라인 세상은 실제가 아니에요!

(B) ❶ More and more people are using social networks in their daily life. ❷ Using social networks is how you can easily find out personal things about other people. ❸ You can not only read about them, but also see their pictures.

더 많은
방법을 나타내는 관계부사(= the way)
not only A but also B: A뿐만 아니라 B도

(A) ❹ However, there's also a downside to this activity. ❺ According to some research, people who spend too much time on social networks often get depressed. ❻ So what is the reason why they feel depressed? ❼ It means that they feel less satisfied with their own life. ❽ When people were asked about this, most of them said they felt "envy" at others' posts. ❾ They kept comparing their lives with others, and believed that other people were living happier lives.

↔ upside
~에 따르면
선행사   주격 관계대명사
선행사   이유를 나타내는 관계부사
접속사   과거분사
수동태   that
명사절 접속사

(C) ❿ ▼ Now let's find out how you can prevent those negative feelings. ⓫ First, don't draw conclusions about other people from the web. ⓬ Be sure to step away from your computer and get the full story about the other person.

관계부사(= the way)
반드시 ~하다   ~로부터 떨어지다

(B) ❶점점 더 많은 사람들이 일상에서 소셜 네트워크를 사용하고 있다. ❷소셜 네트워크를 사용하는 것은 당신이 다른 사람들에 관한 개인적인 것들을 쉽게 찾아낼 수 있는 방법이다. ❸당신은 그들에 관해 읽을 수 있을 뿐만 아니라 그들의 사진들도 볼 수 있다.

(A) ❹그러나 이 활동에 바람직하지 않은 면도 있다. ❺어떤 연구에 따르면, 소셜 네트워크에 지나치게 많은 시간을 보내는 사람들은 자주 우울해진다. ❻그렇다면 그들이 우울한 원인은 무엇일까? ❼그것은 그들이 자기 자신의 삶에 만족감을 덜 느낀다는 것을 의미한다. ❽사람들이 이것에 대해 질문을 받았을 때, 그들 대부분은 다른 이들의 게시물에 '부러움'을 느낀다고 대답했다. ❾그들은 계속해서 그들의 삶을 다른 사람들과 비교했고, 다른 사람들이 더 행복한 삶을 살고 있다고 믿었다.

(C) ❿이제 당신이 그러한 부정적인 감정들을 막을 수 있는 방법을 찾아보자. ⓫먼저, 웹사이트로부터 다른 사람들에 대한 결론을 이끌어내지 마라. ⓬반드시 컴퓨터에서 떨어져서 다른 사람에 대한 충분한 이야기를 입수하라.

⓫어떤 노예들은 심지어 매우 열심히 공부해서 역사, 경제학, 수학, 그리고 과학에 대해서도 많이 알았습니다. ⓬노예의 주인들은 보통 이러한 교육 받은 노예들을 아주 잘 대우했습니다.

❸You can also <u>try to meet</u> the people in real life. ❹When you are
actually with others, you'll recognize <u>that</u> all of them live a <u>normal</u>
life just like yours.

---

1 이 글은 소셜 네트워크를 사용하며 부정적인 감정이 드는 현상을 설명하고 그것을 해결할 수 있는 해결방안을 이야기하고
있으므로 ③이 알맞다.

2 소셜 네트워크는 다른 사람들에 관한 개인적인 것들을 쉽게 찾아낼 수 있다는 장점이 있지만(B), 자주 사용하면 우울해질 수
있다는 단점도 있다고 알려주면서(A), 이러한 부정적인 감정을 막는 방법을 제시하는(C) 순서로 글이 전개되는 것이 가장
자연스럽다.

3 소셜 네트워크에 등록된 친구의 수가 대인관계를 말해준다는 내용은 본문에 언급되지 않았으며 소셜 네트워크를 지나치게 많이
하는 사람들은 자신의 삶에 덜 만족한다고 했다.

4 이유를 나타내는 관계부사 why에 유의하여 해석하도록 한다.

04 미낭카바우 부족 사회

❶▼**There was a time <u>when</u> most societies were dominated by men.**
❷**Men still hold most of the power in family and public life.**

❸**For example, it was only a short time ago when women could**
not vote in most Western countries. ❹Also, in many developing
countries, women are still not equal to men.

❺However, the Minangkabau tribes, who live in the highlands of
West Sumatra in Indonesia, have another way of running things.

❻This is a society <u>where</u> women have traditionally held a lot of
power. ❼Most importantly, <u>the oldest</u> woman in the family is
usually the head of the household. ❽She controls the family's
money and possessions. ❾<u>After</u> she dies, her money and land <u>are</u>
<u>passed on to</u> her daughter. ❿But the Minangkabau society is <u>not</u>
<u>exactly</u> <u>the opposite of</u> a traditional society. ⓫That's because
women do not completely control society.

❶대부분의 사회가 남성에 의해 지배되던 때가 있었습니다. ❷여전히 남성들은 가정이나 공적 생활에서 대부분의 힘을 가지고 있습니다. ❸예를 들어, 대부분의 서구 나라에서 여성들이 투표를 할 수 없었던 때가 불과 얼마 전이었습니다. ❹또한 많은 개발 도상국에서 여성들은 아직도 남성들과 동등하지 않습니다.

❺그러나 인도네시아의 서부 수마트라의 고지대에 사는 Minangkabau 부족은 일들을 운영하는 또 다른 방식을 가지고 있습니다. ❻이곳은 전통적으로 여성들이 많은 힘을 가지고 있는 사회입니다. ❼가장 중요한 것은 가족 안에서 가장 나이가 많은 여성이 보통 가정의 우두머리가 된다는 것입니다. ❽그녀는 가정의 돈과 소유물들을 통제합니다. ❾그녀가 죽은 후에, 그녀의 돈과 땅은 그녀의 딸에게 상속됩니다. ❿그러나 Minangkabau 사회가 전통적인 사회와 완전히 반대되는 것은 아닙니다. ⓫그것은 여성들이 사회를 완전하게 지배하지는 않기 때문입니다.

❷Minangkabau men can't own land, but still have important roles to play. ❸They usually take care of most of the religious and political affairs.

형용사적 용법   ~을 돌보다

❷Minangkabau의 남성들은 땅을 소유할 수 없지만, 여전히 해야 할 중요한 역할을 가지고 있습니다. ❸그들은 보통 종교적이고 정치적인 일의 대부분을 맡습니다.

---

1 이 글의 중심 소재는 무엇인가?
① Minangkabau 부족에서 여성의 역할
② 대부분의 사회에서 남성의 역할
③ 인도네시아의 전통 사회
④ 공적 생활에서의 남성의 힘
⑤ 엄마와 딸의 관계

2 이 글의 내용과 일치하지 <u>않는</u> 것은?
① 남성이 대부분의 사회를 지배해왔다.
② 몇몇 나라의 여성들은 여전히 불공평하게 대우받고 있다.
③ Minangkabau 부족의 우두머리는 가장 나이가 많은 여성이다.
④ Minangkabau 부족 사회는 전통적인 사회와 유사하다.
⑤ Minangkabau 부족의 남성들도 중요한 역할을 한다.

3 이 글의 내용과 일치하도록 빈칸에 알맞은 말을 본문에서 찾아 쓰시오.
Minangkabau 가정의 우두머리인 여성이 사망할 때, <u>그녀의 딸</u>이 돈을 상속받는다.

4 이 글의 밑줄 친 <u>affairs</u>와 의미가 가장 가까운 것은?
① 관계
② 사건, 일
③ 믿음
④ 편
⑤ 수익

1 이 글은 여성들이 많은 힘을 가지고 있는 Minangkabau 부족에 대한 이야기이므로 중심 소재로 ① 'Minangkabau 부족에서 여성의 역할'이 알맞다.
2 본문에서 Minangkabau 부족 사회는 전통적인 사회와 완전히 반대되는 것은 아니라고 말했으므로 ④는 일치하지 않는다.
3 본문 12행의 After she dies, ~ to her daughter.로 보아 가정의 우두머리인 Minangkabau 부족의 여성이 죽으면 그녀의 딸에게 유산이 상속됨을 알 수 있다.
4 종교적, 정치적 사건들을 돌본다는 문맥이므로 affairs가 events(일)의 뜻으로 쓰였음을 알 수 있다.

UNIT 09 Hobbies

01 퍼즐을 통해 집중력을 향상시키세요! 02 여러분의 아름다운 손 글씨를 뽐내 보세요! 03 여러분의 스타가 집에서 무엇을 하는지 알고 싶나요? 04 별나고 독특한 취미들을 말해 보세요.

Before Reading pp.90~91

1 나는 궁금하다 / David가 올지 안 올지 2 나는 밖에 나갈 수 있었다 / 내가 숙제를 끝낸 후에 3 비록 Ann은 어릴지라도 / 그녀는 매우 용감하다 4 만약 네가 서두르지 않는다면 / 너는 버스를 놓칠 것이다 5 Tom은 화가 났다 / Emily가 그의 휴대 전화를 고장 냈기 때문에 6 Susan과 Lea는 둘 다 / 수영을 잘한다

Basic Test

1 whether(if) 2 Unless 3 when 4 Both, and 5 Although(Though)

Preview Test

01 It's because / both sides of your brain work / when you do jigsaw puzzles. 이것은 ~ 때문이다 / 양쪽 두뇌가 활동하기 / 당신이 조각 그림 퍼즐 맞추기를 할 때 02 It is the art of / both writing symbols beautifully by hand and arranging them well. 이것은 ~의 예술이다 / 손으로 아름답게 상징들을 쓰는 것과 그것들을 잘 배열하는 것들 둘 다 03 Do you play / either the guitar or the piano? 너는 연주하니 / 기타 또는 피아노 중에 하나를 04 It is a high-tech treasure hunt game / because it is a game to find a hidden thing / using GPS. 그것은 첨단 보물 찾기이다 / 왜냐하면 그것은 숨겨진 물건을 찾는 놀이이기 때문에 / GPS를 이용하여

Real-Life Reading pp.92~97

01 1 ③ 2 당신은 또한 퍼즐을 맞추는 데 애쓰는 동안 집중력을 향상시킬 수도 있다 Words form 형성하다 instructive 유익한, 교훈적인 improve 향상하다 02 1 ⑤ 2 ⓒ, ago → before 또는 when Words related to ~에 관련된 brush 붓 curve 곡선 03 1 ③ 2 ⓐ interesting ⓑ knitting 3 ⑤ 4 ③ Words spare time 여가 시간 pirate 해적 whole 전체의, 모든 hang out 시간을 보내다 04 1 ① 2 ④ 3 ③ 4 ① Words cruel 잔인한 extreme 극한, 극도의 compete 경쟁하다 precious 귀중한

01 재미있는 조각 그림 퍼즐　　　　　　　　　　　　　　　　　　　　　　　　　　　　　　p.92

❶Have you ever done / a jigsaw puzzle? ❷It's a game / in which
<u>현재완료(경험)</u>　　　　　　　　　　　　　　　　<u>전치사 + 관계대명사</u>
pieces fit together / to form a picture. ❸Perhaps you've
　　　　　　　　　<u>부사적 용법(결과)</u>
wondered / how jigsaw puzzles were first started. ❹A printer from
　　　　　　<u>간접의문문</u>
England, John Spilsbury decided / to stick a map onto a thin piece
　　　　　　　　　　　　<u>decide는 to부정사를 목적어로 취함</u>
of wood. ❺And he cut it / into strangely-shaped pieces. ❻His idea
　　　　　　　　　　<u>→ a map</u>
enabled children / to have a lot of fun. ❼Later, / other printers began
<u>enable + 목적어 + to부정사</u>　　　　　　　　　　　　　　　　<u>= began to make</u>
making jigsaw puzzles as well. ❽Now people of all ages / <u>enjoy</u>

❶당신은 해 본 적이 있는가 / 조각 그림 퍼즐 맞추기를 ❷그것은 게임이다 / 조각들이 (그 안에서) 맞물려 / 하나의 그림을 이루는 ❸아마 당신은 궁금할 것이다 / 어떻게 조각 그림 퍼즐이 처음 시작되었는지 ❹영국의 인쇄공 John Spilsbury는 결심했다 / 얇은 나무판 위에 지도를 붙이기로 ❺그리고 그는 그것을 잘랐다 / 이상하게 생긴 조각들로 ❻그의 아이디어는 아이들이 ~할 수 있게 했다 / 재미를 느낄 수 있게 ❼후에 / 다른 인쇄공들도 조각 그림 퍼즐을 만들기

putting jigsaw puzzles together. ❾ Putting puzzle pieces together is/
enjoy는 동명사를 목적어로 취함   동명사(주어)
a pleasant and instructive way of relaxing. ❿ It is good for your
brain. ⓫ ▼It's because/both sides of your brain work/when you do
                                                      ~할 때
jigsaw puzzles. ⓬ You can also improve your concentration/while
                                                        ~ 하는 동안에
you work on a puzzle.

시작했다 ❽현재 모든 연령의 사람들은 /
함께 조각 그림 맞추기를 즐긴다 ❾함께 조
각 그림을 맞추는 것은 ~이다 / 휴식을 취
하는 즐겁고 유익한 방법 ❿그것은 당신의
두뇌에도 좋다 ⓫~ 때문이다 / 당신의 양쪽
두뇌가 활동을 하기 / 당신이 조각 그림 퍼
즐 맞추기를 할 때 ⓬당신은 또한 집중력을
향상시킬 수도 있다 / 당신이 조각 그림을
맞추는 데 애쓰는 동안

 **해설**

1 조각 그림 퍼즐은 성취감을 느낄 수 있다는 내용은 본문에 언급되지 않았다.
2 시간을 나타내는 접속사 while은 '~하는 동안'이라는 뜻이므로 이에 주의하여 해석하도록 한다.

 02 캘리그라피; 시각적 예술

p.93

❶ Calligraphy, which means "beautiful handwriting," is a kind of
         관계대명사의 계속적 용법   동사
visual art related to writing. ❷ Actually, calligraphy is more than that.
          과거분사   → a kind of visual art related to writing
❸ ▼It is the art of both writing symbols beautifully by hand and
                      └─── both A and B: A와 B 둘 다 ───┘
arranging them well. ❹ In calligraphy, you need skill to position
                                                    형용사적 용법
words so that they show harmony, rhythm and creativity. ❺ Would
~하도록(= in order that)
you like to try calligraphy? ❻ You need a few tools to get started.
                                약간의, 몇몇의   부사적 용법
❼ You need a broad-tipped brush and ink, and of course paper to
write on. ❽ Make sure you are sitting comfortably before you begin.
❾ Start by making a vertical stroke straight down. ❿ Then try
making letters. ⓫ Write anything you like such as the alphabet or
try+-ing: ~을 시도하다   that
your name. ⓬ Once you build some confidence, try changing the
          일단 ~하면
feel of your writing. ⓭ You can add curves. ⓮ Even small changes
will change the feel of your writing. ⓯ Don't be afraid to get
                                        명령문
creative and remember to have fun.
        remember+to부정사: ~할 것을 기억하다

❶'아름다운 손 글씨 쓰기'를 의미하는 캘리
그라피는 쓰기와 관련된 일종의 시각적 예
술이다. ❷실제로 캘리그라피는 그것 이상
이다. ❸그것은 손으로 상징들을 아름답게
쓰는 것과 그것들을 잘 배열하는 것 둘 다에
관한 예술이다. ❹캘리그라피에서 여러분은
단어들이 조화, 리듬, 그리고 창의성을 보여
주도록 그것들의 위치를 정하는 기술이 필
요하다. ❺캘리그라피를 해보고 싶은가? ❻
시작하기 위해서 여러분은 몇 가지 도구가
필요하다. ❼여러분은 끝이 넓은 붓, 잉크,
그리고 물론 (글씨를) 쓰기 위한 종이가 필요
하다. ❽반드시 시작하기 전에 편안하게 앉
아라. ❾수직으로 곧게 한 획을 그어 내리는
것으로 시작하라. ❿그리고 나서 글자를 만
들어 봐라. ⓫알파벳이나 여러분의 이름과
같이 여러분이 좋아하는 어떤 것을 써 보아
라. ⓬일단 자신감이 약간 생기면, 글자를
바꾸는 것을 시도해 봐라. ⓭곡선을 추가할
수도 있다. ⓮심지어 작은 변화들도 여러분
이 쓴 것의 느낌을 바꿀 수 있다. ⓯창의력
을 발휘하는 것을 두려워하지 말고 즐겨야
한다는 것을 기억하라.

---

1 이 글은 캘리그라피가 무엇인지에 대한 정의와 초보자들이 어떻게 시작하면 좋을지에 대한 정보를 주는 글이므로 빈칸에 들어갈 말로 가장 적절한 것은 ⑤ '정의'이다.

① 근원 　　　　　② 장점 　　　　　③ 인기

④ 진화 　　　　　⑤ 정의

2 ⓒ는 문장과 문장을 연결하고 있으므로 '~전에' 의미를 가지는 접속사 before 또는 '~할 때'의 의미를 가지는 when으로 고쳐야 한다.

03 유명인들은 집에서 무엇을 할까?

❶ What do you usually do in your spare time? ❷ ▼**Do you play either the guitar or the piano?** ❸ Do you dance or draw? ❹ Celebrities also have some interesting hobbies. ❺ Everyone knows Johnny Depp who stars in *Pirates of the Caribbean*. ❻ He usually shows a tough image, but at home he sometimes plays with dolls! ❼ Playing with Barbie dolls helped him develop the voices of Jack Sparrow and Willy Wonka in the movie. ❽ Academy award-winning actress Meryl Streep enjoys knitting. ❾ The hand-knit shawl she wore in the movie, *Doubt*, was made by herself. ❿ She has said that she gathers her thoughts while knitting. ⓫ Furthermore, former CEO of the social network company Dick Costolo also has an interesting hobby. ⓬ One of his favorite hobbies is beekeeping. ⓭ He said to Bloomberg, "The whole way the hive works is fascinating. ⓮ I love just hanging out and watching them." ⓯ A lot of celebrities also build a collection as a hobby. ⓰ Tom Hanks collects typewriters, Celine Dion collects shoes, and Nicolas Cage collects comic books. ⓱ Celebrities have a wide variety of hobbies, and there are probably some who share your hobbies!

❶ 여러분은 여가 시간에 주로 무엇을 하는가? ❷ 기타를 치거나 피아노를 연주하는가? ❸ 춤을 추거나 그림을 그리는가? ❹ 유명인들 또한 몇 가지 흥미로운 취미를 가지고 있다. ❺ 조니 뎁이 〈캐리비안의 해적〉에서 주연을 맡은 것은 누구나 알고 있다. ❻ 그는 주로 거친 인상을 보여 주지만, 때때로 집에서는 인형을 가지고 논다! ❼ 바비 인형을 가지고 노는 것은 그가 영화에서 잭 스패로우와 윌리 왕카의 목소리를 만들어 내는 데 도움을 주었다. ❽ 아카데미 상을 수상한 여배우인 메릴 스트립은 뜨개질을 즐긴다. ❾ 그녀가 영화 〈다우트〉에서 입었던 손 뜨개질로 만들어진 숄은 그녀가 직접 만들었다. ❿ 그녀는 뜨개질을 하는 동안 생각들을 모은다고 말한 적이 있다. ⓫ 뿐만 아니라 소셜 네트워크 회사의 이전 CEO인 Dick Costole 또한 흥미로운 취미를 갖고 있다. ⓬ 그가 가장 좋아하는 취미 중 하나는 양봉이다. ⓭ 그는 Bloomberg에게 "벌 떼가 일을 하는 전체 방식은 매혹적이에요. ⓮ 나는 그저 시간을 보내면서 그것들을 지켜보는 것이 좋아요."라고 말했다. ⓯ 많은 유명인들은 또한 취미로 수집품을 모은다. ⓰ 톰 행크스는 타자기를 수집하고, 셀린 디옹은 신발을 수집하며, 니콜라스 케이지는 만화책을 수집한다. ⓱ 유명 인사들은 매우 다양한 취미를 가지며, 아마도 여러분의 취미를 함께하는 사람들도 있을 것이다.

1 유명인들의 취미를 소개하는 글이므로 중심 소재로 가장 적절한 것은 ③ '유명인들의 취미'이다.

① 영화 사업　　　　　　　　　　　　② 인형 가지고 놀기
③ 유명인들의 취미　　　　　　　　　④ 상을 받은 여배우들
⑤ 가장 인기 있는 취미

2 ⓐ 수식을 받는 hobbies가 감정을 유발하는 요인이므로 현재분사 interesting으로 고쳐 쓰고 ⓑ enjoy는 동명사를 목적어로 취하는 동사이므로 knitting으로 고쳐 쓴다.

3 셀린 디옹은 신발을 수집한다고 했으므로 일치하지 않는 것은 ⑤이다.

4 빈칸 다음에 수집을 하는 유명인들의 예시가 나오고 있으므로 빈칸에 들어갈 말로 알맞은 것은 ③ '수집품을 모으다'이다.

① 책을 읽는다　　　　　　　　　　　② 글쓰기를 좋아한다
③ 수집품을 모으다　　　　　　　　　④ 취미를 갖는 것을 싫어한다
⑤ 패션에 관심이 있다

04 특이한 취미들

❶ Have you ever seen beetles fighting? ❷ Some people feel excited watching the fight. ❸ Their hobby looks a little cruel, but unique.
❹ Here are some other unique hobbies from foreign countries.

❺ **1. Tree Shaping:** Gardening is a household chore, but many people enjoy shaping trees. ❻ Imagine a tree shaped like a dinosaur.
❼ As the tree is growing taller, the dinosaur is, too. ❽ It would be so interesting to see!

❾ **2. Extreme Ironing:** Extreme ironing sounds funny, but it is an extremely active hobby. ❿ Some people climb mountains or surf waves as they iron something. ⓫ It looks like a wonderful circus performance.

⓬ **3. Stone Skipping:** Actually, this is a world-wide hobby. ⓭ Have you ever thrown stones by a river or a pond? ⓮ In Scotland, a stone skipping championship takes place every year. ⓯ They compete how many times a stone skips before sinking.

⓰ **4. Geocaching:** Geocaching is a compound word; "geo" means "earth," and "cache" means "a hiding place" or "a precious thing."

❶ 여러분은 딱정벌레들이 싸우는 것을 본 적이 있는가? ❷ 어떤 사람들은 그 싸움을 보면서 흥분이 된다. ❸ 그들의 취미는 다소 잔인해 보이지만, 특이하다. ❹ 여기 외국의 몇 가지 다른 특이한 취미들이 있다.

❺ 1. 나무 깎기: 정원을 가꾸는 것은 허드레 가사일이지만, 많은 사람들이 나무 다듬는 일을 즐긴다. ❻ 공룡 모양으로 다듬어진 나무를 상상해 보라. ❼ 그 나무가 커지면, 그 공룡도 커진다. ❽ 그것은 보기에 매우 재미있을 것이다!

❾ 2. 극한 다림질: 극한 다림질은 우습게 들리겠지만, 그것은 극히 활동적인 취미이다. ❿ 몇몇 사람들은 무언가를 다림질하면서 산에 오르거나 파도타기를 한다. ⓫ 그것은 멋진 서커스 공연처럼 보인다.

⓬ 3. 강가에서 돌 던지기(물 수제비뜨기): 사실, 이것은 전 세계적인 취미이다. ⓭ 여러분은 강가나 연못에서 돌을 던져본 적이 있는가? ⓮ 스코틀랜드에서는 물 수제비뜨기 챔피언 대회가 매년 열린다. ⓯ 그들은 돌이 가라앉기 전까지 몇 번이나 튀어 오르는지를 경쟁한다.

⓰ 4. 지오캐싱(GPS 보물찾기): Geocaching 은 합성어이다. geo는 '땅'을 의미하고 cache 는 '숨을 곳', 혹은 '귀중품'을 의미한다.

⓱ ▼It is a high-tech treasure hunt game because it is a game to find
　　　　　　　　　　　　　　　　　　~ 때문에　　　　　　　형용사적 용법
a hidden thing using GPS.

⓱그것은 GPS를 이용하여 숨겨진 물건을 찾는 놀이이기 때문에 첨단 보물찾기이다.

⓲ What is your unique hobby?

⓲여러분의 특이한 취미는 무엇인가?

1 이 글을 쓴 목적으로 알맞은 것은?
  ① 다양한 독특한 취미를 소개하기 위해서
  ② 위험한 취미에 대해 설명하기 위해서
  ③ 독특한 그들의 경험을 공유하기 위해서
  ④ 동아리 활동을 홍보하기 위해서
  ⑤ 독특한 취미를 비판하기 위해서

2 이 글을 읽고 유추할 수 <u>없는</u> 것은?

	취미	장점
①	딱정벌레 싸움놀이	몇몇 사람들은 그것이 흥미롭다고 **생각한다.**
②	나무 깎기	당신은 상상력을 표현할 수 있다.
③	극한 다림질	그것은 매우 활동적이다.
④	강가에서 돌 던지기(물 수제비뜨기)	그것은 배우기 어렵다.
⑤	지오캐싱(GPS 보물찾기)	그것은 GPS사용자에게 매력적일 수도 있다.

3 이 글의 빈칸 ⓐ에 알맞은 것은?
  ① 재미있는 숨바꼭질
  ② 쉽고 재밌는 스포츠 대회
  ③ 훌륭한 서커스 공연
  ④ 유명한 오프라인 보드게임
  ⑤ 클래식 음악 콘서트

4 이 글의 밑줄 친 <u>precious</u>와 의미가 가장 가까운 것은?
  ① 소중한　　　　　　　② 공공의　　　　　　　③ 흔한
  ④ 인기 있는　　　　　　⑤ 유용한

1 이 글은 다양하고 독특한 취미를 소개하기 위해 쓰인 글이므로 ①이 알맞다.
2 물 수제비뜨기가 배우기 어렵다는 말은 본문에 언급되지 않았다.
3 다림질을 하면서 산에 오르거나 파도타기를 하는 것은 마치 '**훌륭한 서커스 공연**'처럼 보인다는 말이 **자연스러우므로 ③**이 알맞다.
4 precious는 '귀중한, 소중한'의 뜻으로 valuable과 뜻이 가장 가깝다.

01 홈스쿨링이 무엇인지 추측해 보세요.   02 봉사활동을 해 본 적 있나요?   03 K-Culture가 전 세계적으로 인기를 누리고 있어요!   04 어떻게 가상현실을 교육에 활용할 수 있을까요?

Before **Reading**   pp.100~101

1 컴퓨터는 수리될 수 있다 / 기술자에 의해   **2** 음식은 요리되고 있는 중이다 / 주방에서 / 지금   **3** 나는 차가 ~ 기대한다 / 판매되기를 / 머지 않아   **4** 나는 좋아하지 않는다 / 요청 받는 것을 / 연설을 하라고   **5** 강아지는 / 돌보아진다 / 내 남동생에 의해

Basic Test

1 can be delivered   **2** is being built   **3** to be bothered   **4** like being watched   **5** is being held

Preview Test

01 You will be protected / from school violence. 너는 보호될 것이다 / 학교 폭력으로부터   **02** While they were being taught, / we helped them / with various subjects. 그들이 가르침을 받는(배우는) 동안 / 우리는 그들을 도왔다 / 다양한 주제로   **03** We hear about lots of non-Koreans / to be taught Korean / in Korea. 우리는 많은 비 한국인들에 대해 듣는다 / 한국어를 가르침 받는 / 한국에서   **04** VR technologies can be made use of / in many areas. 가상현실 기술은 이용될 수 있다 / 많은 영역에서

Real-Life **Reading**   pp.102~107

01 1 ②   2 전통적인 학교에서는 학생이 너무 많아서 각각의 학생들이 선생님들로부터 관심을 받는 것은 거의 불가능하다. **Words** advantageous 이로운, 유리한   violence 폭력   disadvantage 단점   **02** 1 ⑤   2 ②   **Words** curiosity 호기심   desire 열망   worthy 가치 있는   **03** 1 ①   2 ⑤   3 ③   4 요즘 한국어 과정이 주목을 받고 있다. **Words** language 언어   demand 수요   apply 지원하다   private 사설의, 사립의   improve 향상시키다   **04** 1 ④   2 현실감을 만들어냄으로써 그들이 배우는 것을 생생하게 기억하도록 도와준다. / 모두에게 교육이 가능해지도록 돕는다.   3 ②   4 ① **Words** fantasy 공상, 상상   vividly 생생하게   drag 끌다   separate 분리하다   supply 공급하다

01 홈스쿨링   p.102

❶Homeschooling is so advantageous/that many people are becoming interested in it. ❷It has many advantages. ❸First, you'll get individual attention/in every class. ❹Traditional schools have such a lot of students/that it's nearly impossible/for each student/to get attention from teachers. ❺Second, you can learn/at your own speed. ❻In this way,/you'll be less bored and distracted. ❼▼Third, you will be protected/from school violence. ❽However,/

❶홈스쿨링은 매우 유익합니다 / 그래서 많은 사람들이 그것에 관심을 가지고 있습니다 ❷그것은 장점이 많습니다 ❸먼저, 여러분은 개별적인 관심을 얻게 될 것입니다 / 모든 수업에서 ❹전통적인 학교에서는 학생이 너무 많아서 / 그것은 거의 불가능합니다 / 각각의 학생들이 / 선생님들로 부터 관심을 받는 것 ❺둘째로 여러분은 배울 수 있습니다 / 여러분만의 속도로 ❻이런 방식으로 / 여러분은 덜 지루해지고 주의가 덜 산만해질 것입니다 ❼셋째로 여러

homeschooling also has its disadvantages. ❾ You may have trouble making friends/because you will not have enough chances/to interact with other students. ❿ Also,/you may have trouble/comparing your academic ability/with others'. ⓫ Therefore, you have to think about/how you like to study. ⓬ Then you'll be able to choose/what will work best for you.

~일지도 모른다 / have trouble -ing: ~하는 데 곤란을 겪다 / 형용사적 용법 / 간접의문문 / 관계대명사

분은 보호받게 될 것입니다 / 학교 폭력으로부터 ❽하지만 / 홈스쿨링 또한 단점을 가지고 있습니다 ❾여러분은 친구를 사귀는 데 어려움을 겪을지도 모릅니다 / 여러분은 충분한 기회가 없을 것이기 때문에 / 다른 학생들과 교류를 할만한 ❿또한 / 여러분은 곤란을 겪을지도 모릅니다 / 자신의 학업 능력을 비교하는 데 / 다른 사람들의 그것들과 ⓫그러므로 여러분은 ~에 대하여 생각해 봐야 합니다 / 여러분이 어떻게 공부하는 것을 좋아하는지를 ⓬그러면 여러분은 선택할 수 있을 것입니다 / 자신에게 가장 잘 맞는 것을

해설

1 자신의 속도에 맞추어 학습을 할 수 있기 때문에 덜 지루하고 덜 산만하다고 했으므로 ②는 글의 내용과 일치하지 않는다.

2 〈such(so) ~ that ...〉 구문과 가주어, 진주어에 유의하여 해석하도록 한다.

02 교육 자원봉사 경험

p.103

❶ When our group stepped into the classroom in Kenya, my heart started pounding. ❷ There were no desks and not even a blackboard. ❸ There were so many students in the classroom that I couldn't count them all! ❹ I was so shocked that I was speechless. ❺ There was curiosity on their faces. ❻ It was my first overseas volunteering experience, and I wanted to do my best. ❼ I met the group of children I was going to help. ❽ I was impressed by their interest and desire to learn. ❾ ▼**While they were being taught, we helped them with various subjects.** ❿ We also taught them about the culture and customs of Korea. ⓫ They enjoyed learning and playing traditional Korean games. ⓬ After just a week, it was time to leave. ⓭ Was it easy? ⓮ Of course it wasn't. ⓯ Was it a worthy experience ⓰ Sure! ⓱ They waved goodbye with smiles and tears. ⓲ It was a meaningful experience that I will never forget.

start의 목적어 / so ~ that 주어+can't: 너무 ~해서 …할 수 없다 / 너무 ~해서 …하다 / whom / 수동태 / 형용사적 용법 / 접속사 / 진행형 수동태: be동사+being+p.p. / 시간의 접속사 / easy / 목적격 관계대명사

❶우리 단체가 케냐의 교실로 들어섰을 때, 내 심장이 마구 뛰기 시작했다. ❷책상도 없었고 심지어 칠판도 없었다. ❸교실에는 너무 많은 학생들이 있어서 나는 그들 모두를 셀 수도 없었다! ❹나는 너무 충격을 받아 말을 잇지 못했다. ❺그들의 얼굴에는 호기심이 있었다. ❻그것은 나의 첫 번째 해외 자원봉사 경험이었고, 나는 최선을 다하고 싶었다. ❼나는 내가 도움을 줄 한 무리의 어린이들을 만났다. ❽나는 배우려는 그들의 관심과 열망에 감명을 받았다. ❾그들이 배우는 동안 우리는 다양한 주제로 그들을 도왔다. ❿우리는 또한 그들에게 한국의 문화와 관습에 대해서도 가르쳤다. ⓫그들은 한국의 전통 놀이를 배우고 해보는 것을 즐겼다. ⓬딱 1주일 후에 떠날 시간이 되었다. ⓭쉬웠냐고? ⓮물론 그렇지 않았다. ⓯가치 있는 경험이었냐고? ⓰물론이다! ⓱그들은 미소와 눈물로 손을 흔들며 작별 인사를 했다. ⓲그것은 내가 결코 잊지 못할 뜻깊은 경험이었다.

1 필자가 자신이 처음으로 경험한 해외 자원봉사 활동에 대해 쓴 글이므로 글의 주요 소재로 가장 적절한 것은 ⑤ '해외 자원봉사 경험'이다.

① 한국 전통 놀이   ② 배우려는 관심과 열망
③ 교실에서 모둠 활동   ④ 한국의 문화와 관습
⑤ 해외 자원봉사 경험

2 교실에는 너무 많은 학생들이 있어서 그들 모두를 셀 수도 없었다고 했으므로 일치하지 않는 것은 ②이다.

03 한국어의 인기

❶Have you ever heard that many K-pop fans are learning the Korean language? ❷Maybe you have, because it's true. ❸These days, the Korean language courses are paid attention to. ❹Now in China, it's not difficult to see not only people learning Korean but also posters written in Korean. ❺The popularity of the Korean music and entertainment has led to a great demand for the Korean language courses. ❻The popularity of TOPIK is soaring across the world thanks to the Korean Wave. ❼When the test was first introduced in 1997, about 2,700 people from four countries (Korea, Japan, Uzbekistan, and Kazakhstan) applied. ❽Now, the scale grew by more than 70 times over the last 20 years. ❾▼We often hear **about lots of non-Koreans to be taught Korean in Korea or in other foreign countries.** ❿For example, the Korean classes in universities are filled with the students who want to learn Korean as exchange students. ⓫Also, they go to private academies to improve their Korean speaking skills. ⓬Now, we can easily meet foreigners saying greetings in Korean or singing songs in Korean.

❶많은 한국 대중가요 팬들이 한국어를 배우고 있다는 것을 들어 본 적이 있는가? ❷아마도 당신은 들어 본 적이 있을 텐데, 왜냐하면 그것이 사실이기 때문이다. ❸요즘 한국어 과정이 주목을 받고 있다. ❹이제 중국에서는 한국어를 배우는 사람들뿐만 아니라 한국어로된 포스터를 보는 것도 어려운 일은 아니다. ❺한국 음악과 엔터테인먼트의 인기는 한국어 과정의 큰 수요로 연결되었다. ❻TOPIK(한국어능력시험)의 인기가 한류 덕분에 전 세계적으로 치솟고 있다. ❼그 시험이 1997년에 처음 소개되었을 때, 네 개의 국가(한국, 일본, 우즈베키스탄, 그리고 카자흐스탄)에서 약 2,700명이 응시했다. ❽지금은 지난 20년 동안 그 규모가 70배 이상이 증가했다. ❾우리는 한국이나 다른 외국에서 한국어를 가르침 받는 많은 비 한국인들에 대해 자주 듣고 있다. ❿예를 들어 대학에서의 한국어 수업은 교환학생으로 한국어를 배우기를 원하는 학생들로 가득 찬다. ⓫또한 그들은 한국어 말하기 능력을 향상시키기 위해 사설 학원에 간다. ⓬이제 우리는 한국말로 인사하는 외국인 또는 한국말로 노래를 부르는 외국인들을 쉽게 만날 수 있다.

1 이 글은 한류 열풍으로 인해 증가하고 있는 한국어의 인기에 대해 이야기 하고 있으므로 ①이 알맞다.

2 요즘 외국인들이 한국어를 많이 배우고 쓴다는 내용이므로 ⑤ hardly(좀처럼 ~않는)가 아닌 easily(쉽게) 정도로 바꿔 쓰는 것이 알맞다.

① 인기 ② 수요 ③ 한국인이 아니 사람들
④ 교환 ⑤ 진지하게

3 이 글에서 한국 음악과 엔터테인먼트의 인기는 한국어 과정의 큰 수요로 연결되었다고 하고 있으므로 ③ '한국 가수는 한국어의 인기에 영향을 미친다'는 글을 통해 알 수 있는 사실이다.

① 한국 문화의 인기가 거세지 않다.
② TOPIK은 1997년 중국에서 개최되었다.
③ 한국 가수는 한국어의 인기에 영향을 미친다.
④ 한국 대학은 훌륭한 교수진을 가지고 있다.
⑤ 한국어 말하기 능력은 다양한 방법으로 향상될 수 있다.

4 동사구 pay attention to가 수동태로 바뀐 형태로 '주목 받다'로 해석한다.

04 교실에서의 가상현실 사용 pp.106~107

❶ Virtual reality(VR) was once regarded as a science fiction fantasy.
regard A as B의 수동태
❷ But now a virtual environment is a very possible future. ❸ With the help of VR, the way students learn is expected to change dramatically.
how 생략 / 선행사를 포함한 관계대명사
❹ First, it will help them vividly remember what they've learned by creating a sense of presence.
help+목적어+목적격보어(원형부정사) / by+-ing: ~함으로써
❺ Let's take science classes as an example. ❻ Students raise their hands in the real world. ❼ Within a VR simulation, their avatars would make the same movement. ❽ In a chemistry class, they could interact with the molecules by dragging them into position.
~와 상호작용을 하다 / by+-ing: ~함으로써
❾ In a biology class, they could separate tissues with their hands and explore the human body. ❿ Second, VR will help make education available to everyone.
사역동사+목적어+목적격보어
⓫ VR hardware will become cheaper, so it can be supplied to the developing countries.
개발도상국 / 조동사+be+p.p.
⓬ This will allow students around the world to benefit from the same level of experience.
allow A to B: A가 B하게 하다
⓭ ▼VR technologies can also **be made use of** in many areas other than education. ⓮ Try to imagine how they will change your lives in the near future.
try+to부정사: ~하려고 애쓰다 / 명사절(imagine의 목적어)

❶ 가상현실은 한때 공상 과학 소설에 나올 법한 공상(상상)으로 여겨졌다. ❷ 하지만 이제 가상 환경은 매우 가능성이 있는 미래이다. ❸ VR(가상현실)의 도움으로, 학생들이 학습하는 방식이 급격히 바뀔 것으로 예상된다. ❹ 첫째, 그것은 현실감을 만들어냄으로써 그들이 배우는 것을 생생하게 기억하도록 도와줄 것이다. ❺ 과학 수업을 예로 들어 보자. ❻ 학생들은 현실 세계에서 그들의 손을 든다. ❼ VR(가상현실) 시뮬레이션 내에서 그들의 아바타가 같은 동작을 할 것이다. ❽ 화학 수업에서 그들은 분자들을 끌어다 제위치에 둠으로써 그것들과 상호작용할 수 있다. ❾ 생물 수업에서 그들은 손으로 조직을 분리시키고 인체를 탐험할 수 있을 것이다. ❿ 둘째, VR(가상현실)은 모두에게 교육이 가능하게 되도록 도울 것이다. ⓫ VR(가상현실) 장비는 더 저렴해질 것이므로, 개발도상국에 제공될 수 있다. ⓬ 이것은 전 세계 학생들이 똑같은 수준의 경험으로 혜택을 받도록 해 줄 것이다. ⓭ VR(가상현실) 기술은 또한 교육 외에 많은 영역에서 사용될 수 있다. ⓮ 그것들이 가까운 미래에 여러분의 생활을 어떻게 바꿀 것인지를 상상해 보라.

1 이 글의 중심 소재로 알맞은 것은?
① VR(가상현실)의 흥망성쇠
② 상호작용하는 미디어의 미래
③ 수업에서 VR(가상현실)을 사용하는 것의 단점
④ VR(가상현실)에 의해 발생된 교육의 변화
⑤ 교실에서 상호작용의 중요성

2 VR(가상현실)을 교육에 사용함으로써 얻는 두 가지 장점을 무엇인가? 우리말로 쓰시오.

3 이 글의 빈칸에 알맞은 것은?
① 더 작아질
② 더 저렴해질
③ 더 어려워질
④ 더 안 좋아질
⑤ 더 단순해질

4 이 글의 밑줄 친 movement와 의미가 가장 가까운 것은?
① 행동
② (사회·정치적 목적의) 운동
③ 이동
④ 진전
⑤ 성장

해설

1 글의 중심 내용은 VR(가상현실)의 도움으로 학생들이 배우는 방식이 크게 바뀔 것이며 어떤 방향으로 바뀌게 될지를 설명하고 있으므로 주제로 가장 적절한 것은 ④ 'VR(가상현실)에 의해 발생된 교육의 변화'이다.

2 First와 Second로 시작되는 두 문장에서 VR(가상현실)을 교육에 적용했을 때의 장점을 설명하고 있다.

3 개발도상국에서는 사용 가능 하려면 VR 장비가 '더 저렴해질' 상황이 문맥상 적절하다.

4 movement는 '동작'의 의미를 지니는 표현으로 ① action과 의미가 가장 가깝다.

기본서 	 All that	중학 영어 학습에 필요한 모든 것 **올댓 중학 영어**	중등 1~3학년
영역별 	**TAPA**	영어 고민을 한 방에 타파! 영역별·수준별 학습 시리즈, **TAPA!**	중등 1~3학년
독해 	**READER'S BANK**	초등부터 고등까지 새롭게 개정된 10단계 맞춤 영어 전문 독해서, **리더스뱅크**	(예비) 중등~고등 2학년
독해 	중등 **수능 독해**	기출문제를 통해 독해 원리를 익히며 단계별로 단련하는 수능 학습서, **중등 수능독해**	중등 1~3학년
문법·구문 	**마법같은 블록구문**	마법같이 영어 독해력을 강화하는 구문 학습서, **마법같은 블록구문**	중등 3~고등 2학년
문법 	**Grammar in**	3단계 반복 학습으로 완성하는 중학 영문법, **그래머 인**	중등 1~3학년
문법 	**악마의 문법책을 찢어라**	알맹이 4법칙을 통해 문장을 쉽게 이해하는 **악마의 문법책을 찢어라**	중등 1~고등 2학년
듣기 	중학영어 **듣기모의고사** 22회	영어듣기능력평가 완벽 대비 듣기 실전서, **중학영어 듣기모의고사**	중등 1~3학년
어휘 	 **VOCA PICK**	주제별로 한 번, 빈출도순으로 또 한 번, 중등 내신 및 수능 대비, **완자 VOCA PICK**	중등 1~3학년